Constructing Constructive Theology

Constructing Constructive Theology

An Introductory Sketch

Jason A. Wyman Jr.

Fortress Press
Minneapolis

CONSTRUCTING CONSTRUCTIVE THEOLOGY

An Introductory Sketch

Cover design: Rob Dewey

Print ISBN: 978-1-5064-1860-5

eBook ISBN: 978-1-5064-1861-2

The paper used in this publication meets the minimum requirements of American National Standard for Information Sciences — Permanence of Paper for Printed Library Materials, ANSI Z329.48-1984.

Manufactured in the U.S.A.

This book was produced using Pressbooks.com, and PDF rendering was done by PrinceXML.

Contents

Preface

This book itself is a work in constructive theology. Because no clear definition or definitive account of constructive theology as a movement has been written, the actual constructive work of arguing for what the method is and what its importance has been remains an open construction site. This book is a contribution to that construction.

Constructive theology is pluralistic and dialogical. Hopefully this book will simultaneously offer current students of theology the opportunity to understand what the term "constructive theology" means as they find their own theological voices as well as encounter the under known history of one of today's most prominent and important theological approaches, all the while gaining familiarity with many of the most influential theologians and their constructive arguments. For currently working and retired constructive theologians, this book is intended to celebrate this important tradition, with certain critiques, and to offer a framework for situating and understanding what constructive theological work has been, is, has done, and continues to accomplish today.

My work in this book is constructive. It takes historical occurrences and confluences, paired with research and interpretation, and works to offer both a narrative and a conceptualization of a span of time and a variety of work. Like constructive theologies themselves, accounts of the formation of a theological community and its shared assumptions, tasks, and methods involves choices about what counts as defining, what aspects to include, who or what counts as representative and what doesn't. There is already so much building material available in constructive theology that the task, from my own constructive role in this book, has been to shape an abundance of material into something with a definite shape and ideally some appeal to the observer. Construction holds it together, and the intended effect is to hold together construction, or constructive theologies, as a widely disparate group of theologies and work by a wild diversity of theologians in both embodiment and viewpoints, to show the common links, assumptions, and methodological tendencies in approach. It is an imaginative construction of a theological movement meant both for people who have been working within it and for people who are first encountering it.

Seeing as constructive theology is always done in collaboration and conversation, I would like to especially thank a number of people who have read and offered their comments on what follows, including Gary Dorrien, Catherine Keller, Paul Lakeland, and John Thatamanil. I also want to be sure to acknowledge and thank people who have taken time to talk to me personally about their contributions to constructive theology over the years, including Peter C. Hodgson, Robert H. King, Rebecca Chopp, Mark Lewis Taylor, Serene Jones, Laurel C. Schneider, and Stephen G. Ray. All of these people, constructive theologians themselves, have helped shape and improve what follows.

Introduction

Theology, as an academic discipline, has found a comfortable place as a "systematic" endeavor. Responding to the rigors of the academy, historical philosophies, and the Enlightenment and modernity, theology has for the most part produced works systematically, using classic theological doctrinal loci one by one in order to arrive at a coherent, rigorous whole, either through dogmatic theology or systematic theology. Yet in recent years, such a preoccupation hasn't sustained talk about God as it has in the past. Within theological work, there has always been a constructive element or phase of doing theology; recently, however, a methodological trend has emphasized the "constructive" aspect of theology. This "constructive" theology has not emerged through a completely linear, straightforward process, and though many contemporary theologians claim the moniker of "constructive theologian," definitions of the movement and understanding of its history have been inconsistent and ambiguous.

The most comprehensive attempts to make sense of constructive theology have come as the result of several collaborative efforts on the part of the Workgroup on Constructive Theology. This Workgroup meets yearly at Vanderbilt University, and as a collective of theologians who claim to be "constructive," it has produced four separate textbooks that make both doctrinal and methodological claims about contemporary theology. These textbooks, written from the perspective of constructive theology, reflect the times at which they were written (which is itself an intentional and acknowledged characteristic of constructive theology) and offer views from various constructive theologians in a dialogic vein (another persistent characteristic of constructive theology). To date, constructive theology hasn't been viewed or conceptualized as a movement or trend in theology on its own as a whole. Questions arise as to what constructive theology is, where it came from, why it considers itself "constructive," and why constructive is something different from the ways in which theology has been done in the past. Constructive theology may not always make claims to being a new method. At the same time, it has taken upon itself a redefinition of theology in certain ways, and there's something important, at least, in insisting upon a new label within such an old and established tradition.

Theologians who claim constructive in their title or method differ greatly in what the word seems, at first glance, to mean. Some claim to be systematic constructive theologians, or both systematic and constructive theologians. Others reject "systematic" outright as an outdated way of doing theology. The term also varies according to tradition, Catholicism still largely preferring "systematic" because of church structure and history, while mainstream liberal Protestant theologians seem more likely to adopt "constructive" as a new, though intrinsically related, method entirely. Popular descriptions of constructive theology call it a "redefinition" of systematic theology in light of contemporary cultural and political critiques, and constructive theologians more often than not hold positions at institutions that historically belonged to systematics.[1] To say the least, systematic theology and constructive theology are still entangled. The questions then become: What is constructive theology, where did it come from, what is its relationship to theology in the past, especially systematic theology? What realities is it responding to and why is a constructive method more appropriate than a systematic one? And ultimately, is constructive theology something different entirely, or simply a reorientation of systematic theology that nonetheless remains within systematic theology itself?

This book traces the overall historical arc of constructive theology, from proto-movement through the present. Inklings of constructive theology emerged well before it began to take any formalized shape. At the same time, an important shift occurred when a group of theologians decided to create the Workgroup on Constructive Theology. Further, even as the Workgroup continues to work collectively, producing textbooks and influencing trends in theology, many theologians who are not part of the Workgroup or may not even know it exists have adopted the title "constructive theologian." The book also considers

1. Joerg Rieger, "Constructive Theology," in *Encyclopedia of Sciences and Religion,* ed. Anne L.C. Runehov and Lluis Oviedo (New York: Springer, 2013), 483–86.

the term "constructive" itself, offering possible reasons and historical contexts that led to this distinction being made in contrast to "systematic" theology and its subcategories. Constructive theology speaks to a very specific, historically situated emergence in the academy generally and in theology's attempts to engage those shifts specifically. It's important to identify exactly what makes constructive theology "constructive," how that term serves the discipline and what the possible drawbacks may be, and whom it implies as conversation partners.

After and alongside tracing the history of constructive theology, in relation to and outside of the Workgroup on Constructive Theology, the core motivations for constructive theology must be analyzed thoroughly. From the start, those who have done constructive theology have held as a primary concern doing theology that is relevant and speaks to contemporary issues and problems. This preoccupation has been expressed in two ways, or in a mix of the two. The first is to try to reconcile theology with the contemporary forms of other academic disciplines. The second is to make theology have something to say with respect to social justice issues. Neither of these things is new in theology as a result of constructive theology. However, constructive theology never works in the absence of one or both of these.

Finding "Constructive" Theology

There has always been a "constructive" aspect or phase of theology. Constructive theology, however, takes that work as primary rather than as a step along the way to a systematic realization of theology. The primary task and argument of this book will be to show how this tradition was built and what questions it answers. Constructive theology is an attempt to create an open-ended, context specific variety of theology that is an ongoing conversation made up of many voices rather than a single systematic description of the nature of God and the world's relation to it. Constructive theology tacitly recognizes the idea behind the often casually overused phrase "socially constructed" (though it predates this term and its popular acceptance): it is a quiet admission in the midst of Christianity's historical complicity with injustices and exclusive normatization that this is not the way things inherently *have* to be, indeed, that things could be otherwise. It is, as well, an ongoing search for that otherwise, relating the historical discipline to new emergences in a contiguous, open way. This book will argue that its history and proponents have made this so, and make an argument for its future development.

Because constructive theology is not a single coherent movement, and in fact resists such homogenization, the best way to approach it is by reading and presenting widely. Though there are many different takes within constructive theology on each central issue, there is yet a discernible range of concerns and approaches, although that range is open to expansion. This book will confront the constructive theological tradition both chronologically and by issue; understanding both is necessary to make sense of its history and contributions. Primarily, the method of this book prioritizes textual evidence as it speaks for the differing evolving concerns throughout the history of constructive theology, supplemented in key historical points by interviews with theologians who were present along the way. In the interest of discourse building it will take self-naming as a constructive theologian or use of the term "constructive theology" as its basis for deciding who is or isn't a constructive theologian. Obviously, this becomes easier with the formation of the Workgroup on Constructive Theology: anyone included in that workgroup at any period in its history will be considered a constructive theologian and his or her work as reflecting some aspect of its tasks. Proto-constructive theologians obviously didn't identify themselves as constructive theologians per se, but use of the term "constructive," even in its amorphous origins, is significant in establishing what constructive theology would become. Recent and contemporary theologians, who are not part of the Workgroup itself but do identify as constructive theologians, will also be considered in the umbrella term. Theologians who explicitly identify as another variety of theologian, such as a systematic theologian or a dogmatic theologian, will not be considered a constructive theologian unless they identify as both.

The history of the emergence of constructive theology formally will largely be established through the self-referential history of the textbooks produced by the Workgroup on Constructive Theology. The issues and concerns of constructive theology will also be presented by reading and analyzing representative, influential examples within the constructive theological tradition. Within the two biggest concerns identified within constructive theology, that of being an authentically interdisciplinary theology and as a type of activist theology, examples will be given of works that go almost exclusively with one or the other, as well as those that do both or authors who started in one and switched to the other later in their careers. This book, ultimately, is one part description, one part interpretation, and one smaller part prescription. It seeks to illuminate what constructive theology is from the perspective of someone viewing its origins and early stages in hindsight, and to describe its history. This allows for an interpretation of what constructive theology has developed into either consciously or unconsciously, and observations concerning what is good and what is lacking in constructive theology, as well as potential future work that could be done.

Constructive theology needs a comprehensive narrative and analysis of what makes it something new. Part of constructive theology's appeal and strength is that it doesn't pretend to offer exhaustive, finalized theologies. At the same time, in order to maximize its effectiveness and reach further in the theological academy and, just as if not more importantly, the church, its history and claims need to be interpreted and presented. That is to say, this book is an accounting of the place of constructive theology within theology at large. It will gesture toward more of a "movement" mentality for constructive theology, suggesting ways in which constructive theology is unique and new, a direction within theology that may have an exciting future. At the same time, as much as I admire constructive theology, this book will also offer critiques based on context, history, and content. In particular, as it stands, constructive theology runs into difficulties in terms of evaluating its contributions with respect to traditions and Christian theological norms, and the effectiveness with which it has taken up liberation despite its proclaimed intentions to do so. Despite these critiques, the book will ultimately explore the many good reasons for doing theology in this constructive manner, suggest some ways it has been successful, look forward to new areas constructive theology can expand into, and analyze the results to this point within the theological academy as a consequence of its emergence.

Dogmatic Theology, Systematic Theology, Constructive Theology

If this book is about delineating constructive theology as its own entity, knowing to what it's being contrasted is key. All varieties and ways of doing theology have a history. There is no single practice or method of theology. Theological reflection throughout the history of Christianity has included the writings of the New Testament, the early church's organizing and writing, the creeds, and more formalized versions of theology like those of Origen and Augustine. Theology has always held a prominent place within the academic tradition of Christianity. The emergence and development of universities historically is closely bound up with the explication of Christian faith, practice, and church or canon law. That's to say, deep thinking about the content of theology, as well as the how of theology, has been an important issue for centuries or even millennia.

The circumscription of constructive theology is largely conducted with respect to dogmatic and systematic theology—closely related traditions of doing theology that are indebted to the full history of theological reflection. As Wolfhart Pannenberg details in *Theology and the Philosophy of Science*, systematic theology and its related dogmatic theological tradition also has a definite starting point, first named explicitly in 1600: "The concept of systematic theology came into theology in the seventeenth century after the introduction of the concept of system into theology to describe the theology known as 'scholastic,' 'academic' or 'acroamatic.'"[2] The term "dogmatic" as a technical designation of theology, according to Pannenberg, emerged around the same time, the earliest known mentions being in 1634, and the first theology to be titled a dogmatic one being in 1659.[3] Systematic theology and dogmatic theology, as a historical subset, emerged as a combination of an attempt to offer a coherent summary of the theological propositions found narratively in the Bible and as a move to split ethics off from theology (a distinction that often persists today and which constructive theology strongly resists).

The primary modes of theology since the seventeenth century, as a result, have been through systematic and dogmatic approaches. Theology before then naturally resembles the theology that comes after, as the entire tradition, even through constructive theology, claims important unity through its concern for explicating Christianity, as faith, as a code of living, as a system of beliefs, as an important story, or any number of ways that Christianity has been viewed throughout history. Constructive theology does not refute systematic theology or dogmatic theology any more than systematic or dogmatic theology refute the various forms theology took before them. The history is a continuum. Constructive theology is an extremely important continuation and expansion of the tradition today.

2. Wolfhart Pannenberg, *Theology and the Philosophy of Science*, trans. Francis McDonagh (Philadelphia: Westminster, 1976), 404.
3. Ibid.

Dogmatic Theology

Dogmatic theology is done to ask questions concerning matters of belief and faith in Christianity. As recognized categories, systematic theology and dogmatic theology arose about the same time. As mentioned above in Pannenberg, descriptions of dogmatic theology often view dogmatic theology as one of two constitutive parts of systematic theology, the other being moral theology or ethics. Dogmatic theology is the mode of theology that deals with questions of belief or faith within the church, making propositional statements about the classically accepted theological dogmas. It is often confessional, and it is particularly intended for the church as an audience. Looking at modern examples of what dogmatic theology has become—in some of its most paradigmatic manifestations of the twentieth century—helps to distinguish the category.

The most well-known and influential expression of dogmatics as it reached its apex in the twentieth century is Karl Barth's *Church Dogmatics*. Barth specifically defines dogmatics as "the scientific self-examination of the Christian Church with respect to the content of its distinctive utterance concerning God." The underlying assumption of Barth's dogmatics is that there is in fact an inherent truth to be reflected upon and unearthed, however imperfectly, through theological investigation. He carefully notes that human speech about God should not be equated with God. Barth writes,

> Theology follows the utterance of the Church to the extent that in its question as to the correctness of this utterance it does not measure it by an alien standard but by its own source and object. Theology guides the utterance of the Church to the extent that it concretely reminds it that in all circumstances it is fallible human work which in the matter of relevance or irrelevance lies in the balance and must be obedience to grace if it is to be well done. Theology accompanies the utterance of the Church to the extent that it is itself no more than human 'utterance concerning God,' so that with this utterance it stands under the judgment that begins at the house of God and lives by the promise given to the Church.[4]

Nonetheless, he also cautions, "The Christian is not free to adopt any current religious idea, to espouse his own private philosophy, and then to urge this upon the community." While constructive theologians

4. Karl Barth, *Church Dogmatics: A Selection with Introduction* (Louisville: Westminster John Knox, 1994), 85.

agree that theology is not free to offer just any theological formulation, the reasons are different. For Barth, the veracity of theological claims is grounded upon divine revelation; the task of dogmatics as a critical testing and theological investigation illuminates for theologians how faithfully their theologizing has been to the actual structure of Christianity and the grace of God. There is a fundamental assumption that a stable Christian message exists, which theologians have a responsibility to bring to light no matter how (infinitely) futile their attempts to do so are.

Christopher Morse in *Not Every Spirit* attempts to revivify the tradition of dogmatics, with close attention to what it means to do dogmatics at all. He explains, "Dogmas are those teachings deemed to be essential to the community's identity." He continues, "When the call not to believe every spirit leads communities to confront questions about where dividing lines of identification are to be drawn between faithful and unfaithful confession of God, theology in practice becomes 'dogmatic,' whether or not the term itself is used. Since the seventeenth century the study of what the church has decreed and should decree as being of God and as not being of God has generally come to be known in the curriculum of theological disciplines as dogmatic theology, or dogmatics."[5] Dogmatics, like constructive theology, in Morse's definition, is premised upon the reexamination of dogmas or doctrines. However, unlike constructive theology, it nonetheless sees an "essential" quality to the doctrines and their content. The question is what Christians are called to confess in order to be faithful to God, to Christ's message, to a deposit of truth that is faithful witness to Christianity. Dogmas must be reexamined in light of new challenges in lived Christian experience and with respect to greater inclusiveness of the varieties of experience in history. Dogmatism, the antidote of which Morse claims is dogmatics, runs the risk of creating idolatrous rigidity, viewing theological formulations as higher than the Gospel itself. Dogmatics is intended to be a recursive return to the Gospel message, to hear afresh the Good News in new circumstances, against new challenges, and resisting idolatrous self-worship. Constructive theology, though it continues to work with the doctrines of traditional theology, does not assume that those doctrines are themselves essential. In fact, the doctrines that constitute the nodes in the lattice of theological reflection are themselves contingent, constructed, and open to change. They can

5. Christopher Morse, *Not Every Spirit: A Dogmatics of Christian Disbelief, 2nd Edition* (New York: Continuum, 2009), 17.

be expanded or consolidated, prioritized or de-emphasized, or in some cases as will be pointed out later, done away with entirely (although that is not the norm). Dogmatics—though it should not be confused with dogmatism or rigid enforcement of right belief without regard to context or history—is built around dogmas, which are considered fundamental building blocks of Christianity and of the Christian community. The intentional examination and investigation of those dogmas, agreed upon and unchanging, is the task of dogmatics.

Dogmatics is most often considered a part, or subset, of systematic theology. However, dogmatics can be usefully extracted. In their beginnings, systematic theology and dogmatic theology were more intimately linked than they would become in the twentieth century. Barth, in his dogmatics, pushes back against the idea of Christian theology being a system. As an influence on a number of constructive theologians, his resistance to systematization is an important development. He writes, "All theology is *theologia viatorum.* It can never satisfy the natural aspiration of human thought and utterance for completeness and compactness. . . . It is broken thought and utterance to the extent that it can progress only in isolated thoughts and statements directed from different angles to the one object. It can never form a system, comprehending and as it were, 'seizing' the object."[6] Most dogmatics are systematic. However, there is the possibility, at least the leaning in dogmatics like Barth's, to resist systematization because of the radical humility Barth claims human beings must acknowledge. The fact that all theology is *theologia viatorum* speaks to the limits of human rationality to express the fullness of theological truths against the rational human mind's desire to do so. Perhaps ironically, Barth nonetheless developed his own *Church Dogmatics* systematically. His widely acknowledged magnum opus works much like other systematic theologies do. But his caveat contains a reservation for the growing resistance to systems as the proper form for speech about God, a trend that held sway for four hundred years.

Dogmatics has an especially prominent place in the German tradition and Reformed traditions generally. Later dogmatics, especially after Barth and leading into the formal origin of constructive theology in the '70s, begin to show a breakdown that more and more resembles the fresh theological start embodied in constructive theology. Dogmatics *may* be systematic theology, and in line with its historical devel-

6. Karl Barth, *Church Dogmatics, Vol. III: The Doctrine of Creation* (New York: T&T Clark), 293.

opment, usually is. Barth, in the twentieth century, is a key and very important exception. Barth's theology is a variety of dogmatics that resists systematization, and yet isn't constructive theology either.

Dogmatic theology, in final observation, is confessional. As Barth and Morse make clear, dogmatic theology is done by the church, for the church. It is often, though not always, even denominationally specific (Barth's situatedness within the Reformed tradition is crucial to understanding his development of doctrines as well as the relative weight he gives their propositions). For Barth, only the church, in the light of God's revelation and judgment, can set the criteria for evaluating the legitimacy or usefulness or truth of any given theological reflection. Dogmas are something to be believed or confessed. As the formulation in Morse goes, through his own spin on the idea of confession, dogmatics is about formulating "faithful disbeliefs." What is to be believed and confessed is honed by determining what is not faithful to the essential character of Christianity and the Gospel. In dogmatics, for Barth, Morse, and others, the task is to subject beliefs to examination in order to compare them with eternal or revealed Christian truths. Human beings have a responsibility to *investigate* or interrogate their beliefs, not to construct them.

Systematic Theology

Both dogmatic theology and constructive theology are often subsumed under the heading "systematic theology." There are good reasons, including the proximity of their origins in time and place, for the former to be considered an element of systematic theology. Nonetheless, systematic theology and dogmatic theology maintain their own tensions, which defines them with respect to each other and helps to define constructive theology even further. As mentioned above, there are important cases where dogmatics explicitly breaks from the system of systematic theology. Because of the connotations of "dogma," often misconstrued as dogmatism, apart from occasional pleas for a more prominent place for dogmatics, its prominence has waned in the twentieth century. The growing skepticism regarding authority, especially church authority, and the credibility of revelation after the Enlightenment made dogma and dogmatics, especially when viewed as dogmatism, suspect. "System," on the other hand, nicely echoed the increasing concern with science, models, and comprehensible and reasonable explanations for the phenomena encountered in the world.

Systematic theology is done to test the internal coherence and consistency of Christianity. Again, consulting Pannenberg's historical analysis of varieties of theology in *Theology and the Philosophy of Science*, he claims,

> The function of theology is to study and describe Christianity understood as the history which receives its impetus from the investigation of the truth of the Christian faith, or of the reality of the kingdom of God made present in Jesus. Theology would not do justice to the historical reality either of Jesus or of the Christian Church if it did not pick out the open question of the truth first of Jesus's Gospel and then of the first Christians' Gospel of Christ as the driving force which creates the historicality of Christianity out of the gap between the truth which has already appeared and the truth that has not yet emerged in its universality.[7]

In his own *Systematic Theology*, Pannenberg writes, "From the 18th century the term 'systematic theology' came into common use to describe the task of offering a comprehensive and coherent presentation of Christian teaching. . . . A presentation of theology can be called systematic if it meets two conditions: (1) it deals with its subject matter comprehensively, which means . . . that it takes into consideration all that is necessary to salvation; (2) it also explains, proves, and confirms its content in detail." He continues,

> The proof and confirmation [of theological claims] come chiefly by way of the form of systematic presentation itself as a connection is shown between the various Christian doctrinal statements, and also between these statements and whatever else is regarded as true. Hence the systematic presentation of the content of Christian doctrine is already related as such to its truth claim. . . . If truth can only be one, the things that are regarded as true will not contradict one another, and they can be united with one another. To this extent a systematic presentation of the articles of faith directly involves their truth and the ascertainment of their truth.[8]

And, while not every theological effort will be able to address every single doctrine, systematic theology "found its most appropriate form in the *Summas* as independent and comprehensive presentations of Christian teaching."[9] A system is not *necessarily* a *summa*. But a *summa*

7. Pannenberg, *Theology and the Philosophy of Science*, 417–18.
8. Wolfhart Pannenberg, *Systematic Theology*, vol. 1 (Grand Rapids: Eerdmans, 1991), 19.
9. Ibid.

is the ideal and greatest expression of the aim of systematic theology, according to Pannenberg. And crucially, systems are unities.

The same cannot be said for constructive theology. Constructive theologians have by and large abandoned the project of a theological *summa*, as will be explored and explained below. In large part, this is because constructive theology values the importance of dialogically constructed theologies, where there are no final systematic presentations of Christian truth. Where Pannenberg and others search for a noncontradictory, coherent truth, constructive theology looks for a messy but ongoing, in flux, revisable approach to theology. This isn't to say that constructive theology embraces contradiction or noncoherence in itself. Instead, the finality of a perfectly logical, inherently unified system is considered a nonstarter for Christian theology from the outset because of the variety of witness that must bear account in Christianity, the reconsideration of authority in Christian theology, the vast plurality in historical and contemporary perspectives, and most basically because of a different view of the permanence or essence of Christianity or Christian truth in theology apart from constructed discourses rooted in human exposition.

Paul Tillich offered perhaps the most famous and most discussed systematic theology of the twentieth century (barring the conflation of systematic and dogmatic outlined above). Of systems, he writes, "The doctrine of the theological circle has a methodological consequence: neither the introduction nor any other part of the theological system is the logical basis for the other parts. Every part is dependent on every other part. The introduction presupposes the Christology and the doctrine of the Church and vice versa. The arrangement is only a matter of expediency."[10] The order of the inclusion of doctrines doesn't matter for Tillich because the form of the system is so strongly interrelated. Individual doctrines do not and cannot exist on their own in Tillich's conception. Every formulation of a doctrine, as a symbol in Christianity, implies the entire system. By saying that introductions or other parts are not the logical basis, Tillich does not mean that they are not logically bound to one another. In fact, he claims that all of the parts of a theology are so logically bound that the order in which they are presented doesn't matter. The system is a tight circle, in which all parts of any theology imply and necessitate logically and coherently linked doctrines around the entire circle. Therefore, theologies, according to

10. Paul Tillich, *Systematic Theology*, vol. 1 (Chicago: University of Chicago Press, 1951), 10.

Tillich, are still the production of single theological thinkers, even if the entire system is not presented in its fullness. Any one doctrine, theologized, is meaningless without considering its implications for every other part of the presumed system. Theologies are formulated in specific contexts and circumstances. The systematically conceived circle of doctrines must answer specific questions of existential importance in particular times and places. But the system, nevertheless, holds.

Interestingly, Tillich disagrees strongly with Pannenberg's assertion that *summas* are the purest expression of systematic theology. Drawing a tripartite distinction, Tillich says, "system stands between *summa* and essay. The *summa* deals explicitly with *all actual* and many potential problems. The essay deals explicitly with *one actual* problem. The system deals with a group of *actual* problems which demand a solution in a special situation. . . . Today a need for systematic form has arisen in view of the chaos of our spiritual life and the impossibility of creating a *summa*."[11] Tillich and Gordon Kaufman, discussed more below, both initially set out on systematic paths for the same reason, namely, to bring order to what they perceived as a cacophony in theology. Foreshadowing the coming constructive theological emergence, Tillich writes, "One could say that in each system an experienced fragment of life and vision is drawn out constructively even to cover areas where life and vision are missing. And, conversely, one could say that in each fragment a system is implied which is not yet explicated."[12] Constructive theology, however, leaves behind the need for full systems, explicit or implied. In Tillich, questions brought by the world, by culture, to the system of Christian theology receive answers that fit in the moment. For constructive theology, systems themselves, and not only *summas*, are untenable. The structures and raw materials of Christianity must be reexamined and reconstructed. That is to say, Tillich reexamines the context, the situation, or the questions brought to theology. Constructive theologians reexamine the theology itself. Tillich's idea of system reflects concerns that constructive theology takes up, even using the word "construction." But, as Pannenberg pointed out, the truth-value of systematic theology is shown in its system. His description of theological "essays" more closely reflects the format that constructive theologies take, but with a specific methodological spin that this book will lay out. Ultimately, constructive theology is premised on the rejection of a "system" at all.

11. Ibid., 59.
12. Ibid., 58.

Finally, Tillich's conceptualization of "system" is relatively novel, thus why he must defend it in his *Systematic Theology*.[13] Systems, for Tillich, are internally coherent in correlating specific historical circumstances to Christian faith and witness. But he rejects *summa* style, deductive systems—anticipating Paul Lakeland, a key constructive theologian, who rejects deduction for his own inductive approach to theology, specifically ecclesiology. Tillich anticipates constructive theology, but doesn't throw himself fully into imaginatively constructed theologizing, as will be described below. In order to defend his use of "systematic," Tillich identifies three points of confusion on the part of critics: "confusion between 'system' and 'deductive system'"; that "system . . . seems to close the doors to further research"; system "seems like a prison in which the creativity of spirit is stifled."[14] Constructive theology responds to these same concerns. It rejects systematic theology in order to prioritize induction, centralize the reiterative nature of theological work, and maximize creativity and relevance. It makes the constructive aspect of theology, the actual building of Christian doctrine, central, rather than the application of theology to offer "solutions."[15]

Tillich recognizes that there will be reinterpretations of Christian theology in order to accommodate new times and new experiences. He writes,

> Attempts to elaborate a theology as an empirical-inductive or a metaphysical deductive 'science,' or as a combination of both, have given ample evidence that no such an attempt can succeed. In every assumedly scientific theology there is a point where individual experience, traditional valuation, and personal commitment must decide the issue. This point, often

13. Alongside Pannenberg's relation between system and *summa*, Sallie McFague, a key early constructive theologian, in discussing her own methodological evolution, rejects "grand systems," which she views as having been constitutive of systematic theological work. The first Workgroup on Constructive Theology textbook, *Christian Theology: An Introduction to Its Traditions and Tasks*, contrasts its format to "full blown" systematic theologies. *Summas* may have been primarily a medieval Christian theological form, but the sense that a complete exposition of the Christian faith, something that deals with "*all actual* and many potential" problems, is an ideal for systematic theology (which Tillich rejects) is well represented in Christian theology since the earliest systematic theologies in the 1600s.
14. Ibid.
15. Different interpretations of Tillich and how to respond to the idea of "system" are visible in constructive theology. Peter C. Hodgson expressed an affinity with Tillich's "system," though he departs from it in certain respects. David Tracy, however, though sharing similar language, clearly critiques and departs from Tillich's idea of "system," even while using his own version of "correlation." See Peter C. Hodgson, *Winds of the Spirit: A Constructive Christian Theology* (Louisville: Westminster John Knox, 1994), 37–40; and David Tracy, *Blessed Rage for Order: The New Pluralism in Theology* (New York: Seabury, 1975), 45–46.

> hidden to the authors of such theologies, is obvious to those who look at them with other experiences and other commitments.[16]

However, he nonetheless maintains that these are different perspectives on a deposit of truth that is Christianity. While he accepts the shortcomings of situated, finite perspectives on Christianity and Ultimate Concern, he stops short of calling the doctrines of Christianity themselves, in their collection and in their individual realizations, impermanent, contingent, and constructed. Reformulations in Tillich's famous method of correlation are not reconfigurations or reconstructions of doctrines. Rather, they are intended as the revisiting of the existent structure of doctrine and saving work of God in Christianity, to be correlated with changing circumstances and experiences, a crucial difference between Tillich's system and constructive theology. His recognition of the role of human experience and perspective, however, gestures toward the insights of constructive theology. The role human judgments necessarily play makes no system the final say in Christian theology for Tillich. Yet, Tillich sees theology as a system, nonetheless.

Systematic theology is about completeness, and ultimately about the individual effort on the part of a theologian to discern and describe as faithfully as possible Christianity and its effects. As Pannenberg very nicely and succinctly puts it, "In systematic theology . . . coherence itself is the object of the investigation and presentation of the doctrinal content."[17] It arose as the preferred term and approach to doing theology in the academy as theology sought to keep up with the systematization of other academic disciplines that grew in prominence, especially in the Enlightenment. Even though the term didn't exist, as Pannenberg and others point out, theology had been done in a more or less systematic format even before the seventeenth century.[18] But a special emphasis on the importance of the systematic nature of theological work grows to the point that the coherence itself, alongside the faithful expression of Christian truths, becomes the point of Christian theology.

Barth, Tillich, and others (including Pannenberg) point toward the advent of constructive theology. As Barth says, "Whether we can call theology a science depends on what we mean by science. If we do not mean a systematic world-view, but strict objectivity and method, then

16. Ibid., 8.
17. Pannenberg, *Systematic Theology*, vol. 1, 19.
18. Ibid.

theology must also, though not exclusively, be pursued in scientific terms."[19] However, constructive theology is not strictly objective, or strict about method, *per se*. In Tillich, this is revealed in the method of correlation, which emphasizes the importance of contingent understandings of Christian doctrines, though not the contingency of the doctrines themselves. For Pannenberg, the development is betrayed in his recognition of the historicist nature of theology. Even if doctrines are permanent, their theological expressions must be read in a historically sensitive way.[20] Immediately preceding the formalization of constructive theology, the need for a nonsystematic, relevant theology that fully acknowledges the constructed nature of the theological project was acutely felt and began to be expressed in many different ways in systematic and dogmatic theologies themselves. The peculiarly North American (to this point) way of taking up these emerging insights was constructive theology.

Contemporary expressions of dogmatic and systematic theology reach their height in Barth and Tillich, although many excellent examples of dogmatic and systematic theologies have continued to be produced since. Gordon Kaufman, a crucial figure in early constructive theology, first wrote *Systematic Theology: A Historicist Perspective*, as an encapsulation of his thoughts on theology. He writes that, for many, "In our own time of religious doubt and cultural pluralism the most that we can, or should, attempt, are pieces of occasional theology, tracts for the times, hortatory or critical essays."[21] He counters at this stage in his thinking that "What is required is exposition of Christian faith in its wholeness, enabling us to see how our entire modern existence . . . looks when grasped in Christian terms. Only systematic theologies, drawing on the vast linguistic and conceptual resources of Christian doctrine which was developed to interpret all sides of human experience, can speak to such needs."[22] Like the other systematic and dogmatic theologies beginning to lead toward constructive premises, Kaufman's early systematic theology is explicitly historicist. He writes,

> We are now in a position to state fairly concisely what systematic theology is and what the procedure to be followed in the present work will be. From what has been said it should be clear that theological work involves a dou-

19. Karl Barth, *Church Dogmatics: An Introduction*, ed. Helmut Gollwitzer, trans. Geoffrey Bromiley (Louisville: Westminster John Knox, 1994), 82.
20. Ibid., 418–19.
21. Gordon Kaufman, *Systematic Theology: A Historicist Perspective* (New York: Charles Scribner's Sons, 1968), vii.
22. Ibid., vii–viii.

> ble reference: to meanings in the present situation, and to a historical norm. Each must be brought into relation to the other in such a way that, on the one hand, the present meaning becomes decisively informed and transformed by the historical norm, and, on the other hand, the almost forgotten normative meaning becomes once again a living and effective reality in the present.[23]

He continues,

> Systematic theology, in the two thousand years of its history, has found it necessary to develop a special conceptuality making it possible to grasp and understand the entire world of our experience as under the sovereign lordship of the God-defined-by-Christ: built into the very logical structure of Christian theological language is reference to the historical Christ as normative. . . . Systematic theology—the attempt to come to an adequate understanding of the meaning of the word "God"—must finally lead, if its goal is to be achieved, to a new and more profound understanding of all reality experienced and known by man.[24]

The systematic theology of Kaufman at this point is meant to reflect all experience and reality. Despite its emphasis on historicity, it nonetheless tries to illuminate an objective "all reality" as encountered through Christianity.

Kaufman, however, as will be expanded upon further on, is a crucial early constructive theologian. He disavowed systematic theology, most dramatically his own. "The question of whether theological claims are *true*, and if so in what respects has not been straight-forwardly addressed in this essay. This is because this question, as usually understood, presupposes what I have called the 'perceptual model' of reality, where the correspondence of our ideas with the real 'out there' is a proper issue." He continues, "We can scarcely avoid being interested, of course, in the question whether our ideas of world and God are valid or true, i.e. how well they represent what is the case. However, since these ideas are imaginative constructs not directly grounded on perceptual receptivity, the usual way of checking this matter is not open to us."[25] Kaufman and others acknowledge that the realities of faith are inaccessible in an ordinary empirical way, and that the diversity of voices and seeming instability of theology in their contemporary moment arise in result, what Edward Farley, another important early

23. Ibid., 10.
24. Ibid., 11–12.
25. Gordon D. Kaufman, *An Essay on Theological Method* (Missoula, MT: Scholars Press, 1975), 75.

constructive theologian, in *Ecclesial Man* calls the "problem beneath the problem of theological method."[26] Constructive theology, as an approach or even a method, does not prescribe a single procedure for arriving at theological propositions. The human element of interpretation and theological construction, in polyphonic, pluralistic, historicized complexity, characterizes constructive theology. Constructive theology rejects both the possibility of a system to be revealed, or one procedure by which it can be. As a method, constructive theology allows for a plethora of procedures, for the purpose of imaginative construction.

Kaufman stands as an evocative hinge between systematic theology and constructive theology. His historicist theology began to move away from the idea of Christianity as a deposit of truth to be explicated. His later work explicitly rejects systematics for theology as imaginative construction. His rejection of his own *Systematic Theology* becomes itself symbolic.

Constructive Theology

Kaufman's description of the constructive activity of theology will serve as a preliminary view into the foundationally different perspective of constructive theology compared to systematic and dogmatic theology:

> Although it may be obvious to us that the constructive work of the imagination has in this way always been constitutive of theological activity, theologians have seldom understood themselves to be engaged primarily in imaginatively constructing a theistically-focused worldview; on the contrary, they have largely regarded themselves as attempting to express in human words and concepts what the divine King had objectively and authoritatively given the church or synagogue in revelation. The fact that their work was thoroughly imaginative and constructive in character was simply not recognized. However, with the aid of the contemporary theory of worldviews and conceptual frameworks, and of contemporary theory of the imagination, we are enabled to gain a fuller understanding of the human function and the logical standing of our religious and theological language; and this makes it possible for us to reconceive the theological enterprise as *explicitly* and *essentially* imaginative construction. Theological work now, therefore, can be carried on as a fully critical and

26. Edward Farley, *Ecclesial Man: A Social Phenomenology of Faith and Reality* (Philadelphia: Fortress, 1975), 6.

> self-conscious constructive activity, in a way that has never before been possible.[27]

The details of this assumption about the imaginatively constructive nature of theology are worked out in different ways by different theologians. But it points to the fundamental shift in the way constructive theology looks at the task and subject of theological reflection. Constructive theologians will agree to differing degrees with Kaufman's pragmatic view of Christian theology, and seemingly near abandonment of the knowability of God. But the character and understanding of Christianity, themselves seen as constructions, putting the responsibility for their analysis, reconstruction, and recognition of their contingency on human beings, underlies constructive theology in a profound way. The latest iteration of the Workgroup on Constructive Theology frames its critique and separation from systematic and dogmatic theology in its publication *Awake to the Moment* by asserting that, "constructive theology is a distinctive form of Christian theology that does not separate heavenly concerns from worldly ones. Some theologians see their work to be a careful stewardship and reiteration of sacred doctrines handed down by church authorities, and they strive to keep those doctrines as pure as possible of the messy world of politics and social struggles."[28] The Workgroup rejects such presumed purity even being possible. Systematic theology and dogmatic theology, all historical varieties of theology, have a constructive element to them. Constructive theology makes that the focus, and makes the constructed and constructive nature of theological work explicit. By keeping the constructed and constructive nature of theological reflection in the fore, the need, even the possibility, of a monolithic system falls away. For constructive theology, grand systems are inherently fallacious when faced with the actual pluralistic lived experiences of Christianity, across cultures and people as well as across history.

Constructive theology is indebted to both dogmatic and systematic theology. Interestingly, many of the works cited as important for its initiation are works in dogmatics, including *Abriss der Dogmatik* by Horst Georg Pöhlmann and *Reformed Dogmatics* by Heinrich Heppe. Likewise, even today, many constructive theologians, lacking a clear historical and theoretical basis for claiming a new role, claim system-

27. Gordon Kaufman, "Theology as Imaginative Construction," *Journal of the American Academy of Religion* 50, no. 1 (March 1982), 78.
28. Stephen J. Ray and Laurel Schneider, eds., *Awake to the Moment: An Introduction to Theology* (Louisville: Westminster John Knox, 2016), 19–20.

atic theology, which has continued to cause confusion in the matter of the relationship between constructive and systematic theology. Like systematic theology in the seventeenth century, and relatedly dogmatic theology, constructive theology builds on Christian theological traditions, but finds its place more clearly in having claimed a name as a related but distinct field of theological work. Constructive theology owes much of its vocabulary, including its doctrinal vocabulary, as well as its analytical bent—to systematic theology. To dogmatic theology—especially twentieth century versions of it, it owes a suspicion of systematization and commitment to an investigation of theological claims as a matter that concerns both the academy and the Church. There are theologians working today who claim to be constructive systematic theologians as well as constructive dogmatic theologians. There is no absolute contradiction in these claims, although they are strongly conflicted and often directly at odds. There is a basic view of Christianity and theology that is implied in constructive theology that challenges these older ways of doing theology that is worth keeping in mind when trying to mix and match terms.

If constructive theology is in fact as distinct of a theological movement as this book argues, it remains to be seen what constructive theology has been and is today. A clear description and definition of what constructive theology is, on its own, is needed.

A Working Definition of Constructive Theology

In trying to pinpoint exactly what constructive theology is, it's very easy for the definition to start to creep further than it should. Because all theologies have a constructive component, it can quickly begin to seem as if all theology is constructive theology. For the term to have any real meaning, however, it must actually point to something distinct or risk being a useless buzz word. To start formulating a definition, therefore, it's worthwhile to offer a preliminary survey of the possible theologies that may or may not be "constructive" in the sense this book explores.

The term "constructive theology" is new enough basically to rule out anything before 1900. There are rare mentions of theology being constructive, or the constructive aspects of theology before then, but nothing like a programmatic statement concerning a specific way of doing theology. The earliest uses of the exact phrase "constructive theology" that seem to have any discernible content are in 1902 and

1907. I've called these instances, and other early sightings, "proto-constructive" theology because they aren't self-consciously creating or making a case for a label. At the same time, how closely these early uses of "constructive theology" relate to what it has come to mean are striking. In a 1904 book review titled "Current Essays in Constructive Theology," Herbert Alden Youtz writes:

> Current essays in theology may be roughly classified in two groups: first, those which are seeking for an 'essence,' a 'finality,' or an 'ultimate principle of unity' which expresses an unresolvable *quantum* in all religion, or 'essential religion' seen in its lowest terms; second, those which take current religious doctrines and try to translate them into the terms of the thought-life of today. They ask: What is the meaning or 'reality' of this or that doctrine for this age and generation? Or, What form will this truth take, consistently with the scientific and philosophical convictions of today?[29]

In what may be the moment in which constructive theology becomes a formalized though unnamed category, Bernard Meland, beginning to depart from his mentor Henry Nelson Wieman, writes,

> All roads beyond liberalism, however, do not lead back to some new form of orthodoxy. . . . This may be the place to point in a direction where fresh illumination on the human problem is emerging, presaging rapport with the Christian Faith. To find a name suitable for designating this vast new complex of insight on the horizon which towers before us like new accumulations of the mind, would be somewhat taxing. I shall not attempt to name it. It does not have the distinctiveness of a movement of thought; and while it has been gaining steadily in force for over two decades, its advances have been almost imperceptible. To enumerate all of the fields in which it has been shaping thought would be tedious.[30]

Though he refuses to try to name this concept, he writes:

Being in the nature of a constructive force, it is not combative; consequently it does not invite discursive champions. Wherever its categories are incorporated, they effect an integrating experience. Facts, in their new context, are not radically changed; they are simply given more depth and perspective by reason of a new sense of relations.

Analyzing Meland's mature constructive theology, Tyron Inbody writes:

29. Herbert Alden Youtz, *American Journal of Theology* 11, no. 4 (October 1907): 694.
30. Bernard Eugene Meland, *The Reawakening of Christian Faith* (New York: Macmillan, 1949), 34–35.

> One way to approach the theology of Bernard Meland is to ask . . . what kind of theologian is he? Some focus for that question can be provided by eliminating some options. Meland is not a dogmatic or a systematic theologian who is concerned about an explication and systematization of the doctrinal heritage of the Christian Church. Nor is he primarily a philosopher of religion who is interested in religion as a system of ideas or the philosophical adjudication of religious ideas and issues. Meland, instead, is a Christian theologian, who is interested in the religious sensibilities, symbols, and practices of historic Christian communities and cultures and in the reconstruction and reappropriation of that broad inheritance of sentiment and symbol for the vitality of contemporary communities and cultures.[31]

Much more will be offered below concerning each of these tentative descriptions of constructive theology. It's important to note that none of these is trying to *define* constructive theology, only to describe retrospectively a way theology is being done.

It is true that the idea of "construction" is tough to pin down. It is, in any case, distinctively modern, fallibilist, and equally loyal to both tradition and contemporary criticism of past theological formulations. I propose a preliminary working definition for constructive theology that will be developed historically and conceptually through the course of this book:

Constructive theology is a method of doing Christian theology that takes seriously theological and church tradition as well as modern critiques of that tradition being something universal, eternal, or essential; it employs traditional themes and loci of theology in order to formulate useful, inclusive, fallible guidance for living as Christians in the contemporary world, against descriptions of a systematic theological system that pretend to unveil any true essence or essential reality of Christianity; and takes as its mode a good-faith engagement with parallel academic disciplines, often religious studies; an activist/crisis confrontation; or, ideally, both.

This definition rejects theologies that see themselves as radical departures from the past in terms of the language one uses to talk about theology. Almost every constructive theology makes a grandstanding claim about the contemporary world needing a radically new way of doing theology, and I believe each author believes this claim. At the same time, constructive theology almost always harkens back to the traditional doctrinal loci of systematic theology. Rather, construc-

31. Tyron Inbody, *The Constructive Theology of Bernard Meland: Postliberal Empirical Liberalism* (Atlanta: Scholars Press, 1995), 222.

tive theology is a new attitude about what good theology is, what it does, and whom it serves. This in turn implies a way of doing theology that over the course of the last century has inadvertently become a method and a movement. Constructive theology has never self-consciously been about movement or school building. The closest it has come to that is the Workgroup on Constructive Theology, but even in that instance every collaborative Workgroup book balks at making an overarching methodological claim about how all constructive theology should be done. The distinctive theological method of constructive theology is to develop traditional theological doctrines, but rather than engaging all of them, that is systematically, constructive theologies engage limited and specific loci for the purpose of illuminating one metaphor, one context, or one important crisis from the perspective of contemporary philosophy and critical theory intertwined with inherited theological vocabulary.

This book specifically considers theologies and theologians who have identified themselves as being constructive. These will naturally include theologies that are usually considered to be in the process and liberal traditions. Much of the early work in constructive theology, because of its link with Meland and Chicago style liberalism, is explicitly process in nature. The tradition is still heavily influenced and very much occupied by process theologians in the tradition of Alfred North Whitehead. Process theology is usually considered within the liberal tradition. Whether constructive theology successfully departs from liberal theology will be an important issue throughout. At this point, it's sufficient to acknowledge that process theology and liberal theology are the immediate historical theological sources for the beginnings of constructive theology.

A radical shift happens with the irruptions of liberation theology, and constructive theology would never be exactly the same after it tried to take adequate account of liberation theologies in the second Workgroup textbook, *Reconstructing Christian Theology*. Constructive theology as a whole, in my view, has never fully reconciled with liberation challenges. At the same time, constructive theology and liberation theology are deeply related. Given liberation theology's redefinition of so many traditionally white, Eurocentric, affluent, heterosexist categories for theological reflection, the question arises whether liberation theology is not itself an important branch of constructive theology, but one that has never been comfortably internalized by the historical center of constructive theology, related as it is to liberalism which has its own historical white male majority problem.

Liberation theology has naturally led to what is often called contextual theology. Contextual theologies are not always strictly liberation theologies, but rather take as their primary source and norm the experience of traditionally marginalized groups. These have included feminist theologies, immigrant theologies, post- and anti-colonial theologies, "third-world" theologies, and many more. The term "contextual theology" is often criticized for being a catch-all for any theology done from a perspective that falls outside a hegemonic norm. Again, the prevailing concern for reworking traditional theological doctrines makes contextual theology a natural conversation partner for constructive theology.

Indeed, all of the traditions above include theologies and theologians who consider themselves to be working in the constructive tradition. Constructive theology in the end doesn't have specific content. It, above all else, has become a methodology based in a specific attitude or "mood" about what purpose theology serves in the world. It has specific concerns that appear in all works done in its vein, but the doctrines, subjects, and crises to which these concerns are applied vary so widely that the only initial basis for establishing who is or isn't a constructive theologian, or what is or isn't constructive theology, will be self-naming. Over the course of this book, especially chapter five, more specific criteria will be offered that will be expansive, inclusive, and hopefully offer some coherence to the disparate works and figures that have been part of this relatively young tradition.

The history of constructive theology starts subtly. Its earliest appearances don't make much of a claim for being anything new. For the most part, it pops up sporadically within the context of other established movements and methods for doing theology. As the idea of culture being something constructed and not innate emerged—and eventually religion within it—different theologies began to incorporate this insight in a haphazard way that only begins to coalesce over the course of several decades. It's important to note that the claim isn't being made that theology suddenly becomes constructive in the early twentieth century. In some sense, theology has always recognized that each new interpretation of the themes of theology is a new effort in making theology relevant to a current age. Constructive theology specifically participates in the modern insight that all social structures are ultimately contingent, could be otherwise, and often perhaps should.

Myths, metaphors, institutions, sacraments, beliefs, practices, doctrines, dogmas, all of the things that make up Christianity slowly come to be recognized as beams making up a larger structure that is "Christianity." In order for that structure to remain standing and to be a place that can stand up to new eventualities and crises it becomes necessary, in the eyes of constructive theology, to employ new materials in new configurations that not only recognize but embrace the new technologies available that can ensure a structure that will withstand newly recognized vicissitudes and potential calamities. The metaphor of theology as a building is a frequent one throughout constructive theology. Like a skyscraper near a fault line, the frame constructive theology takes as its aim is deeply anchored but flexible, neither shying away from the challenge nor assembling to limitless, hubristic heights at the peril of those who trust the architects and engineers. And crucially, it is built with the capability to have old parts swapped out as they become fragile or corrupted.

Early constructive theology is clearly related and indebted to emergent structuralism in the early twentieth century and its argument that all cultural phenomenon are interrelated in a way that makes it necessary to understand the constructed parts in order to have a better understanding of the whole: our human understanding of the structures of culture is always mediated through language, and is therefore always subject to contingency, change, and variability. As the tradition developed, it also came to reflect later post-structuralist critiques of the rigidly formed cultural structures posited by structuralism. In both cases, the affinity is betrayed by constructive theology's persistent interest in culture, starting even before Meland, for whom culture became the dominant informant for doing theology. Most importantly, this emphasis and incorporation of linguistic and social science insights leads to the defining conceit of constructive theology that, though traditional doctrinal loci may still be the most expedient way to propose theological ideas, the contents of these loci, or even the loci themselves, are ultimately historically contingent, constructed, and changeable. Christian theologians in fact do not reveal or explicate pre-existing religious truths but construct in the mode of Christianity for historically situated, crisis confronting, culturally bound communities.

This incorporation begins in the earliest years of the twentieth century. In order to understand how this came to be a method for doing theology, this book begins by examining the collaborative efforts of the first few theologians, most of which are relatively unknown, who claimed to be doing explicitly "constructive" work in theology. Next comes a recovery and presentation of an obscure theologian, James Ten Broeke, who did most of his work in Canada. Though Ten Broeke never made a huge splash in the academy nor appears to have directly been cited by later constructive theologians, his methodological proposals are shockingly relevant for what constructive theology is in its first days and what it becomes throughout its history. Ten Broeke is an unheralded harbinger of a flourishing tradition that is usually traced specifically to Meland. Nevertheless, after Ten Broeke, it's necessary to turn to Meland who gives constructive theology a much broader profile, a character, its recognizable method, and the impetus to grow into a much wider acknowledged and practiced way of doing theology. These are what I call the "proto-constructive" theologians who may not have recognized a new method emerging (for the most part, they struggle to make their theologies fit into systematics), but in a very profound way set the agenda for all of the constructive theology that would come after them, continuing through today.

1

The Emergence of Constructive Theology

> Though no system of the remote or recent past can be said to be the theology of the present, no successful rival exists that I can find. Indifference prevails, for only a few seem to care for systematic theology.
>
> —James Ten Broeke, *A Constructive Basis for Theology*

The very earliest mentions of "constructive theology" appear in unlikely places and earlier than one might expect. In 1902 a book titled *Contentio Veritatis: Essays in Constructive Theology* was published, written by "six Oxford tutors," H. Rashdall, W.R. Inge, H.L. Wild, C.F. Burney, W.C. Allen, and A.J. Carlyle. This is the only early mention of "constructive theology" outside the United States, but it's important because it's the first apparently anywhere. *Contentio Veritatis*, so early on, sets the tone for what constructive theology in some ways still tends to be, and introduces a key question, the relationship between liberal theology[1]

1. Throughout this book, when discussing theological liberalism, I use Gary Dorrien's definition from the third volume of his exhaustive, authoritative trilogy, *The Making of American Liberal Theology*: "Liberal theology reconceptualizes the meaning of Christianity in the light of modern knowledge and ethical values. It is reformist in spirit and substance, not revolutionary. Specifically, it is defined by its openness to the verdicts of modern intellectual inquiry, especially historical criticism and the natural sciences; its commitment to the authority of individual reason and experience; its conception of Christianity as an ethical way of life; its advocacy of moral concepts of atonement or reconciliation; and its commitments to make Christianity credible and socially relevant to contemporary people." Gary Dorrien, *The Making of American Liberal Theology: Crisis, Irony, and Postmodernity* (Louisville: Westminster John Knox, 2006), 2–3. Dorrien distinguishes, as this

and constructive theology. In a strikingly prescient turn, the introduction to the book says,

> Among younger men and women of fair education, there is a widespread unsettlement and uneasiness. There is a vague feeling that the old Orthodoxy is impossible; people suspect that much that was once commonly believed is no longer tenable, but they do not know how much, nor by what it is to be replaced. The writers of the present work are well aware that the needed reconstruction must take a much more solid and substantial form than a volume of Essays by different authors. The most that such a volume can do is to call attention to the need of such a reconstruction, to show that the need is felt, and to indicate some of the lines on which they believe it ought to take place.[2]

The early instigator for constructive theology is the same as that as for liberal theology, namely, the fact that biblical criticism and a new prevalence of scientific reasoning had forced theologians to reimagine how theology would remain important for the contemporary world. Prefiguring the Workgroup on Constructive Theology by seven decades, however, this group of Oxford tutors introduces the need for a "reconstructed" Christian theology in response to the realization that Christian thinking had become untenable for many who accepted the criticisms that the Enlightenment and liberalism had brought to Christianity.

Structurally, *Contentio Veritatis* is also anticipatory of later constructive theology. It typically forswears any pretention to being a final account of theology, suggests that it is meant to influence others to engage in their own reconstructions of Christian theology, and compiles its constructive chapters collaboratively. Aside from being separated by time and historical situation, *Contentio Veritatis* very much resembles the concerns and form that the textbooks of the Workgroup on Constructive Theology would take.

William Sanday, one of the few reviewers, if not the only, of *Contentio Veritatis*, notes the new term, observing, "Two things have struck me more particularly in their book . . . these are on the one hand a pleasing candor which gives the impression of great sincerity, and on the other hand a certain cheerful optimism which is everywhere more sensible of gain than of loss and which does not take pleasure in the mere act of

book does, between liberalism and liberationism. The specifics of the differences between liberal theology and constructive theology will develop throughout.

2. Six Oxford Tutors, *Contentio Veritatis: Essays in Constructive Theology* (London: John Murray, 1902), vi.

destroying. The essays are described as 'in constructive theology,' and they really are constructive."[3] At the end of his review, Sanday notes that the content of the individual essays is less important than the overall claim of the title of the book. "'Constructive Theology,' as the name implies, is a process and not a finished work. 'Essays in Constructive Theology' is an appropriate title. What we have been discussing are essays or attempts, some of which really build—and the building has beauty as well as strength."[4] This is the start of the method or mood of constructive theology. Most importantly, the unfinished nature of constructive theology is immediately evident. Each of the six tutors tries to offer a new reading, a reconstruction of a Christian theological doctrine, with differing levels of success according to Sanday. But they all participate in the project of offering tentative, structural elaborations of Christianity in the wake of what was seen as an extended period of destruction or deconstruction.

Another early spotting of constructive theology occurs in 1907 in *The American Journal of Theology*. Herbert Alden Youtz, in a review titled "Current Essays in Constructive Theology," observes,

> Current essays in theology may be roughly classified in two groups: first, those which are seeking for an 'essence,' a 'finality,' or an 'ultimate principle of unity' which expresses an unresolvable *quantum* in all religion, or 'essential religion' seen in its lowest terms; second those which take current religious doctrines and try to translate them into the terms of the thought-life of today. They ask: What is the meaning or 'reality' of this or that doctrine for this age and generation? Or, What form will this truth take, consistently with the scientific and philosophical convictions of today?[5]

Youtz is reviewing *The Realities of Christian Theology: An Interpretation of Christian Experience*, written by Clarence Augustine Beckwith, a professor at Chicago Theological Seminary, in 1906. Beckwith doesn't refer to his theology as a "constructive theology," but he does write, concerning his method and the reason for it, "We are advised that the time is ripe for a reconstruction of theology, and are treated to fruitful suggestions along this line; on the other hand, we are warned that a reconstruction of theology is hopeless, since, without an accepted cosmology

3. William Sanday, Review of *Contentio Veritatis: Essays in Constructive Theology*, by Six Oxford Tutors, *Journal of Theological Studies* 4, no. 13 (October, 1902): 2.
4. Ibid., 16.
5. Herbert Alden Youtz, "Current Essays in Constructive Theology," *The American Journal of Theology* 11, no. 4 (October 1907): 694.

or metaphysics, it provides no material for the system builder. . . . It cannot . . . be wholly in vain to attempt a fresh interpretation of Christian experience in terms of modern intelligence."[6] Once again, the key theme of "reconstruction" emerges, bringing theology into conversation with contemporary science and especially philosophy.

The final very early glimpse of constructive theology comes in a periodical called *The Constructive Quarterly*. Founded in 1913 by Silas McBee, a layperson in the Episcopal Church, the journal brings together an astonishing number and variety of voices from a wide range of traditions. In the introduction to its inaugural issue, McBee writes, "The destructive method has had its full opportunity and will continue to have it and ought to have it. But it has developed no power to unite and is most effective at promoting division. The plan is to bring together members of all Communions who will write constructively of the Christianity they profess and practise in order that others may know their Communion as they themselves would desire to have it known."[7] Again, the same themes as those above emerge: the need for reconstruction in the wake of a prolonged period of destruction, a collaborative effort, and engagement and redefinition of typical theological themes. *The Constructive Quarterly* adds an overarching ecumenism along with a respect for unresolved and perhaps unresolvable differences between the theological voices included. The common agreement is not doctrinal or confessional, but in the commitment to constructing Christianity for new purposes and in the wake of "destruction."

William Porcher DuBose, in the first article contained in the quarterly, illustrates the tension that constructive theology raises with other methods of doing theology. DuBose explains,

> Before venturing upon a construction, or even a constructive treatment, of Christianity, let me first carefully limit and define the term, as I purpose to use it. 'Constructive' and 'construction' may attach either to the verb to construct or to the verb to construe, and these two, though the same in origin, have a very different force in use. I do not undertake to construct but only to construe Christianity. Christianity *is*, and is what it is: I cannot conceive it as at this late day either needing to be or capable of being 'made' or 'made over.'[8]

6. Clarence Augustine Beckwith, *The Realities of Christian Theology: An Interpretation of Christian Experience* (New York: Houghton, Mifflin and Company, 1906), vii.
7. Silas McBee, "Introduction" in *The Constructive Quarterly: A Journal of the Faith, Work, and Thought of Christendom*, vol. 1, ed. Silas McBee (March to December, 1913), 1.
8. William Porcher DuBose, "A Constructive Treatment of Christianity" in ibid., 5.

Constructive theology, as it develops, does in fact push back against the very idea that "Christianity *is*, and is what it is." Early proto-constructive theology seized on the emerging recognition of the constructedness of human institutions, including religion. But it was hesitant to admit that Christianity might be constructed all the way down. DuBose, despite writing for the *Constructive Quarterly*, prefers the term *construe* because it presumes a reality to be construed, rather than something that's a total construction. In fact, the opposite becomes normative for most of constructive theology. Through today, some constructive theologians view their work as construal, but most represent their projects as wholesale construction or reconstruction within the basic framework of Christianity. The extent of the rebuilding needed varies according to the starting doctrine for each theologian and each author's respective tolerance for the extent to which Christianity is viewed to be a cultural construction.

Even though *The Constructive Quarterly* is relatively unknown, the number and variety of contributors, as well as their influence, is impressive. The first volume, March to December 1913, includes articles from important liberal theologians like William Adams Brown, Newman Smyth, Rufus Jones, Shailer Mathews, and others. It is also impressively ecumenical. It includes works from Protestants of many varieties, Roman Catholics, and Eastern Orthodox theologians. There is no one theme to the quarterly. It expresses both doctrinal thinking and engagement with current events along with Christian responses to them. Foreshadowing later developments in constructive theology, *The Constructive Quarterly* establishes a collaborative, ecumenical, positive, theologically constructive tradition in the United States, incorporating disparate theological voices committed to laying a new foundation for Christianity and building a new edifice out of Christian theology.

These early instances of proto-constructive theology never developed into a coherent program. They indicate the emergence of themes that would remain important throughout the constructive theological tradition. Two theologians, James Ten Broeke and Bernard Eugene Meland, offered extended treatments of the advent of "construction" in theology. Turning to their most important works and engaging the evolution of their thought, first Ten Broeke and then Meland, will put into clearer view what defines proto-constructive theology and how those features persist throughout constructive theology's history while evolving into the movement that it is today.

James Ten Broeke

James Ten Broeke is a virtually unknown figure who nonetheless plays a very important part in proto-constructive theology. Most influential in his lifetime as a professor at McMaster University in Ontario,[9] he earned his doctorate at Yale and taught a combination of theology, philosophy, and psychology classes. Ten Broeke only published two books and a handful of articles, most of them reviews of others' work. At McMaster, Ten Broeke was known for being a passionate teacher who gained the admiration of students and offered a much-needed progressive sensibility at a place that was otherwise quite conservative. As Leslie Armor and Elizabeth Trott write in one of the few mentions of Ten Broeke in print, "In spite of McMaster's Baptist biases he was not, in spirit, the evangelical preacher that some of his writing would at first glance suggest. His position, were it fully understood, might have raised the eyebrows of many of his colleagues. . . . He was not a dogmatist. And he was far too interested in the human side of being to let God become just an abstract symbol."[10] In fact, his interest in the human side of things led Ten Broeke to claim that God, at least God in theology, is a constructed symbol, though an important and concrete one with implications for human beings in specific contexts in need of constant revision and reconstruction.[11] His work is firmly based in the liberalism of his time, specifically a Hegelian idealist variety. Yet he emphasizes symbol, interpretation, and above all else, the constructed nature of Christianity and a call for modern human beings to take charge of embracing their own involvement in the construction of Christianity that serves the historical moment.

A Constructive Basis for Theology

Ten Broeke's first and most important book, *A Constructive Basis for Theology* published in 1914, is the inaugural extended treatment of theology that takes construction as its methodological starting point. Ten Broeke does not use the term "constructive theology" to refer to his work. It is transitional. He introduces a constructive element as constitutive of his method of doing systematic theology. At the same time,

9. Leslie Armour and Elizabeth Trott, *The Faces of Reason: An Essay on Philosophy and Culture in English Canada 1850–1951* (Waterloo, Ontario: Wilfrid Laurier Press, 1981), 354–60.
10. Ibid., 359.
11. James Ten Broeke, *A Constructive Basis for Theology* (London: Macmillan and Co., 1914), 51.

he notes that systematic theology has already in many ways fallen out of favor, as the epigraph above attests. The central claim of *A Constructive Basis for Theology* is one that persists as a question throughout the history of constructive theology. In the preface, Ten Broeke states, "The attempt is made to show that modern as compared with ancient thought affords a superior constructive basis for Christian faith, making it possible to form a theology that shall effectively promote present religious life."[12] The question arises again and again, at least implicitly, whether contemporary forms of thought, especially philosophy, provide a better basis entirely as the foundation of Christian theology. The answer specific constructive theologians give to this question varies, some opting for classical philosophical underpinnings while incorporating modern insights, others completely replacing the traditional "orthodox" philosophical basis of theology.

Part I of *A Constructive Basis for Theology* offers a cursory history of Christianity and Christian theology. Much of the narrative Ten Broeke offers has been revised, revisited, or completely rejected in studies of church history that have happened since. His claims are interesting but not overall that useful, most being overly reductive. Ten Broeke, after all, was not primarily a church historian. The second two parts, however, offer his own method. Most basically, Ten Broeke argues for revealing the theological already inherent in certain of his contemporary philosophical and academic movements. He characterizes Christianity as nothing more than a "conception" that is "a sort of mental tool or instrument constructed by the individual thinker for dealing with experience." "A conception arises in connection with the needs of life and becomes a rule of acting; it is both a formulation of the modes of former conduct and an anticipation of the future, a map, a chart of life, trustworthy so long as it successfully serves us in our activity but always leaving the way open for a new and unique experience."[13] These seemingly unassuming statements in fact lay the foundation for constructive theology. Ten Broeke, in claiming Christianity to be nothing more than a "conception," a useful construct, throws open the possibility of a complete refashioning and reworking of Christian theology. Using imagery that would be echoed by the Workgroup on Constructive Theology in 2005, he likens Christian theology to a map that is meant to guide modern experience instrumentally. He somewhat boldly, in calling Christianity a conception, proposes that

12. Ibid., v.
13. Ibid., 51.

for him Christian theology should be largely pragmatic in nature. He recognizes that doctrines as encountered in Christianity are wholly constructed and human-made, the content of which is ultimately dispensable when it ceases to be useful.

Seizing on the contemporary philosophy of the early twentieth century, Ten Broeke quietly introduces the claim that Christian theology doesn't necessarily describe an externally existent reality. Against DuBose's idea of a "construal" above, Ten Broeke goes so far as to suggest that construction is in fact the right word. Dogmatic and systematic theology before sought to reveal a structure that objectively exists apart from human mental activity. The task of the theologian was to discern the structures of Christianity that were already there because they were created by God and are eternal. The constructive basis for theology, as Ten Broeke argues for it, embraces the constructed nature of Christian theology. He puts it more strongly later, arguing, "Let it be remembered, however, that every meaning is necessarily the personal interpretation of some thinker reflecting upon what is given for constructive thought. . . . In the nature of the case, Christianity, as a system of objective judgments called theology is man's product; it is even a personal construction, serving as a guide, primarily of the individual, but also of the religious community."[14] Not only Christian theology, but Christianity is "man's product." Reinterpreting Christianity for new times and new contexts is not only necessary but inevitable. He pushes specifically for marrying Christian theology with contemporary philosophy in a way that accepts its synthetic nature and reinvigorates theology as a useful endeavor for his contemporary Christian compatriots.

Situated in the early twentieth century as he was, Ten Broeke identifies four bases on which his own personal constructive theological method relies. The first is a Hegelian inflected absolute idealism. Hegelianism is evident throughout *A Constructive Basis for Theology*, providing both the justification for interrogating knowledge about Christianity and Christian theology and its constructedness as well as the model for many of its most problematic historical hypotheses. The second is pluralism, which he defines obscurely. The third, theism, he claims as a synthesis of the first two, and the fourth is an emphasis on "limiting knowledge to phenomena and putting in the place of knowledge of God symbols of values which arise from a reflection upon feel-

14. Ibid., 74.

ing, while thought continually strives to formulate these symbols of values that shall be the most useful and effective in the conduct of life."[15] This final point, the most important, argues for an empirically based theology, insofar as the material for interpretation are symbols and values rather than any objective knowledge of God. The orientation is pragmatic in nature and fallibilist, calling for constant reevaluation and reformulation of these symbols and values used to capture changing understandings of God. The importance of culture and especially symbol will carry over into Bernard Eugene Meland, who worked throughout his career to establish these things as central to his own constructive theological project, the one that would come to be identified as the origin of constructive theology as we know it today.

The most important thing for constructive theology to emerge in *A Constructive Basis of Theology* is the idea, paired with the constructed nature of Christianity and its theology, that *re*construction is needed in the wake of an extended period of *de*struction.

> Negations and destructive criticism are comparatively easy, but what is being done towards a really new theological construction of a systematic character? Shall we simply continue to pull down the old house without being sure that we are able to build a better? Or shall we make not too radical changes and live in the old house still? It seems as though the most one may reasonably hope to do is to form some temporary abode, using whatever material is at hand. In the present condition of things, it is to be expected that a good working hypothesis serviceable in the conduct of the individual and social religious life is about all that can be obtained without becoming dogmatic. Whether theology can ever be more than such an hypothesis is itself a problem. There is also good ground for expecting that the present affords much that is favourable to the construction of a theological view that will serve the religious life of the present, for the theology of each generation springs out of its complex life, and that life itself is largely the fruit of what has gone before.[16]

In many cases throughout its history, the term "constructive" theology is a bit of a misnomer. In fact, within representative texts, it is very often more appropriate to talk about "reconstructive" theology. This terminology carries through the tradition from *Contentio Veritatis*, *The Constructive Quarterly*, and this extended formulation in *A Constructive Basis for Theology* all the way through to contemporary constructive

15. Ibid., 291.
16. Ibid., 248–49.

theologies. Constructive theology is not accommodationist in the same way as liberal theology. Even though early constructive theology holds much in common with liberal theology, and in many cases may be considered a branch of it, the foundation is laid for a reengagement and rewriting of the doctrines of Christianity rather than an attempt at linking up the liberal cultural project with Christianity. This is an important distinction.

Ten Broeke writes against the backdrop of systematic theology. Yet he claims that the systematization of theology makes it less faithful to Christianity. "It should be remembered, however, that in proportion as a theological system becomes all-inclusive, it becomes in part at least unfaithful to the concrete religious experience which is the true reality. There must be, then, a proper relation between theology and life."[17] Ten Broeke sees himself as in the systematic tradition not because it accurately represents his method but because the theological context had accepted systematic reflection as the way one does theology. The constructive basis for theology resists all-inclusive systematization because it doesn't accurately reflect either life or Christianity. While Ten Broeke doesn't go so far as to deny absolutely that there may be an objective reality to Christianity, he does argue that theologians betray it when trying to force thinking about Christianity into one comprehensive container. One of the most important results of this rejection of theological comprehensiveness is an openness to alternative, perhaps even contradictory, claims within theology itself: "The different results of theological thinking are not regrettable, for they may be regarded as signs of real and varied experiences which cannot be entirely embodied in fixed objective formulas. It is rather a condition of vital religious experience that the theological activity of the mind should be made constantly to serve, however variously, in subordination to the living faith."[18] Within the constructive theological method of Ten Broeke, plurality of theological opinion is a good thing. Theology that doesn't leave room for such disagreements is dishonest and, importantly, not Christian, or at least not faithful to Christian religious experience. In the wake of so much "destruction" of Christianity, theology faces a remarkably potent moment. With old "orthodoxies" gone, a fresh platform for constructing theology that relates to the contemporary world and accounts for pluralistic Christian experience reveals itself. The constructive basis for doing theology, accord-

17. Ibid., 377.
18. Ibid.

ing to Ten Broeke, is an important and powerful moment for Christian theology, not a liability.

Features of Ten Broeke's Proto-Constructive Theology

Assembling the various parts of Ten Broeke's proposed new philosophically based Christian theology gives a general idea of what his constructive theology turns out to be. First, and most importantly, Ten Broeke argues that Christianity is a "conception," not an objective reality itself. Casting Christianity as a conception rejects the descriptive nature of systematic theology. As a conception, then, Christian theology is "man-made." Of course, all Christian theology has always been made by human beings, and theology has acknowledged that fact throughout its history. The concept of *analogia fidei* embodies the concession that all theology is ultimately insufficient human speech about the divine. Second, Ten Broeke's idea of Christian theology being a human endeavor, linked with Christianity being a conception, gives human beings greater license in deciding what theology must do and how it can do it. In particular, Ten Broeke's emphasis on the synthetic nature of Christian theology aligns it with other cultural manifestations that lent themselves to humanistic intellectual interrogation. Building on the first two principles, Ten Broeke's constructive theology is fallibilist and pragmatic. This fallibilism in turn creates not only an acceptance of pluralistic theological expressions but the absolute need for it. If no single theology can possibly be right in every way, if theology never truly encapsulates the whole of the conception of Christianity, then multiple perspectives and opinions will be not only a fact, but absolutely necessary to do justice to Christianity itself. In a sense, theologies do not compete against one another. No single system can claim to be the central explication of Christianity. Christian theology must be constructed by many voices that are in tension with one another, yet building upon each others' claims and discourses. Seeing Christian theology as pragmatic also emphasizes the importance of Christianity remaining relevant and engaged with ongoing cultural developments and crises. Finally, Ten Broeke's constructive basis for theology asserts that "reconstruction" is needed after an extended period of "destruction." For him, which will not be true of all constructive theologians, contemporary philosophies provide a better foundation upon which to build Christian theology than ancient ones. In any case, reconstruction after destruction is an ecumenical, progressive, intentional project that accepts the criticism that has been levied against Christianity but still sees value in the doctrinal loci upon which Christianity has traditionally been built.

The acceptance of the ongoing "destruction" of parts of Christianity is crucial. Constructive theology is not reactionary in the sense that it tries to defend against such destruction. Instead it embraces it and sees the potential for stronger, more inclusive, more relevant Christianity to be reconstructed in its wake. Extended periods of "destruction," later called "deconstruction" in a postmodern context, are frequently noted in constructive theologies. Sometimes, but not usually, this is lamented. Usually, constructive theology heralds it as an opportunity to rethink Christianity from the bottom up, structurally rethinking theology from the perspective of human beings, and later specifically marginalized human beings and creation. Constructive theology makes deconstruction an internal project. Destruction, therefore, holds as crucial a place in constructive theology as construction, whether undertaken internally or externally. The tutors from Oxford, Silas McBee and the *Constructive Quarterly*, and Ten Broeke all realize this fact and, rather than lamenting the assault on Christianity, dive into the potential.

Finally, in concluding with Ten Broeke and turning to Meland, the cruciality of culture and symbol must be recognized. Ten Broeke refers to what he calls "social consciousness" as the site at which people construct religion, in his case, specifically Christianity. They do this within language and in conversation with the various other aspects of culture in which they are immersed. Importantly, the social consciousness or culture of different groups of believers inevitably results in many different kinds of Christianity. Ten Broeke praises this fact, saying, "whatever this Christian social consciousness accepts and acts upon is, for that community, the truth which must be accepted by him who would be accounted as holding the truth 'as it was once delivered to the saints.'"[19] Faith isn't ultimately accountable to the experiences of the early church. Ten Broeke claims that contemporary philosophy is in some sense closer to the philosophy of the early church before it was infiltrated by ancient Greek philosophy, and this is one of his weaker and more dispensable arguments. But the claim that Christian theology should be held responsible to its contemporary culture and never accepted as a completed project, a done fact, is crucial for Ten

19. Ibid., 262.

Broeke, as it is for Meland and other constructive theologians. Just as culture and circumstances construct communities in contingent ways that are always in flux, a modern insight at the time of Meland, culture constructs Christianity through the interaction of symbols, signs, authority, experience, and interpretation.[20] These things, as delivered to contemporary human beings, are as legitimate for the reconstruction of Christian theology as the context of the early church was for the "saints."

Ten Broeke was not a great writer. *A Constructive Basis for Theology* lapses from cogent prose into half-finished ideas that are obscurely and unhelpfully summarized. Partly, this may have had to do with his location at a Baptist school in rural Canada that had a strong interest in retaining what had come to be called "orthodoxy," stifling Ten Broeke's more radical leanings. It also may be that his greatest talents were as a teacher rather than a researcher and writer of books. He brought a cosmopolitan and progressive sensibility to McMaster, an attitude that was apparently much needed and appreciated by students as evidenced by his only serious posthumous analysis being in the context of how he personally affected others who would go on to be more influential. He has an interest in Christian history but uses it somewhat haphazardly and superficially. Ten Broeke matters because he raises the question of a constructive basis as the controlling method for doing theology. He challenges systematics, though he doesn't seem to have completely realized he did so himself. Perhaps the conservative environment of rural Canada and pressures not to go too far outside the fray tempered some of his more radical statements. Regardless, despite not gaining much name recognition, Ten Broeke provides the foundation for constructive theology. Whether Meland knew about Ten Broeke's *A Constructive Basis for Theology* is unclear, though he probably didn't. At the same time, the cultural and historical realities to which the two responded are similar. Ten Broeke deserves more credit than he receives, which is presently none. Nonetheless, Meland is the consensus founder of constructive theology.

Bernard Eugene Meland

Bernard Eugene Meland straddles many different worlds in theology. Most basically he stands on the cusp of two generations of Chicago School liberalism.[21] He spent much of the beginning of his career work-

20. Ibid.

ing closely with Henry Nelson Wieman, but makes a distinct break with him on questions of epistemology and with what exactly theology engages. Meland chooses to take up the intersection of culture and Christianity while Wieman sought to establish scientifically empirical ways of confirming God's actions in the universe. Like Ten Broeke, Meland's academic interests ranged from theology and philosophy of religion to psychology and sociology. With his Chicago forebears, Meland initially sought to unite scientific empiricism with theological thought. The scientific theological method of other Chicago theologians like Wieman sought to discern the actions of God as revealed in the workings of the universe. With the right method and attuned to the right sort of phenomena in line with historical attestations to revelation like the Bible, those things that occur in the universe that are a direct result of God's action can be identified, according to the school of theology Meland worked with at the beginning of his career.

Meland and Chicago School Liberalism

Early in his career Meland published widely in theology and religion journals. He wrote his first substantive book with Wieman in 1936, titled *American Philosophies of Religion*. This first book outlines what Wieman and Meland saw as the contemporary philosophies available to be employed in the service of writing theologies that were intellectually viable in the modern age. The overall breakdown includes supernaturalism, idealism, romanticism, and naturalism. Breaking these down further, both Meland and Wieman identify themselves as "empirical theists." Meland writes, "The key insight into this mode of thought lies in the idea that man has been produced by the natural universe, and that through healthful relations with its environing processes, he may fulfill his life."[22] For several books Meland includes himself uncomfortably in the company of his Chicago teachers. Of the four available options, naturally Meland and Wieman identify their own, empirical theism, to be the most important and useful for Christian theology. Yet later in his career Meland's theology would come more to resemble the "eclectic theology" identified in *American Philosophies of Religion*. "If the requirements of the most noble living results in a philosophy which does not fit into a neat system, then so much the worse for the neat

21. Dorrien, *The Making of American Liberal Theology*, 98.
22. Henry Nelson Wieman and Bernard Eugene Meland, *American Philosophies of Religion* (Chicago: Willet, Clark & Company, 1936), 272.

system. While these men want to achieve a coherent system so far as they can, they will sacrifice it if the best interests of human living seem to require it."[23] Notably, Wieman and Meland include Clarence Beckwith in this category; he was mentioned earlier as another proto-constructive theologian. This eclectic theology is described as theology that mediates between three emergent concerns: between traditions of religious living that are shaped by tradition and new perspectives in modern life, between the needs of the church and those who have left it or see it as dispensable within Christianity, and between new moral positions and longstanding modes of action within Christianity.[24] This form of eclectic theology is decidedly liberal. It mediates because it refuses to accept the destruction that has occurred as a result of recent critical work on Christianity and Christian theology. It tries to reconcile rather than reconstruct. Later, Meland would distance himself from the empiricism of his teachers, instead incorporating the concern for the distinctiveness of Christian language and epistemology as embodied by these eclectic theologians, while embracing the insights of the social sciences and psychology that he absorbed through the Chicago School's emphasis on employing modern scientific techniques.

Meland's mature theology is famously eclectic. Later analysis of his work struggles to settle on a single term that captures the wide variety of approaches and concerns that guided his method. This is in large part because later readers inevitably try to place Meland in some way within the liberal tradition. In fact, however, Meland accepts the contributions of liberal theology, but takes up the constructive turn in theology. Meland identified himself as within the liberal tradition, but qualified it with the disillusioned correction of realism in the wake of crisis, and by emphasizing the importance of culture. His distinctive proposition for theology is a method and set of concerns that are thoroughly constructive. This important turn first occurs, fittingly, in *The Reawakening of Christian Faith*, and solidifies in *Faith and Culture*, often considered his most programmatic text.

The Reawakening of Christian Faith: Meland's Split from Wieman

The Reawakening of Christian Faith, published in 1949, collects Meland's Clark lectures at Pomona College given in 1947. From the very start

23. Ibid., 157.
24. Ibid.

of the book, Meland marks his break from the empiricism of Wieman that he identified himself with in *American Philosophies of Religion*: "Once one is seized by the disturbing idea that reason and observation give only truncated accounts of existence, one is no longer able to be complacently empirical, nor content to remain inhospitable to imaginative efforts to comprehend the human problem in its vaster context."[25] One overlaying theme in the book is that of mystery and tragedy. Of course, Meland's liberal theology, like everyone else's, had to be tempered by the Second World War and the advent of the nuclear age. Even apart from that history, though, Meland never fit as snugly in the category of empirical theist as it seemed. *The Reawakening of Christian Faith* finds him repeatedly characterizing empiricism as complacent and superficial. The lectures are aimed at dispelling the enchantment that not only theology, but culture as a whole, had with science as the controlling mode of thought in the United States. He responds by delving into symbol, culture, mystery, and most importantly, their construction. Meland always had a mystical streak and took Christian worship seriously.[26] Combining his critique of empiricism with what he perceives as the importance of the symbolic nature of Christianity, Meland turns to construction.

In the preface of *The Reawakening of Christian Faith*, Meland describes Christianity as an "imaginative adventure."[27] Linking up Christianity with literary expressions at the time, Meland comes around to his theology by first analyzing various contemporary fictional narratives and poems. Like many other constructive theologians who come after him, Meland dips into the cultural well of the literary in order to illuminate or reinvigorate Christian thinking. He writes, "I have come around through this by-path of literary citation, in part, because I see these literary figures as our most eloquent spokesman for the mood that has urged upon us a new theological approach to the human problem."[28] Facing disillusioned liberalism, along with his own disillusionment with empiricism, Meland begins to work out his own theological method. He starts with "mythological naturalism." Mythological naturalism rejects one-to-one correspondence between scientific models and experiential concepts as humans encounter them. Benjamin Miller, a theologian who studied Meland and argued for mythological

25. Bernard Meland, *The Reawakening of Christian Faith* (New York: Macmillan, 1947), viii.
26. Dorrien, *The Making of American Liberal Theology*, 104.
27. Meland, *The Reawakening of Christian Faith*, x.
28. Ibid., 33.

naturalism, writes, "the justification of conceptual thinking is two fold. First, it is an essential medium by which we may have knowledge of the continuity in time of experienced realities. It is by means of concepts that we distinguish the before, the now, and the hereafter. Concepts freeze the moments of our awareness and relate them in a non-empirical context."[29] This idea of concept calls to mind Ten Broeke's assertion that Christianity is a concept. Indeed, Meland and Miller call for the same reenvisioning of Christianity and culture as Ten Broeke. Science and liberalism have led to a spiritual dead end, as well as a possible literal dead end for humanity. Reengaging the myths of Christianity, and reconceptualizing its tenets, provides a theological next step that accepts the damning critiques against liberalism while rejecting "supernaturalism," that is, a return to conservative, authoritative, dogmatic theologies.

His indication of "disillusioned liberalism" is certainly a reference to Reinhold Niebuhr, though he rejects Niebuhr's perceived supernaturalism. Meland comes down somewhere oddly in between liberalism and supernaturalism, even if "supernaturalism" isn't a fair characterization of Niebuhr. Tyron Inbody notes the dramatic shift in Meland's work after 1945, partially in response to tragedy and partially in response to the rise of Christian realism and the challenge of Niebuhr. Early Meland alongside Wieman cast the theology of Niebuhr and other realists as well as that of the Barthians as "new supernaturalism."[30] Meland realized his own place as being between Niebuhrian realism and Chicago school naturalism at this time, first projecting himself in the role of constructive theologian as a result. Drawing on his penchant for mysticism and his interest in evocative language, including literature, poetry, and within the context of religion, myth, Meland moved away from the liberalism of his Chicago mentors. At the same time, he guards against what he sees as a slippage back into authoritative, even tyrannical, and importantly, irrational supernatural theistic Christianity. Constructive theology presents itself as Meland's method that anchors itself in myth, culture, a response to crisis, and an openness to change in theology, manifest in his engagement with process philosophy.

29. Benjamin Miller, "Mythological Naturalism," *Journal of Religion* 22, no. 3 (1942): 281.
30. Tyron Inbody, *The Constructive Theology of Bernard Meland: Postliberal Empirical Realism* (Atlanta: Scholars Press, 1995), 33.

Meland's Early Definition of Constructive Theology

In this shift, constructive theology as it has come to be known is born. The constructive theology that many contemporary theologians trace back to Meland starts with *The Reawakening of Christian Faith,* and is developed through *Faith and Culture*, and finally *The Realities of Faith. The Reawakening of Christian Faith* offers a succinct, though not complete, definition of constructive theology: "Constructive theology, in so far as it pursues a formulation of the cognitive meanings of the Christian faith in the context of structural meanings that provide intelligibility in our time, has no alternative but to follow the procedure that has given rise to systematic theology in former periods of reconstruction—namely, of setting the sentiments of the Christian myth in the philosophical context that elaborates the controlling idea."[31] This packed definition offers a few points worth noting:

1. "Constructive theology . . . pursues a formulation of the cognitive meanings of the Christian faith"—this posits the nature of Christian faith, as expounded in Christian theology, as being anchored in mental, linguistic processes, not an independently existent reality; it is unintelligible otherwise.
2. "In the context of structural meanings that provide intelligibility in our time"—again, this draws on the emergent insight that all important sociological and cultural systems are ultimately constructed and contingent. Constructive theology engages the contingent, structural, discursive facts of the moment in which it is written.
3. "Has no alternative but to follow the procedure that has given rise to systematic theology"—though this sounds like a reluctant reversion to systematic theology, in fact it is the same, often begrudging as here, accommodation to traditional doctrinal loci of Christian systematic theology. It does not, however, ascribe to systematization.

These are the three central conceits of constructive theology throughout its history. Caught between liberalism that didn't work anymore and the specter of reemergent authoritarian Christianity, Meland forges a distinct constructive theological method that seats Christian theology in human-made cognitive structures, couched in the culture

31. Meland, *The Reawakening of Christian Faith*, 89.

and crises of its time. As a method, it resembles but departs from its forebear—systematic theology.

This definition of theology sneaks by so quietly it doesn't at first blush appear to be particularly worth noting. Meland, however, offers a stark analogy that captures how momentous the potential is for such an unassuming method: "One will see from this analysis that the current theological situation has many facets. One who views it simply as a head-on collision between neo-orthodoxy and liberalism is overlooking one of the real intellectual dramas of history. He is missing an earthquake in his preoccupation with a squall of wind. The import of this new constructive mood that is upon us is, I believe, as significant as that."[32] For Meland, the dispute between liberalism and "neo-Orthodox" theologians is mostly a distraction from the real intellectual shift occurring in culture. Indeed, constructive theological method, though keeping a low profile, has supplanted both liberalism and neo-orthodoxy as *the* method for progressive Christian theology. But it has done so unassumingly. Caught between liberal theology and neo-orthodoxy in its early days, constructive theology can resemble both, but its emphases and method are distinctly its own. *The Reawakening of Christian Faith* is the origin of what can officially be called "constructive theology," the first coalescence of the flashes of insight in Oxford, McBee, and Broeke, and the first, but certainly not the last, programmatic statement of one of the most important contemporary theological traditions.

Myth and Construction in Culture and Theology

This first formulation of constructive theology bases itself firmly in myth. Meland argues that myth is the "basic controlling construct" of culture.[33] The recovery of myth as central for theology echoes Niebuhrian and Tillichian critiques of liberalism. Yet his idea of myth expands beyond simply the incredible stories of the Christian biblical tradition. Myths abound in human culture and cultures are governed by mythological "controlling ideas." As Meland explains, "All of culture at any given period of time is shaped and, as it were, is held within an ideological orbit by some luminous insight, out of which forms a distinctive pattern of thinking."[34] Myths are narratives that govern

32. Ibid., 53.
33. Ibid., 87.
34. Ibid.

behavior and the ways a culture, and as a result people within a culture, thinks about itself. Controlling myths can be religious in nature or not. Part of the crisis of liberal theology and the supernaturalist reaction arises because the controlling idea, the myth of culture, changed. Liberalism worked with the myth of what Meland and his peers called scientific empiricism, a variety of crass naturalism that prioritized technological advance and the supremacy of scientific reasoning above all else. This myth proved to be not only morally bankrupt but devastating with the occurrence of two world wars. "Supernaturalists" recovered the importance of religious myth, but according to Meland, problematically lost sight of the human imagination's role in formulating those myths, asserting an uncritical and unhistorical factuality for them. A return to unthinking acceptance of the myths of Christianity as being true in a basic sense, apart from human cognition, is a complete nonstarter for Meland. The proper place for religious myth, then, comes in recognizing its reliance on human reasoning, what would later come to be called discursive reasoning. This recognition in turn leads to a commitment to intentional, reflective, responsible myth constructing in a Christian mode. Meland's concept of myth recognizes the contingency of all cultural norms and proposes that, if Christianity is to be relevant and influential in a post-scientific empiricist age, Christian theology must engage myth and construct around traditional sites of Christian thinking within the controlling idea, the myths of culture.

Controlling myths are always in competition with one another. Constructive theology as developed by Meland tries to develop controlling Christian myths that best confront ongoing realities as they present themselves in the world. Controlling myths do not have to be Christian, or even religious. Though Meland argues that culture has one controlling myth at any given time, postmodern criticism and a growing awareness of marginalization and intersectionality amongst many groups would draw attention to the fact that any culture in fact has many controlling myths, which may or may not apply to any given group within that culture. Meland's idea of controlling myth would come to be developed in later constructive theologies as being specifically for progressive Christians coping with contemporary culture and crises. Contemporary constructive theologies tend to develop certain imaginative developments of doctrines as proposals for controlling myths that allow Christians to orient their beliefs and behaviors in the context of the culture and crises they experience in the place and time they find themselves.

Myths for Meland serve as the narrative embodiment of the constructedness of culture and Christianity. Crucially, though, myth has no definitive meaning.[35] Myths are open to reinterpretation and revision. Myths, as constructs, delineate what has value in a culture, what people should do, and what their most important beliefs are. The onus falls back on the reader or cultural actor as interpreter rather than on the myth as literally true narrative, or even metaphorically but univocally true story. Myths cannot be abandoned in Christian theology because myths persist whether they are recognized as such or not. That is to say, myths are not simply incredible stories that modern reason and rationality reject because of a commitment to the coherent intelligibility of the universe. Myths are the very fabric of culture and society, of religion, and everyone operates under some mythical framework. Meland takes myth and recovers it as the religious, literary, narrative expression of the role Christianity has to play in accepting its responsibility as an important driver of ethical, cultural, and spiritual behavior in his modern into postmodern context.

Faith and Culture sees Meland integrating the language of his lesser-known constructive theology forebears. Reconstruction, destruction, and crisis become the language of Meland. But the destruction to which Meland reacts is not an Enlightenment withering of the incredible or supernatural elements of historical Christianity. Instead, Christian realism as embodied by Niebuhr has destroyed the liberal basis on which progressive theology had been conceived. As the title *The Reawakening of Faith* implies, Meland sees the "re-creation of liberalism" embodied in reclaiming the centrality of faith. The initial liberal preoccupation with taking reason and experience as central sources for doing theology, which remains Dorrien's definition of liberal theology as noted above, fell short. Recovering faith as a central Christian category and recognizing the importance of myth become the hallmarks of Meland's theological method. Drawing heavily on cultural anthropology and psychology, Meland details how faith and religion, unattached from the hostility and bias of recent generations against religious experience as legitimate data for interpretation, have come to be recognized as constitutive parts of the cultural worldview of human beings, as much or more than anything else. Christianity and its myths constitute a major part of the structures of experience. After recognizing this place for Christianity within modern culture, Meland claims

35. Meland, *The Reawakening of Christian Faith*, 69.

theologians have an immense task before them: analyzing the state of Christian faith through its deep historical resources, reasserting the importance of mystery and holistic complexity to Christian experience, and offering a complete reconception and reconstruction of Christianity through its theological tradition.

In *Faith and Culture*, Meland declares that he seeks to institute "sanity" in Christian theology, not "reasonableness."[36] Sanity, he argues, does not require the same strict adherence to restricted rationality that he thinks has pervaded and corrupted the generation before him. "Sanity," he writes, "does not presuppose a completely rational order of existence. It simply implies a margin of rationality in the midst of irrational and unpredictable factors which, nevertheless, assures sufficient order and meaningfulness to enable us to function intelligibly in a context of related disciplines."

When speaking of the constructed nature of Christianity, it is important to note that this does not mean that the structures are always rationally or cognitively known; quite the opposite in many cases. Constructive theology, as Meland illustrates, purports to engage with irrational societal structures, the affective or precognizant discourses that govern our behavior in everyday life. The non-rational nature of the structures of Christianity as Meland proposes them relates to insights in other disciplines at the time *Faith and Culture* was written, especially the social sciences and psychology. He introduces the concept of "depth" as a metaphor for the structural analysis he seeks to bring to Christian theology. He likens it to "*gestalt*" theory in psychology and analogizes it to new varieties of philosophy. In short, "depth" asserts the non-rational relationality of human beings and human experience. Discernible structures do govern human experience, not least in Christianity. But these structures are complexly and inextricably intertwined in a way that science and rationalism cannot adequately account for and which demands openness to ambiguity, irrationality, and revision. All levels of experience overlap and influence one another. Christianity must recognize itself in this web of interactions and learn to self-reflexively participate constructively.

In order to work out the nonrational nature of Christianity in a way that lends itself to reconstruction, Meland takes up the question of the "immanence" of God. Rejecting the reaffirmed transcendence of God as encountered in neo-orthodoxy, Meland believes the liberal assertion of

36. Bernard Eugene Meland, *Faith and Culture* (Carbondale: Southern Illinois University Press, 1953), 33.

the immanence of God should be reaffirmed but rethought. The immanence of God does not mean that God is only experienced in rational ways in history, however. He speaks of properly uniting "depth" and "rationality." He draws extensively on Whitehead to develop this view of the complexity of experience and relationality in the world, buying into his "new metaphysics" that calls to mind Ten Broeke's insistence that new philosophies can serve as a better foundation for Christian theology than ancient ones. Indeed, this is an overarching assertion of process theology, and much of process theology falls within the constructive domain. At the same time, Meland affirms that process theology is not the only manifestation of the recovery of the irrational interrelatedness of reality in the structures of human experience. The overall academic *geist* at the time, and into ours, reasserts the complexity of human structures and experiences against the clean modernist discursive project. Meland recovers the messy, open-ended nature of human experience and insists that Christian theology must recover this sense in its overall effort to reconstruct a liberal, as Meland calls it, theology.

Meland's Constructive Theology and Theological Liberalism

In Meland, constructive theology is born out of tragedy as a repudiation of liberalism. *The Reawakening of Christian Faith* presents this repudiation rather unequivocally. *Faith and Culture* reigns in Meland's departure from liberalism, claiming his own work as a contribution to a "renascent liberal spirit in a chastened and realistic mood."[37] Meland retains liberalism because he finds supernaturalism completely intolerable. Though in retrospect those he has in mind, like Reinhold Niebuhr, are themselves best viewed as within the liberal tradition, the passion with which they blasted their liberal predecessors gave the initial and much repeated feeling that they sought to return to some variety of Christianity that relied on old doctrine and external authority like the Bible and tradition. The departure, in my view, of Meland from liberal theology arises because of his explicit abandonment of reason and experience as the normative sources for doing Christian theology. Constructive theology has a penchant for recovering tradition and scripture in ways that liberal theology had abandoned, to a greater or lesser extent, throughout its history. Meland and many constructive theologians may not necessarily agree with the characteriza-

37. Ibid., v.

tion of constructive theology as having left the sphere of liberalism. Though Meland sought to rehabilitate liberalism, I believe he initiated a new tradition altogether. That tradition is not, however, unrelated to liberalism. This is in part the reason Meland has sometimes even been described as "post-liberal," including in Inbody's monograph. Like other "post" movements, the implication is that, though it moves beyond, it is in many ways still anchored in answering the questions raised by the movement before it. As Dorrien points out, the more famous postliberalism associated with Yale is a different, though related, variety of theology entirely.[38] Postliberalism has a conservative or recovery strain that doesn't sync with constructive theology, though the two share many similarities and there is sufficient room for crossover and sharing. Postliberalism seeks to recover tradition and reassert its primacy within Christian culture. Constructive theology recognizes the potential of constructing anew on the foundations of Christian tradition.

Meland both is and is not a liberal theologian. He oscillates throughout his career. Clearly he began as a liberal, specifically a Chicago school empiricist liberal. With *The Reawakening of Christian Faith* he breaks with his immediate predecessors. Yet in *Faith and Culture* he recovers the term liberalism, but abandons the methodological assumptions of liberalism as well as its conclusions. This ambivalence is key. Meland founds constructive theology, coins the term as one that would stick for many generations after him. Yet he couldn't himself imagine the liberal project to be over, which indeed it wasn't and still isn't. Constructive theology, as it develops in Meland and since, is a friendly competitor with liberal theology. They share political concerns, and important critiques of the "orthodox" Christian tradition. But they deviate crucially in method and sources, as well as, ultimately, their conclusions. To conclude that liberal theology is modernist and constructive theology is postmodernist doesn't quite summarize the divide either. Both liberal theology and constructive theology have modern and postmodern expressions. But constructive theology takes postmodernism further and incorporates it more fully. Meland sits right on the cusp, between liberal theology and constructive theology, between modernism and postmodernism, between liberalism and neo-orthodoxy. Because Meland sits both so uncomfortably and so fluently between all of these competing theological starting points, he holds a

38. Dorrien, *The Making of American Liberal Theology*, 530.

special place in constructive theology. Like many foundational figures, he is transitional, having a foot both in what he departs from and what he starts. Meland sows what the Workgroup on Constructive Theology and later constructive theologians would reap in terms of the mood and method of constructive theology.

Meland writes poetically, if not always terribly clearly. His interest in myth itself stresses the importance of poetics and narrative in reconstructing Christian theology. He warns against theology's propensity to over exaggerate its own importance, but he asserts the absolute centrality of theology being "in part, a poetic enterprise."[39] Christian theology cannot content itself with being dry rhetoric that has no appeal to the broader community of Christians, or truly, to culture at large. In taking up questions of the intensities of human experience and interpreting it, giving meaning and value to structures of experience, Christian theology cannot shy away from proposing theological arguments in deep, literary language. Symbol, metaphor, and analogy are the proper language of theology and do a better job of capturing the non-rational character of theology, even while relating it to the intelligible aspects of the structure as analyzed by theology and other disciplines. Myth is the primary language of religion, whether Christianity or other religions. Even supposedly non-religious controlling metaphors of culture are examples of myth. Constructive theology must be doubly poetic. It must engage with this primary language as well as other narrative testimonies to the structural experiences of human beings both within and without Christianity (mostly within for Meland, though Sallie McFague and others will emphasize the necessity of those without) while also employing poetic language in rebuilding the theological edifice of Christianity. Constructive theology is a literary, language-based creative process that doesn't shy away from poetic license, in fact asserts its centrality in constructing meaningful, deep theology that accurately and unreductively represents the potent ambiguity of Christian experience and belief.

Proto-Constructive Theology: Method and Legacy

These early instances of constructive theology clearly do not have a coherent project in mind. It seems that for the most part the various projects that claim constructive nomenclature were unaware of one another, even though there is significant overlap of certain individuals

39. Meland, *The Reawakening of Christian Faith*, 50.

involved in the conversation. But they are united by concerns and commitments in method. This arose from the broader intellectual environment of the early twentieth century, especially in its liberal expressions, but also in the modern insight of the contingent, constructed nature of all human institutions, especially in psychology and the social sciences. Proto-constructive theology can be summarized as the early insights that Christian constructive theology should:

1. Acknowledge the ongoing, unfinished nature of Christian theology.
2. Accept, without indignation, the "destruction" that has been wrought by various movements both inside and outside Christianity of traditional Christian theological structures and beliefs.
3. Refuse to be satisfied with the state of Christianity in ruins, incredible and irrelevant to the present.
4. Likewise refuse to retreat into authoritarian "orthodoxy."
5. Be primarily non-confessional, unlike dogmatic theology.
6. Be more than descriptive, like systematic theology tends to be.
7. Be ecumenical, open to engaging the same themes across denominational lines without defensiveness (ideally).
8. Consider understanding the structures of experience, in a potent way manifest through myth though not solely so, a first step in the effort to reconstruct theology.
9. Acknowledge that reason and experience cannot sustain Christian theology alone as primary theological sources.
10. Acknowledge that (re)Constructing theology must be an intentional project.
11. Be fallibilist in realizing that any theology that currently seems true may ultimately be proved to be less so, relating back to number one.

These early concerns remain remarkably consistent throughout the rest of constructive theology's history through the present. Meland names constructive theology, but the foundation for it was laid twenty years before he received his doctorate. Capitalizing on advances in knowledge about the structures of human culture and society while viewing Christianity as having undergone a period of destruction, proto-constructive theologians, including Ten Broeke and Meland, introduced the basic characteristics that would infiltrate in various guises the next hundred years of doing theology.

The relationship between constructive theology and liberal theology is conflicted. All of these early instances of constructive theology react in some way against liberal theology. Constructive theology, like neo-orthodoxy and Christian realism, recognizes liberal theology as a spiritual and cultural dead end for Christianity, especially in light of crisis and tragedy. Ten Broeke and *The Constructive Quarterly* have less of the pall of tragedy throughout them because they explored the possibility of constructive theology before the spell of liberal theology seemed to have been utterly destroyed by the World Wars. Meland's justification for breaking with his liberal teachers and developing a constructive theological method arises directly from the profound cultural experience of tragedy. In *Faith and Culture,* Meland claims a place within the liberal tradition—albeit a variety of new liberalism, chastened by Christian realism—that incorporates the historical sense for the depth of the tragic within Christianity, mediating between liberalism and Christian realism/Niebuhrianism. At this stage, constructive theology seems best characterized as a straying descendant of liberalism. Certainly born of liberalism, its critiques of liberalism run too deep and too wide to fall comfortably within the liberal umbrella. Meland, the anchoring figure for early constructive theology, explicitly rejects reason and experience as primary sources for theology. Like "neo-orthodoxy," constructive theology has minimal interest in historical criticism of the Bible or materialist/empiricist scientific reasoning as they relate to reconstructing Christian theology. If anything, historical examination of the theological and ecclesial tradition provides a more important basis for rethinking Christian theology. Constructive theology's primary contradiction is not the challenge of science and reason, but the weakness of the Christian tradition itself. Liberalism responded to the accusation that Christianity couldn't hold up against the critiques of the Enlightenment and the rising prevalence of reason as the most, if not only, legitimate way of understanding the world. Constructive theology acknowledges that critique but doesn't preoccupy itself with it. Instead, it takes up the structural weakness of Christian witness and reinterprets the tradition.

For the same reason, constructive theology isn't, for the most part, apologetic in nature. Paul Tillich characterized his *Systematic Theology* as a work of apologetics. If Christianity could be shown to be reasonable and accommodating to modern culture, it could be seen as feasible to modern human beings who had other pulls on their allegiance that were equally legitimate. Tillich's apologetics insists that Christian theology must offer a response to culture. Constructive theology, on the other hand, insists that religion is endemic to culture itself, while also being more than culture. To put it overly simply, Tillich's method of correlation seeks to answer the questions culture raises, cyclically as those answers raise new questions. Constructive theology, on the other hand, intends to construct culture itself, or at least Christianity as a religious expression within culture.

Meland introduces cornerstones that run throughout the rest of the constructive theological tradition after him, namely, culture and crisis. The question of theology and culture runs in various streams in all of the work of the Workgroup on Constructive Theology as well as in many constructive theologians' individual works. It becomes a touchstone for the relevance of theology as well as a primary adjudicator of the success of any specific constructive theology. Crisis also pervades the development of constructive theology, but reaches its apex in the second textbook composed by the Workgroup on Constructive Theology. The proto-constructive theologians each had their own engagements with these two key concepts.

For Ten Broeke, culture proper plays a lesser part, caught up in the controlling philosophy of the different periods in Christian theology he describes. Philosophy plays close to the same role for Ten Broeke that myth does for Meland. Contemporary philosophy, for Ten Broeke, offers a better foundation for Christian theology, more in line with Jesus' intentions and truer to the core of Christian faith than the philosophies that have carried it historically. For Ten Broeke, the problem of culture is still heavily tied up with the problem of rationalist challenges to Christianity, best answered by finding the theological in contemporary philosophy. For Meland, culture becomes of utmost importance. It runs deep. Governed by myth, culture and Christianity mutually critique, construct, and control one another. Culture becomes both a source for theology and an expression of it. In *Write Your Own Ten Commandments*, an odd book by Meland that falls somewhere between theology and self-help, Meland highlights the importance, for him, of starting with narrative and poetic articulations of Christian values. These more closely represent present formulations of Christianity, for Meland, and offer reevaluation of classical Christian myths.

Crisis reemerges throughout the history of constructive theology as a definitive category. Its original confrontation with modernity is not a crisis, yet *The Constructive Quarterly* and Ten Broeke manage the raw materials of Christianity after a period of "destruction." The call is to move beyond this destructive period without defensiveness. Meland started his career working with the same challenges of liberalism, but made a sharp turn to critiquing liberalism as an ally who still saw value in the project. For constructive theology, crisis makes a claim for the call to action in Christianity. That is, crisis demands Christian praxis.

Liberalism deals with progress, not crisis. At various points, history forces it to rethink its idea of progress in the light of historical tragedies, but its commitment to Enlightenment idealism remains a defining feature throughout the tradition. But for Meland, crisis is imminent, and demands the redefinition of Christian theology from the standpoint of humans who accept Christianity's nature as a constructed tradition. Meland's idea of crisis, contrasted with the way it might be formulated by Barth, remains within the immanent and cognitive, that is, with human beings. It forsakes the absolute demand of rationalism, however, insisting on the irrational nature of human experience and of the way in which crisis reveals the shortcomings of liberal theology. Meland does not go for neo-orthodoxy and its persistent insistence that only God can decide true faith or reveal the nature of real faith. Neither does he continue in liberalism. Deep, irrational religious experience is real. But it participates in the greater irrational, communally constructed myths of culture as a whole. Crisis in constructive theology signals its departure from liberalism, but at the same time it is not the crisis of neo-orthodoxy. The crises that guide constructive theology and its method are crises of structure and history, not of God's breaking into history. This in part happens because of the importance of process theology to constructive theology, which precludes an omnipotent God, and in part because of constructive theology's continued affinity with liberalism. Constructive theology recovers the language of myth and doctrine while integrating the critique neo-orthodoxy brought to liberalism. It doubles down on immanence and the role human beings play in constructing religious experience, albeit in a complex, interrelated, irrational way that transcends human reason.

Fallible Forms and Symbols, published by Meland in 1976, creates an interesting overlap chronologically between Meland and the formation of the Workgroup on Constructive Theology in 1975. Referring to the structure of the Christian faith, Meland asserts that Christianity has never "assumed absolute certainty." In place of certainty, it has established a level of trust. Meland offers a mature definition of constructive theology as he sees it at the moment of handing over its legacy. By this point he has a clear idea that constructive theology is something like but different from systematic and dogmatic theology. "Since the mode of inquiry is that of constructive theology, as contrasted with systematic study of doctrine or dogmatics, the concern in focus is that of attending the problem of faith within contemporary culture and within the lived experiences of people as they participate simultaneously in the culture and in the legacy of faith that persists within these experiences."[40] Constructive theology unifies tradition and future, faith and culture. It doesn't reconcile or mediate between them, though Meland for a while imagined it that way. Instead, the two become part of the same project. Faith and culture aren't separate. Instead, both are ambiguous, ongoing, constructive projects. Constructive theology "explores dimensions of the witness of faith which relate to the historical legacy transmitted through the church and to the accumulative thrust of the mythos."[41] The mythos, as the controlling discourse of present culture, offers both a strength and a pitfall for theology. It offers resources for reinvigorating theology and establishing a new and vital structure of experience for Christian faith. At the same time, all theologies are culturally bound and will inevitably contradict and challenge one another even while building upon what has come before. This challenge, though, is in itself a strength. The acceptance of this fact and the boldness to continue to construct theology nonetheless is a defining feature of constructive theology.

Systematic and dogmatic theologies seek to stand outside this cultural situatedness. Dogmatics, as the name implies, seeks incontrovertible veracity. A dogma is held on faith because its objective truth is held to be absolute. A system cannot tolerate ambiguity or the sudden realization that some part of the system has been false all along. By nature of being a system, it relies on all parts being internally consistent and logically consistent with all other parts. Even Tillich's embrace of culture as the interrogator of Christianity demands that the system itself stay the same, despite cultural contingencies. The materials that go in and out change, but the process and the parts stay the same. Constructive theology as Meland conceives it is unequivocally culturally

40. Bernard Eugene Meland, *Fallible Forms and Symbols: Discourses on Method in a Theology of Culture* (Philadelphia: Fortress, 1976), 121.

41. Ibid.

invested and circumscribed. Not only the answers theology gives, but the makeup of Christian theology and Christian faith will change over time in response to changes in mythos or changes in cultural structures.

Meland takes a different tack on the use of philosophy in theology than Ten Broeke. By this point in constructive theology, culture, mythos, structure, social sciences, and others have all become sources for constructing theology. Meland admonishes theologians to maintain "indifference" toward their philosophical systems.[42] Ten Broeke sought to integrate modern philosophies as better bases for Christian theology. Meland encourages the use of philosophy, in his case especially process philosophy, but not as a controlling structure. Theology cannot simply try to make one to one correspondences between philosophy and theology, as Ten Broeke seems to imply, or even as early Meland with Wieman seems to have argued for in *American Philosophies of Religion*. Theology must, according to Meland, reemerge as a self-sufficient discipline in conversation with other disciplines, philosophy included. Ideally, other disciplines will be able to receive insights from theology back into them. This thrust identifies constructive theology's preoccupation with becoming an interlocutor with religious studies (as it emerges) and other academic disciplines on equal footing. Theology is not simply an instance of recognizing the inherently religious nature of certain philosophical systems. It incorporates insights from philosophy in order to construct its own structure of Christian faith and experience.

Essays in Constructive Theology brings together work from across the span of Meland's career in 1988. By this point the Workgroup on Constructive Theology had produced one textbook and its reader in historical Christian theology. Constructive theology had a presence in the academy but its definition was just beginning to be worked out. *Essays in Constructive Theology* acknowledges the significant and important contribution of Meland in introducing a distinct theological method and his unique incorporation of the insights of outside disciplines alongside culture.

Not everything in Meland's definition, or that which appears in *Contentio Veritatis*, *The Constructive Quarterly*, or the work of Ten Broeke defines all constructive theology. *Contentio Veritatis* formulates a collaborative, tentative way of doing theology that foreshadows constructive

42. Ibid., 133.

theology. Its context at Oxford and its heavy dose of the Church of England hinder it from participating fully in what constructive theology becomes. It above all else incorporates "fragmentary and provisional" thinking into theology in an unapologetic way, an important characteristic of constructive theology. Ten Broeke emphasizes the unification of contemporary philosophy with Christian experience more heavily than most constructive theologians after him do. He essentially sees theology as an endeavor to reveal the already religious dimensions of contemporary philosophy. Constructive theology as a tradition incorporates the embrace of modern modes of thought, including philosophy but also other social sciences and academic disciplines. But it retreats from the assertion that theology is simply a religious expression of philosophy. In fact, with Meland onward, the wholesale adoption of any one philosophy is rejected. Nonetheless, Ten Broeke introduces the basic constructed nature of theology and proposes construction (or reconstruction) as a mode for doing theology. Meland overemphasizes culture as compared to many of the constructive theologians who emerge after him. Culture remains important in all constructive theology, but not all constructive theology takes culture as fundamentally constitutive of or definitive for theology. All constructive theology demands that theology be held responsible to contemporary culture and crises. Further, Meland asserts the break of constructive theology from systematic and dogmatic theology. Other proto-constructive theologians sensed the fissure, but nonetheless sought to fit constructive theology awkwardly into the category of systematics.

All of these proto-constructive theologians see the clash between orthodoxy and liberalism as falsely magnified against the historical intellectual backdrop. Seeing the fundamental contradiction of the theology of their times as a disagreement between liberalism and orthodoxy, or later, liberalism and neo-orthodoxy, is to miss the forest for the trees. For them, as liberalism and orthodoxy or supernaturalism fought a turf war over issues of historicity and the reliability of the Bible as well as the reasonableness of metaphysical realities and miraculous occurrences, constructive theology took an entirely different strategy and proposed a new method. At the same time, its method respects the Christian theological legacy as one that needs to be acknowledged, even in its destructed state, and self-consciously rebuilt to reflect contemporary Christian experience better and call for a renewed commitment to being Christian in the modern and postmodern world that is neither naïve nor indistinguishable from other cultural systems.

By the time *Fallible Forms and Symbols* was published, other theologians had begun talking about what constructive theology is. He references a number of emerging definitions and offers his own. Of course, this is also the moment the Workgroup on Constructive Theology was formed and began to offer shape to the tradition.[43] For Meland, constructive theology unifies contemporary culture and the legacy of faith in contemporary experience. Constructive theology in Meland isn't a method per se, but, as he calls it, a collection of "directives" for theological method. He is clear about the fact that constructive theology departs from systematic or dogmatic theology, the first to make such a strong distinction. Ten Broeke struggled to situate constructive theology within systematic theology, as did Meland in his earlier works. A wide range of other theologians contributed their own versions of constructive theology at this time, including Gordon Kaufman, Peter C. Hodgson, Edward Farley, Langdon Gilkey, John Cobb, Robert H. King, Sallie McFague, and others. The late '60s and '70s saw an explosion of theologians working in a constructive vein. Religious studies, as a self-contained, independent discipline, also arises around this time. Theology finds itself, because of liberalism, unhinged from traditional Christian authority, chastened by neo-orthodoxy and crisis, and outed as a wholly human-made, constructed endeavor.

43. Ibid., 121.

2

The Workgroup on Constructive Theology

The Workgroup on Constructive Theology, founded in 1975 at Vanderbilt University, has served as an organizational center for the development of constructive theology and a place where its key methodological and thematic proposals have been nurtured and propagated. Most basically, the Workgroup is a collection of prominent theologians that, in various configurations, have gathered periodically over the last forty years and collaboratively published four textbooks and one historical theology reader. Throughout its history, the Workgroup on Constructive Theology has variously defined itself, though never in very stark terms. This is partly intentional as one defining feature of constructive theology is its openness to multiplicity of interpretation within its own tradition. In recognizing the constructedness of theology, it doesn't presume to have final answers to any of the questions of Christian theology (though it does rule out certain things as beyond the pale).

Gary Dorrien, in a short reflection on the Workgroup on Constructive Theology, writes, "Organized in 1975 to celebrate Sallie McFague's inauguration as dean, the group's original Vanderbilt members included [Sallie] McFague, [Peter] Hodgson, [Edward] Farley, [and many others]."[1] McFague and Kaufman played important roles in the

1. Dorrien, *The Making of American Liberal Theology*, vol. 3, 336.

origin of the group. But neither McFague nor Kaufman contributed much to the collective works of the Workgroup. McFague offered a powerful epilogue that briefly suggests constructive theology's method in *Christian Theology: An Introduction to Its Traditions and Tasks.* McFague was one of only two women who participated in the early years of the Workgroup, the other being German liberation theologian Dorothee Soelle. Soelle left the group very early on. She criticized the group for its lack of an adequate engagement with liberation theology. Her departure seems to have been due to a combination of that disagreement and the more practical fact of her return to Germany. McFague participated in very important ways in the beginning, but sometimes she distanced herself for fear of being tokenized as the only woman in the group—a problem the group faced with respect to both gender and race, and wouldn't begin to solve until well into its history. Kaufman never contributed any writing to the books put together by the Workgroup—though he was crucial in its formation, he declined to contribute due to time constraints and disagreement with the format of the book, which he ironically saw as too systematic.[2] Nonetheless, he provided methodological underpinnings for constructive theology as it would come to take shape. His *Essay on Theological Method* appeared the same year the Workgroup was founded, 1975, and so partakes in the intellectual environment that resulted in the formation of the group. And it serves, foundationally, as a prolegomenon, alongside works by Edward Farley and David Tracy, for all constructive theology that would come after it—which would be joined with further developments that have given it a distinct character that builds on and adapts these prolegomena's methodological structures.

Prolegomena for Constructive Theology

Many present day constructive theologians have a hard time pinning down where the term "constructive" comes from when applied to theology. The adjective, introduced to theology with McBee and Ten Broeke, found its formulation as "constructive theology" with Meland. What exactly that meant remained to be clarified, as evidenced by Meland's ambiguous legacy. Building on this growing movement, the term as it is used today primarily comes out of the methodological proposals of Gordon Kaufman, Edward Farley, and David Tracy at the very moment when the Workgroup on Constructive Theology was being

2. Peter C. Hodgson, in discussion with the author, December 21, 2015.

formed. The idea of constructive theology predates these theologians. But the nitty-gritty theoretical justification and analysis of what it means to do theology constructively in a rigorous way had to wait for them.

Gordon Kaufman

In the preface to *An Essay on Theological Method*, Kaufman states bluntly, "I attempt to show that much confusion is introduced into theological work by the failure to recognize that the notion of God (like the notion of the world) is an imaginative construct built up in quite a different way than the concepts of objects known in and through experience. Theology, therefore, is fundamentally an activity of *construction* (and reconstruction) not of description or exposition, as it has ordinarily been understood in the past; and the failure to grasp this fact has led to mistaken expectations for theology and to the use of misleading criteria both in doing theology and in assessing its conclusions."[3] The fundamental qualities of constructive theology are captured in this sentence and developed throughout the rest of the *Essay*. Much anxiety manifested in theology in response to the Enlightenment, and a wide variety of strategies were used to plead the case for theology, and Christianity itself, in its wake. Liberal and fundamentalist strains of Christianity continue this discussion in the United States today. Kaufman claims that the fault of these theologies, and in fact theologies that have predominated throughout theological history, is primarily that they have failed to recognize that theology is inherently made up of "imaginative constructions." Kaufman does not preclude the actual existence of God, but instead argues that human speech about God, and subsequently our beliefs and theological judgments about God and Christianity, are fundamentally language-bound, contingent, and human-made. Like other similar controlling constructs, as in the "world," constructions about God are indispensible for human beings according to Kaufman, serving to orient and assign value to life, existence, and experience.

As a result of this realization, "a far-reaching reorientation of theological work is needed. As such a change is accomplished, theologians should be able to work with greater self-understanding and sophistication and with more promise of success. The view of theology that emerges here is one of a generally significant cultural enterprise with

3. Kaufman, *An Essay on Theological Method*, x.

universal and public standards, not a parochial or idiosyncratic activity of interest only to special groups."[4] Kaufman lays the foundation for what I describe as theology that is interdisciplinary and justice/activist oriented by opening the "idiosyncratic" and "parochial" activity of theologians to wider accountability. Theology should be relevant beyond the small circle of theologians who do it. This includes both other academic fields and the public at large. Kaufman's definition of theology is worth quoting at length:

> Theology . . . is not so much devotion to the symbols of faith as the attempt to *understand* those symbols and the way they function in human life, to criticize and reinterpret them so they will more adequately achieve their purpose, and finally (as I am especially emphasizing in this essay) to reconstruct them, sometimes radically. Theology, thus, like faith, arises out of response to religious symbols and their meaning, but instead of expressing itself in simple trust or devotion it is particularly sensitive to difficulties or problems in the formulation and implications of these symbols. It is a *deliberate human activity* directed toward criticizing and reconstructing the symbols by which faith lives and to which faith responds. If faith is a gift of God, as it has been traditionally understood, theology is clearly human work, and we must take full responsibility for it. But it is human work that emerges out of faith's own need for more adequate orientation and symbolization. Such theological activity may reinforce—or it may weaken further—the religious stance.[5]

Theology, as Kaufman received it and saw it, faced the problem of having naturalized what theology had said about God to the point that it believed those things to be inherently and fundamentally true about God. While the *anologia fidei* is a classic quality of theology, Kaufman and others argue that over time, served by certain power structures and interests in universalizing specific images of God, these analogies have come to be confused with Godself.

Most basically, all human speech about God is metaphorical and analogical. Theologians construct conceptions of God using the languages available to them, the metaphors that they see to be most effective, and in response to the urgencies of any particular time. Nothing a theologian says about God, or the resulting structure of Christianity, can be confused with representing a one-to-one true statement about God. Importantly, this, for Kaufman, doesn't mean Christian theology done

4. Ibid.
5. Ibid., xii.

in this way is any less "Christian," any less religious. Rather, it is more accountable, more humble, and ultimately more effective because it deals in what Christian theology actually is rather than pretending to be making objective statements about God.

Recognizing theological constructs about God as constructs allows theology, then, to reconsider the effects and ramifications of what has been said about God. Theologies that have cast themselves to be describing the essence of the structures of Christianity, a task exemplified in magnum opus systematic works or dogmatic works that assert articles of belief, tend to form rigid structures that, through habituation, come to be seen as the structure of Christianity, and therefore of God. "Despite all claims that we human beings can never come to know God in his essence, what was in fact presented by theologians was an elaborate scheme of interpretation which set out what it was believed God actually was, and what humanity and the world were, and how they were related to each other."[6] Systematic reflection that fits snugly together from beginning to end, in a format that suggests comprehensiveness and revealed to be logically and philosophically consistent, masquerades as objective theological speech. Kaufman rejects his own earlier attempt at such work. The methodological move of working with a single doctrine begins with his insistence on developing the doctrine of God as sufficient for constructing relevant contemporary theology.

What Kaufman accepts from the Enlightenment and modernity is that human reason cannot access direct knowledge about God. This insight, specifically from Kant, demands a reconsideration of what sort of language theology is and what it is meant to do.[7] Early proto-constructive theology considered the legacy of German idealists like Kant and Hegel, arguing for different degrees of incorporation of their philosophies into Christian theology. Later constructive theologies don't often name Kant, but the premise of God as construction largely rests on the argument that human beings can speak about God, but that that speech should not be confused with actual knowledge about God. Constructive theology does not agree with Kant that religion's main usefulness is solely ethics, however. It takes the task of talking about God, conceptualizing God and considering the possibilities of God, as necessities.

Constructing God, without direct knowledge of God, is the basic

6. Ibid., 22.
7. Ibid., 24.

activity of constructive theology, its primary premise, and ultimately its creative driving force. Engaging the theological tradition, with its constructed qualities reclaimed and highlighted, constructive theology creates space for theology that examines, deconstructs, reconstructs, and repeats indefinitely. No construction of God can or should be considered final. Kaufman, therefore, asserts three "moments of theological construction." The first is the "explicit development of a conception of the overall context in which experience falls, a concept of the world."[8] This throughout the constructive theological tradition takes the form of engagement with other disciplines, using their insights to help construct a conception of the "world" that is more nuanced and more rigorous. The second, the "theologian's proper business," is "to construct an adequate concept of God, of that further reality which relativizes and limits the world and all that is in it."[9] The concept of God does not simply conform to the constructed image of the world. Rather, in some way it must stand in contradiction to it, or out of sync with it, in order to be an "adequate" conception of God. God cannot simply be an expression of the "world" or of culture, but must still maintain the qualities of God as being greater than and beyond human works. Finally, "it is necessary to move on to a third moment of theological construction in which the concept of world is reformulated so as to 'fit' intelligibly with the God who is thought to be its ultimate ground and limit."[10] I suggest that this is constructive theology's move to help change the world, to assert that the world must be held accountable to a better conception of God, though one that nevertheless is not an image that conforms to whatever metaphysically real God there may be. The entire process is imbued with the task of imaginative construction.

Kaufman provides the theoretical underpinnings for reconstructive theological projects, as well as an argument for why and how it must account for the rising recognition of the world and human activity in it as itself discursively constructed. His methodological proposals allow for a theology that reflexively changes, or at least suggests change, for the world. He, however, like much constructive theology, comes up short when it comes to liberation theology. *An Essay on Theological Method* was written in part to address what he saw as the murkiness being introduced by contextual and liberation theologies, alongside

8. Ibid., 47.
9. Ibid., 49.
10. Ibid., 59.

the misunderstanding historical theologies had introduced by seeing themselves as talking about God rather than about a conception of God. He argues that liberation theologies may in fact be simply a form of constructive theology—an argument that ultimately falls short of giving liberation theology its full due. As Dorrien notes, according to Kaufman, "Instead of copping an attitude, theologians needed to produce works of enduring intellectual value, affirming that there is no substitute for intellectual seriousness; on occasion he referred to liberationism as 'so-called liberation theology.'"[11] Constructive theology maintained an arm's length relationship with liberation theology for much of the first half of its history. It always maintained that it needed to engage and embrace liberation theology and marginalized and minoritized voices. But it struggled to do so until the group expanded its membership substantially.

Ultimately Kaufman discontinued his involvement with the Workgroup on Constructive Theology partially for lack of time to contribute fully, but also because he disagreed with the methodological direction that the Workgroup took with the insights of his prolegomenon—though not in a combative or hurt way, as Kaufman remained friends and a close colleague with the participants in the group throughout his and their careers. According to Peter C. Hodgson, Kaufman disagreed with the group's commitment to using doctrinal loci in its theologizing, including in *Christian Theology: An Introduction to Its Traditions and Tasks.* The turn in Kaufman's theological work would eventually mean the outright rejection of theologizing around doctrinal loci. Considering his argument that all doctrines fundamentally reflect only one locus anyway—that of the doctrine of God—it makes sense that from his point of view exploring the other loci on their own terms is somewhat futile. He explicitly rejected the take on loci he used in *Systematic Theology: A Historicist Perspective*, reducing all theology to talk about the doctrine of God. His later books would increasingly stress a departure from traditional formats of doing theology, while he nevertheless always characterized his theology as "constructive." He continued to assert the constructed nature of theological concepts of God, and explicitly constructed his own new conceptions.

Edward Farley

Also in 1975, Edward Farley, a theologian at Vanderbilt Divinity School,

11. Dorrien, *The Making of American Liberal Theology*, vol. 3, 315.

published his own methodological text: *Ecclesial Man*. Like Kaufman, Farley doesn't waste time getting to the point of the construction of his constructive methodological project. In the preface, he straightaway includes a quote from Horst Stephan and Martin Schmidt, German Protestant theologians, and his own corrective statement that reveals his constructive intentions: "'Where the path to new construction remains hidden, development can occur only in the sense of evermounting radicalization.' The following chapters fall more on the side of a construction than a mere radicalization."[12] Farley reveals right away two of his underlying presumptions with respect to theology. First, construction will be the focal point and explicit approach of his theology. And second, as will be true of constructive theology from 1975 through today, it is suspicious of "mere radicalization." That is to say, radical options had been open—and have continued to open—for theology in recent history, including traditions that call themselves "radical theology" outright. Objecting to mere radicalization grounds constructive theology in the Christian tradition, both practically and theologically. Farley suggests that construction may be the more difficult and more profound task at hand.

Again like Kaufman, the impetus for a theological prolegomenon emerges from a perceived undirected plurality that was prevalent at the time. The anxiety of the moment around the lack of a single, or even multiple but clearly articulated, methodology is summed up dramatically by Farley: "Given the methodological paralysis bequeathed to us from the past, it is impossible for me to get on with theology's proper business and pretend that, if I do not look in their direction, maybe the problems will just go away. Most theologians would think they had died and gone to heaven if they awakened one morning with their methodological puzzles solved and their procedures ordered." He goes on to suggest that "This work is my struggle to deal with the most paralyzing problem of all. Are there any realities to which we can trace the normative language and the intellective acts of theology and the images resident in faith itself? If there are such realities, where and how are they apprehended?"[13] Once again, cognitive access to the realities that theology speaks about is questioned. According to Farley, theologians have been nervously trying to ignore the reality that the realities of faith have been radically challenged as existing at all. *Eccle-*

12. Edward Farley, *Ecclesial Man: A Social Phenomenology of Faith and Reality* (Philadelphia: Fortress, 1975), xiii.
13. Ibid., xvi.

sial Man is Farley's attempt to offer justification for discussing what have been considered the essential realities of Christian faith, while also recognizing that the "essence" of Christianity, and the sureness with which theology historically discussed it, has been lost after the advent of historical criticism. He does so while also guarding against complete loss of connection with both the lived and theoretical tradition of Christianity.

The key to Farley's prolegomenon on its own is what he calls social phenomenology. He summarizes,

> In recent years the theological community has entertained what might be called a nasty suspicion about itself. The rumor did not arise within the community but, once implanted, it had a certain self-fulfilling effect. Could it be that there are no realities at all behind the language of this historical faith? Could it be that the testimony, the storytelling, the liturgical expressions of this faith refer to entities that have only phenomenal status? . . . With this suspicion at work in the theological community comes a new problematic for theological method. Replacing the traditional disputes over criteriology is the prior problem whether or not faith apprehends any distinctive realities at all.[14]

Drawing on Edmund Husserl, he suggests a phenomenological approach that circumvents questions of the realities of Christian faith, instead focusing on experiences in faith of the "ecclesia," which is a community of faith not to be equated with the Christian church. Historically, Christianity has in fact presumed that faith was directed to actual realities that coincided with what theology said about it.[15] In contemporary thinking, it has lead to "two impossible alternatives":

> Acknowledging that the faith in which [Christian theology] is grounded does, in fact, suspend the axiom of object-evidence correspondence, it can charge this faith with being grounded on a several-thousand-year-long logical fallacy. Theology itself is, therefore, scientifically purified. It's cognitive grounding is no longer suspect, for it now does what all genuine disciplines do; it describes and explains on the basis of evidence. . . . The difficulty with this rather simple and 'honest' alternative is that it reduces historical faith to something other than itself, and, therefore, puts theology out of business. Second theology can make a heroic attempt to do justice to the 'realities' on which this faith insists and to which it testifies. In

14. Ibid., 6.
15. Ibid., 15.

> this case, it must live with the impossible situation of admitting that these realities are arbitrarily asserted.[16]

Farley rejects the most obvious supplement to the problem of the inaccessibility of realities, namely, authority. Unlike other disciplines where laypeople rely on experts to supplement limited knowledge and expertise, church experts, authorities in historical theology and matters of the Church, would themselves be basing their authority on fallacious history viewed from a post-historical-critical perspective. Questioning the house of authority in a historical faith and proposing a new methodological foundation for theology is the crux of Farley's "pre-methodological" prolegomenon.

Farley's solution must be quoted at length:

> Phenomenological theology cannot solve the problem of reality in the concrete sense of making it available. What can it do? We recall that there is "before our eyes" a living historical faith which in its fullness. . . . Is not reducible to any one specific period of its history, including the present period. This implies a distinction between the empirical content and situation of this faith in any specific time and its persistent structures which lie below the surface. It also implies the possibility of penetrating beneath the surface layers of what is specific, visible, and contemporary to what is constitutive and persistent. We may not settle the question whether a particular reality is in fact apprehended in a specific place and time. We can describe the conditions of reality-apprehending distinctive to this historical faith. . . . Phenomenological theology, that initial moment of theological prolegomenon . . . [does] not establish the realities of faith's apprehensions. They are efforts to understand the conditions whereby such reality-apprehensions are possibilities. However, the conditions of faith's apprehensions differ from the conditions of "knowledge as such" in several important respects.[17]

These important "respects" include that theology reaches into the mystery of being and that it is from the perspective of a faith community, or "ecclesia." The realities of faith are beyond ordinary cognition. They are only experienced from the vantage point of faith. Ultimately, Farley rejects what he calls the "criteriology" of previous theology. The criteria of Christian faith must be reexamined, a renewed look cast at the conditions under which the realities of faith, indeed if there are any realities, are experienced.

16. Ibid., 16.
17. Ibid., 21.

Farley does not go as far as Kaufman in establishing the imaginative construction of Christian theology. However, he does prioritize construction above either radicalization or an investigation into the essence of Christianity. He raises the ongoing tension between a "construal" and a "construction" as identified in the *Constructive Quarterly*. Farley seems to gingerly lean toward construal while establishing the basis, alongside Kaufman, of outright construction. The realities of Christian faith are in flux, or at least inaccessible to ordinary cognition or "knowledge as such." Farley raises the possibility and importance for Christian theological projects, in an explicit way that Kaufman doesn't, that the realities about which Christian theology talks, do actually exist in a greater sense. Kaufman's "imaginative construction" may make it seem as if Christianity is nothing but a fictional structure elaborated willy-nilly. Farley keeps the realities of Christian faith in view while acknowledging their inaccessibility by human cognition. He, in bringing his prolegomenon to the question beneath the question of theology, raises the unsure status of the realities of Christian faith, dismisses an essence to Christianity, and introduces an interdisciplinary, phenomenological, recursively investigative approach to the constructive theological method emerging.

Farley's introduction of the thoroughly interdisciplinary quality of theological method as he sees it is especially important. He writes, "Several interests and fields of study converge in this work which would seem to have little relation to each other."[18] The result is that, "although these inquiries are 'theological' in the sense that they are conducted within the bounds of a determinate historical faith, they are pertinent beyond these bounds."[19] They apply as well to "philosophers and historians of religion." In the emphasis on "life-world" and the phenomenological aspects of the Christian faith as they relate to its realities, constructive theology would expand its incorporation of interdisciplinary insights across the academic spectrum. Likewise, today, constructive theology is cultivating ways to be pertinent to all of the disciplines it self-consciously references and assimilates.

Farley insists that his prolegomenon is broadly ecumenical, but he still does so from a Protestant perspective. David Tracy introduces a final prolegomenic voice that embodies a Roman Catholic position on constructive theological method.

18. Ibid., xiv.
19. Ibid., xvii.

David Tracy

Catholic theologian David Tracy rounds out the trifecta of prolegomena for constructive theology. Once again, in 1975, in his flagship methodological text, Tracy acknowledges the key reality of pluralism in his contemporary theological context: "That the present situation in theology is one of an ever-increasing pluralism is by now a truism. That such a pluralist condition enriches the possibilities for theology would seem at least equally clear and true. For a theologian to accept the present pluralism as a state of pure enrichment, of gratuitous and untarnished blessing, is another matter entirely."[20] In the development of constructive theology, David Tracy is a hero for pluralism, a key defining feature in several guises. He develops the theme of pluralism around its effects on theological truth claims and truth making, its challenge to traditional authorities upon which theology based those claims, and finally, in the method of doing constructive theology itself.

Kaufman expressed discomfort with the pluralist character of the moment in theology. Farley approaches it phenomenologically in order to arrive at deeper experiences that can be considered unifying data for theology. Tracy raises up pluralism as the defining feature of the moment that will be persistent, and in the end must be embraced for the opportunity it offers theology. How to approach that pluralism and effectively account for it and employ it in theology is his task. He offers two "principal assumptions": First, "the present pluralism of theologies allows each theologian to learn incomparably more about reality by disclosing really different ways of viewing both our common humanity and Christianity," and second, "Each theologian must attempt to articulate and defend an explicit method of inquiry, and use that method to interpret the symbols and texts of our common life and Christianity."[21] In short, pluralism is a gift, a strength, for theology that takes it seriously and demands "really different ways" of experiencing and articulating the world as experienced by all people. Each theologian must identify and explain their own "method of inquiry." This, in its openness to diverse approaches, is characteristic of constructive theology's openness, indeed demand for, pluralism, expressed through its interdisciplinary variety of inquiry. Different constructive theologians may employ different interdisciplinary techniques, as long as that technique is made explicit and serves to makes sense for the

20. Tracy, *Blessed Rage for Order*, 3.
21. Ibid.

contemporary world of more traditional Christian categories, symbols, doctrines, and texts.

Enlightenment challenges to authority and the rise of rationalism, especially as expressed in the development of other disciplines like the social sciences, undercut the claims of theology to be speaking of a reality at all, and also pointed out the circular logic Christian theology had used to uphold itself historically. If rational inquiry had undercut the traditional authorities of Christian theology, the Bible, church tradition, revelation, then appealing to those authorities as evidence to uphold one's theological conclusions becomes fallacious.[22] Methodological disagreement arose in contemporary theology because theologians are torn between two competing allegiances. On the one hand, Christian theologians feel loyalty to the church and to the theological tradition. On the other, they, as modern components of the academy, feel the ethical and methodological tug of scientific inquiry. As Tracy puts it,

> The modern Christian theologian cannot ethically do other than challenge the traditional self-understanding of the theologian. He no longer sees his task as a simple defense or even as an orthodox reinterpretation of traditional belief. Rather, he finds that his ethical commitment to the morality of scientific knowledge forces him to assume a critical posture toward his own and his tradition's beliefs. He insists, to be sure, that the concept 'critical' does not bear a simply negative meaning. But open-ended inquiry, a loyalty to defended methodological canons, a willingness to follow the evidence wherever it may lead.[23]

Constructive theology embraces the centrality of critical inquiry into traditional Christian doctrines, beliefs, and practices. Tracy makes it an ethical imperative. Critical inquiry, through social sciences, philosophy, literary theory and hermeneutics, religious studies, and others, allows constructive theologians to examine, critique, and reformulate Christian symbols for contemporary crises. Tracy is describing his contribution to what becomes constructive theological method, which embraces multiple methods of inquiry, is enriched by the conversation created by competing theological claims, and authentically places itself in the tense space between the modern academy and the traditional church. Embracing a dialogue in which theologians may make claims as

22. Tracy, *Blessed Rage for Order*, 5.
23. Ibid., 7.

a result of any number of methods of inquiry is central to the approach and method of constructive theology.

Tracy emphasizes, however, that it is not only Christian theology and Christian tradition that need to be revised and rewritten, that is, reconstructed. In fact, modernity itself, the condition in which Christian theology has confronted these issues, needs to be and is in the process of being reexamined and rethought. Tracy says, "neither traditional Christian understanding nor recent modern self understanding nor any combination thereof will suffice to resolve the dual dilemma. Only a basic revision of traditional Christianity and traditional modernity alike would seem to suffice."[24]

By linking up Christian theology with modern modes of inquiry, it at first seems that Tracy is reifying the liberal theological project. That questioning of authority and an emphasis on reason and scientific understandings of the world requires Christianity to learn how to express itself in a mode that satisfies what theologian Friedrich Schleiermacher famously called "cultured despisers." In fact, however, Tracy pushes beyond modernity and beyond liberalism: "In short, the revisionist theologian is committed to what seems clearly to be the central task of contemporary Christian theology: the dramatic confrontation, the mutual illuminations and corrections, the possible basic reconciliation between the principal values, cognitive claims, and existential faiths of both reinterpreted post-modern consciousness and a reinterpreted Christianity."[25] He continues, "revisionist theology, then, is intrinsically indebted to and derived from the formulation of the liberal task in theology classically formulated in the nineteenth century. It is post-liberal in the straightforward sense that it recognizes and attempts to articulate not a new ideal for the theological task, but new methodological and substantive resources for fulfilling that ideal."[26]

Tracy highlights that his method for theology, which would become an important element of constructive theology broadly, is not liberalism as he understands it. It is post-liberal, but not in the Yale school postliberal theology sense. It is post-liberal in that it inherits the problems and issues of the liberal tradition, critiques them and moves beyond them, with new method and new pluralism. Much of the "ideal" of constructive theology is shared with liberal theology—though it moves further from liberal theology as it increasingly

24. Ibid., 4.
25. Ibid.
26. Ibid., 32.

embraces liberation, which will be explored more below—but the method and many of the basic assumptions of liberal theology have been left behind.

Tracy's "correlative" method rings of Tillich's "method of correlation." Crucially, Tracy acknowledges the connection and the apparent similarity with Tillich. However, he draws a distinction in that Tillich brings culture's questions to a theological system that can provide answers. He explains, "The fact is that Tillich's method does not call for a critical correlation of the results of one's investigations of the 'situation' and the 'message.' Rather, his method affirms the need for a correlation of the 'questions' from one source and 'answers' from the other."[27] Christianity simply has answers. In Tracy's reading, Tillich's system of theology does not in fact interrogate the system he presumes. The answers change according to history and the questions that are asked, but not the system that provides those answers. For Tracy, the Christian "answer" itself must be critically interrogated and revised.

Tracy calls his method "revisionist rewriting" of Christian theology. It is a rewriting, reexamination, revisiting, ultimately a reconstruction of Christianity in the view that pluralism has revealed Christian theology's contingent nature. Not only does his method show that Christian theological claims could always be otherwise. At any given moment those "otherwises" participate in the conversation. Tracy's terminology, "revisionist" theology, caught on and was briefly applied (especially by opponents and critics) broadly to a number of theologians who shared many of his stances, including Kaufman and Farley. As the methodological proposals of the three interacted and influenced one another, they formed mutually reinforced prolegomena for constructive theology.

An Essay on Theological Method, *Ecclesial Man*, and *Blessed Rage for Order* were all published in 1975. All three are methodological works, slated specifically as prolegomena that respond to the same collection of questions for theology: pluralism, loss of authority, rejection of a permanent essence of Christianity, the need for theology that is intellectually and critically rigorous as well as responsive to crises. The three, taken together, form the basis for constructive theological method as a formal category. They gather the emerging methodological trends of theologians working in different places on different issues but with

27. Ibid., 46.

a common underlying approach to Christian theology that was just beginning to be articulated: that Christian theology works with contingent doctrines, that Christianity is a human made construct even if it does reflect a relationship with actual revealed divine structures—and many, if not most, constructive theologians do believe so, while accepting that human beings don't have cognitive access to those structures.

1975 is the same year the Workgroup on Constructive Theology formed, creating a community for these like-minded theologians to work within. Kaufman, Farley, and Tracy were all three instrumental to the Workgroup in its early years, helping to guide its early mission and offer a methodological framework. Solidifying the prolegomena framework offered here, Kaufman, Farley, and Tracy all participated in a panel on method at the Annual Meeting of the American Academy of Religion in 1982, the same year the Workgroup on Constructive Theology published its first collaborative textbook.[28] That panel served as a central topic for one of the Workgroup's meetings shortly thereafter. The dialogical method of constructive theology was being solidified and consolidated. Interestingly, the first printing of that textbook did not include a methodological section. The pluralistic, dialogic method is implied. The second printing included a section on method by David Tracy. But that section only offers one of the important perspectives on constructive theological method.

Like constructive theological propositions themselves, the method of constructive theology is developed collaboratively. In order to understand the big picture it is necessary to understand many different voices. Kaufman introduces imaginative constructions, Farley brings the question beneath the question of the realities of Christian faith as well as a phenomenological approach to Christian experience that doesn't rely on bequeathed presumed realities based on authority, and Tracy brings pluralism and revision. They all play into the final outcome of theology that is (re)constructive. The Workgroup on Constructive Theology consolidated and expanded on these methodological premises. The claims of all three of these prolegomena are developed in the subsequent history of constructive theology. But their foundational assertions, in their open-ended, constructive, pluralistic fullness, provide the methodological ground on which constructive theology is built.

28. Peter C. Hodgson and Robert H. King, "The Workgroup on Constructive Theology: A Brief History." Unpublished working paper, 1990.

Founding the Workgroup on Constructive Theology

The Workgroup on Constructive Theology requires a fuller introduction. Composed of a number of highly influential theologians, it has existed in various states since 1975. The membership, both in terms of number and personnel, has varied greatly in that time. It all started in a relatively small way at Vanderbilt University, and has since become a behind the scenes engine in progressive Christian theology in the academy. The Workgroup was organized at the suggestion of Walter Harrelson, who recommended that theologians at Vanderbilt needed to collaborate like biblical scholars at Vanderbilt had. After a number of preliminary meetings, the group came together on the occasion of Sallie McFague's inauguration as Harrelson's successor as Dean of Vanderbilt Divinity School. McFague, of course, is one of the central figures throughout the history of constructive theology, who, at the time, worked with the significance of metaphor and language in representations of God. The suggestion led to informal meetings, which then turned into formal meetings and the formation of an official Workgroup that took as its goal the production, in collaboration, of substantial, useful work under the heading of "constructive theology." At first, this meant conversation within the group about theology and pedagogy as well as about contemporary issues in theology and theological method. Early attendees included Hodgson, Robert H. King, McFague, Walter Lowe, Julian Hartt, Schubert Ogden, and Kaufman. As the group began to take shape, it received funding from the Collegeville Institute for Ecumenical and Cultural Research in Minnesota and had meetings there, as well as at Vanderbilt. Eventually, after several years of mostly informal gatherings that resulted in individual works by members, the group decided that in order to fulfill its mission as a Workgroup, it needed to produce a work in collaboration. As Hodgson stated in an interview, "The original idea was that it would be a Workgroup, not just a discussion group. A group that would work together to produce publications of value to the study of theology. And that's still the purpose of the group."

The Workgroup on Constructive Theology varies in its intention with respect to whether it purposefully set out to develop a method or category of theology. Almost all constructive theologians, when asked, have a hard time explaining where the "constructive" of constructive theology came from, pointing to Bernard Meland if anything.[29] Meland, for all intents and purposes coined the term, though the proto-constructive theologians before him pioneered the constructive view of theology. The way the Workgroup uses the term "constructive" comes quite directly from the constructive prolegomena. Some members of the group, in conversation, protest that the group never truly intended to make a case for a method. Nevertheless, the textbooks include whole sections that reflect on trends and needs in theological method. It is true that the Workgroup has never taken as its aim the promotion or expansion of the constructive theological community, though it has nonetheless inadvertently done so.

The Workgroup on Constructive theology has provided a dialogical and methodological home to a far-reaching and wide-ranging group of theologians—and occasionally bible scholars and historians—that has given a name and a method to contemporary progressive theology. By calling themselves a Workgroup that deals with constructive theology, as well as individually identifying as constructive theologians, they have propagated constructive theology throughout the theological world. The group did not explicitly set out to form a method, but rather to cultivate a conversation around how to do theology and what it should be about. This original conversation took a pedagogical turn, which took a methodological turn, which over its history has influenced any theologian who identifies as "constructive" today. Indeed, it's not an accident that many constructive theologians today who are not part of the Workgroup worked with and earned their doctorates under members of the group. The Workgroup can be read as representative of constructive theology as a whole because, intentionally or not, by amassing theological clout and developing complementary theologies in dialogue, it has influenced an entire generation of progressive theologians, whether or not that new generation knows that the Workgroup popularized—again intentionally or not—the very term constructive, and its accompanying method.

Christian Theology: An Introduction to Its Traditions and Tasks

Soon after the meetings began, Ogden suggested the group collaboratively write a textbook for the purpose of introducing a new generation of students to theology, both historically and in the present. They decided to model its structure very loosely on the book *Abriss der Dog-*

29. Responses in interviews have ranged from "constructive" being a more accessible term than "systematic" to head scratching. The term combines linguistic/social science insights about culture with the active process of revising inherited theological arguments.

matik by Horst Georg Pöhlmann. They also discussed the doctrinal format of *Reformed Dogmatics* by Heinrich Heppe as an influence.

As editors of the first book produced by the Workgroup, Hodgson and King played a directive role in forming the text and shaping its argument. King in an interview expressed that, for him, constructive theology meant "shifting the emphasis to the process rather than the product. When I think of systematic theology I think of completed works like Tillich or Barth. It's all given to you as a system. They no doubt evolved it over time, and that is concealed in the outcome. . . . I think if we called it systematic theology students would think it's an accomplished fact and all we have to do is assimilate it. If you call it constructive theology, it invites people into the process."[30] Hodgson echoed this claim, remarking, "thinking about the various doctrines and topics of Christian theology is an ongoing task and every generation really has to reconstruct these doctrines with a view to its own sensibilities and cultural contexts and interests and so on. There was some objection initially to even using the traditional loci. The word 'constructive' emphasizes the way in which the author's own imagination and interests contributed to the project. It's not as though a system is simply there that can be plucked out of thin air."[31] Both of these descriptions directly echo Kaufman's emphasis on imaginative construction, rejecting systematic approaches that seek to describe a revealed, complete system that exists independently. Further, to the mission of the early Workgroup, they both stress the pedagogical function of constructive theological method. In a sense, showing one's work is as important as showing one's conclusions. Inviting others into the conversation, prioritizing and centering dialogue and collaboration, including with the student or reader of constructive theology, epitomizes the early work of the Workgroup on Constructive Theology and all of the work that has flowed out of it.

With the goal of producing a book that would be useful in classrooms, the Workgroup set about putting together a textbook that ambivalently revolved around the doctrinal loci of earlier methods of doing theology. Though today the importance of Kaufman's contribution to the premise of theology being a "construction" is often overlooked or forgotten, the group very much worked within a method that incorporates proto-constructive insights, brought to theoretical fruition by Kaufman. The textbook, composed of a number of essays,

30. Robert H. King, in discussion with the author, January 5, 2016.
31. Peter C. Hodgson, in discussion with the author, December 21, 2015.

presented its own joys and challenges, according to Hodgson and King. Even as the Workgroup privileged collaboration and sought to show the three moments of theological construction, reworked as history, deconstruction, and reconstruction, it struggled to meet its deadline and to gather all of the needed works. It also left out crucial doctrines, which would be addressed in a second edition. Nonetheless, the book was much more successful than could have been anticipated, earning enough to be reinvested into the group—no individual within the Workgroup profited from the book, with the proceeds being saved and used to support the Workgroup's future work—funding the group for the foreseeable future, into the present.

Christian Theology: An Introduction to Its Traditions and Tasks—the first of the four textbooks published by the Workgroup on Constructive Theology so far—is clearly historically situated as evidenced by its authors and their concerns. Yet at the same time, it's a bit more timid than the later textbooks in making strong claims about what constructive theology is as opposed to other types of theology. The Workgroup was only composed of "fifteen to twenty altogether" at the time, and the project is intended to offer both a look back at tradition and a way forward in theology that emerged over the course of several meetings of the Workgroup.

Published in 1982, seven years after the first meeting of the Workgroup, the introduction makes the first widely disseminated attempt in terms of self-identification of what the Workgroup is and what constructive theology seeks to do. Most important is the way the book purposefully sets up constructive theology and the project of the Workgroup as being between tradition and the future. As the introduction explains, "The purpose of this work is twofold: (1) to introduce the student of theology to the Christian tradition by setting forth in brief compass its primary shape and substance, and (2) to pose the issues for systematic theology in the present day by showing how that tradition has been challenged and transformed under the pressures of modern thought."[32] Throughout the history of the Workgroup on Constructive Theology, a premium has been placed on the importance of finding new ways to teach theology. Even given that all four of these books are "textbooks," the content is often programmatic. Nonetheless, the information contained in the book is identified as an introduction for the "student of theology" that places the big questions of

32. Peter C. Hodgson and Robert H. King, eds., *Christian Theology: An Introduction to Its Traditions and Tasks* (Minneapolis: Fortress, 1985), ix.

systematic theology within the context of modern thought. The question of whether constructive theology is simply a new name for liberal theology is raised by the first textbook; in this instance, the idea of coping with the "pressures of modern thought" gestures toward that conclusion. Indeed, many of the topics taken up in the first book are concerned with the problem of identifying a theological third-way between traditional Christian theology and the challenges of modern skepticism/empiricism/naturalism.

One aspect that most clearly places it historically is its overarching anxiety about Nazism and the communism of the U.S.S.R. This attitude of taking full stock of the crises of each historical situation will continue to be a highly visible theme throughout the texts of the Workgroup. That is to say, a primary concern of constructive theology, from the beginning of its formalization in the Workgroup, is to be historically aware and situated, and making the historical moment in which each theology is formulated known as essential background information. Constructive theology never pretends to do theology in a vacuum or removed from the vicissitudes of the unfolding of history, especially with respect to its crises. This theme, while present in the first volume, will become even more pronounced in *Reconstructing Christian Theology*, *Constructive Theology*, and *Awake to the Moment.*

In the introduction to the book, the editors explain that "Our intent is not to write a history of theology, though it will be evident that we attach great importance to the historical development of Christian thought. Neither are we attempting to set forth a full-blown systematic theology, though there is considerable consensus among the contributors to this volume about what the outstanding issues are. Certainly, the book is not designed simply as a review of past accomplishments. In an important sense it is meant to set the agenda for future theological discussion."[33] The introduction here explicitly contrasts the book that arose out of the meetings of the Workgroup on Constructive Theology to systematic theology. The sense isn't that constructive theology sees systematic theology as illegitimate. Rather, the concession is that while there is "considerable consensus" among the participants, a full-blown systematic theology is largely not possible. Further, and perhaps most importantly for the remaining history of the Workgroup, the book is meant "to set the agenda for future theological discussion." Constructive theology is permanently in the mode of agenda-setting.

33. Ibid., ix–x.

It intends to propose a way of talking about theology. An important part of that purpose, despite this first book seeming to defer to "full-blown" systematic theologies, is to explore theologies that are persistently multiplicitous and incomplete. This sort of theological agenda, which maintains a case-by-case approach to theology and produces theology in conversation and cooperatively, is embodied in this first text, and is perhaps its most important contribution to the idea of theology being "constructive."

A very interesting feature in this first book, which is maintained in the other three books as well, is that despite the rejection of doing theology systematically, the scheme of building theology around traditional theological doctrines is used. Again, in a somewhat apologetic mode, the editors say,

> The way in which the book is laid out may initially strike the reader as anachronistic, for we have adopted a very traditional format: the loci of doctrine. This format . . . rested on assumptions that are now largely discredited, primarily the view of Christian truth as consisting of a deposit of discrete doctrines that have simply to be expounded by the theologian in order to become intelligible. . . . We have adopted the format as a useful way of making contact with the tradition, but within that structure we have attempted to show how fundamental a transformation the tradition has undergone. Were any one of us to set out to write an actual systematic theology this would not be the format we would employ.[34]

Despite the protest, this format remains in the two later textbooks as well, and in a modified format in the fourth. Constructive theology usually maintains a traditional organization. While the individual theologians, in their own books outside the Workgroup on Constructive Theology, may dispense with the use of the loci for constructing their theologies, the cooperative group as a whole employs the organization every time, including in the collection of readings from Christian theology's history. Constructive theology truly seeks to straddle tradition and contemporary exigencies. The third book, *Constructive Theology: A Contemporary Approach to Classic Themes*, will offer a longer, more developed, and more generous explanation for its use of the traditional loci of theology in introducing the reader to constructive theology. The fourth book still uses them, but discreetly. The point being made is that constructive theology does ascribe to the importance of all of the traditional loci of theology; they all must continue to be dealt with

34. Ibid., x.

by *someone*. But no single constructive theology is beholden to try to account for every locus. Constructive theology doesn't demand completeness or total coherence, as systematic theology does. Theology is constructed by a plethora of voices, each of which is affected by and seeks to affect the tradition. The loci of doctrine are preserved in an effort to critique and reconstruct Christian identity and witness.

David Tracy's chapter on method, added to the second edition, gives a clearer idea of many of the overriding concerns that will be central to constructive theology. Tracy writes, "I shall claim that amidst the great differences of contemporary theologies certain methodological constants do appear. That claim can be made more specific by introducing the following definition of a shared theological method in the new paradigm: *theology is the attempt to establish mutually critical correlations between an interpretation of the Christian tradition and interpretation of the contemporary situation*"[35] (italics original). Tracy is arguing for a "new paradigm," and programmatically describing a method for constructive theology, a "sharing [that] . . . helps to constitute postclassical theology as a community of shared inquiry and method." Tracy identifies these things as defining Constructive Theology's method:

1. "Whatever else is true about Christian theology, it is clearly an interpretation of the central symbols of the Christian tradition for some construal of our present situation."[36] That is, constructive theology is primarily a mission of interpretation, and must be attuned to what theology means in the present.
2. "Interpretations cannot be grounded in the older classicist base but must risk new interpretations of both past tradition and present situation."[37] This is the critique of Christianity's past complicity, while also recognizing that Christian theology cannot completely abandon tradition.
3. Overlapping concerns/sensitivity to the arguments of feminist, liberationist, and political theologies that lead to "interpretations that risk envisioning a Christian future."[38] This in turn contextualizes constructive theology as not exactly being liberation theology while making constructive theology an ally to it. It also again situates constructive theology as a new paradigm

35. Ibid., 36.
36. Ibid., 35.
37. Ibid.
38. Ibid.

that takes seriously the constructive nature of making Christianity relevant for the present and future.

4. "Contemporary theologians must engage in the kinds of interpretations now known as both 'hermeneutics of retrieval' and 'hermeneutics of critique and suspicion.'"[39] This is related to the others, and once again emphasizes the tension being held between the past and present. Further, it also draws on feminist and liberation concerns of both salvaging and critiquing the past.

The overarching methodological claim is that constructive theology is held together by the "method of hermeneutics": reading the Christian theological tradition alongside contemporary realities and practices, critiquing that tradition, and reconstructing in a self-conscious and inclusive way. Tracy makes strong claims in this first textbook about the method of constructive theology that will be critiqued in later work, but the mentality of a unity, of a "new paradigm" in theology is clearly present.

In addition to these four features, Sallie McFague's epilogue claims one other: plurality and openness to ambiguity and variety. She writes, "One distinctive note of the essays in this book is the insistence on pluralism and openness regarding what Christianity is and will be. The hesitancy this perspective engenders is seen in our reluctance or inability to engage in monumental systematic theologies as in the past. Theologians today are less certain than in the past about how to present a metaphysical systemization of Christian faith."[40] In fact, this is one of the most persistent and important delineations of what sets constructive theology apart. McFague acknowledges not only a resistance to systematic theology that pretends to be complete and authoritative, but even an "inability." The grand systems of the past have increasingly become untenable, and our postmodern perspective is inherently suspicious of them. The new paradigm is plural and open. And for constructive theology, that is not a liability, but in fact a very good thing.

Many of the founding figures in the Workgroup on Constructive Theology eventually saw their own ways out. Kaufman, according to Hodgson, eventually exited because he was already too busy, but also because he thought the method settled upon by the group ultimately didn't go far enough in departing from the classical systematic approach. Other senior scholars, like Julian Hartt, Ogden, and Langdon

39. Ibid., 35–36.
40. Ibid., 389.

Gilkey, served as transitional figures that helped lend legitimacy to the nascent group, but didn't maintain sustained involvement as it continued to develop its own character and method. Furthermore, as a constructive, ongoing-oriented group, it has always prioritized the incorporation of fresh new rising voices, a drive that continues today. As a result the Workgroup has periodically experienced almost complete turnover in personnel. King found himself preoccupied with administrative work, and though he kept in touch with the group as it evolved, became less and less involved to the point of stepping out. Hodgson kept tabs on the work of the group, but recounted a memory of attending a meeting of the Workgroup in which some of the work presented struck him as not being theology at all, thus ending his involvement. Yet both remain positive about the Workgroup and the importance of its original mission. And most importantly, the method developed in the early years of the Workgroup on Constructive Theology has defined it ever since, even as the Workgroup has both refined the technique and expanded its vision into multiplicitous, pluralistic theological terrain.

This pluralism finds radical expression in *Reconstructing Christian Theology.* The loci of doctrines are still there, but they are purposefully set against contextualization and questions that challenge the theological tradition from many different experiences of oppression.

Reconstructing Christian Theology

The Workgroup, despite the success and popularity of its first textbook, faced a demographics problem, especially as liberation theology demanded that theology at large account for its historical complacence, or even support, for injustice that hurt large groups of people that were beginning to demand a voice in the theological academy. As Dorrien puts it, the group had a "white maleness problem,"[41] and expanded its number to make up for it. As Rebecca Chopp recounts, after a period of fallowness, and a phase of bringing in new voices, the group found itself composed of "three distinct cohorts." The original Vanderbilt group, including those who helped get the Workgroup going but didn't contribute much going forward like Gilkey, Ogden, and Kaufman; the first substantive, contributing group that would continue to consult as the Workgroup developed; and finally, the group that did the primary production of the second book, which took lib-

41. Dorrien, *Making of American Liberal Theology*, vol. 3, 335.

eration for granted as a theological movement that must be taken seriously—though it had great difficulty in bringing this intention to fruition—and had seamlessly incorporated social scientific, philosophical, and other disciplinary techniques into its theologizing. Chopp says, "I think [Sharon] Welch and [Catherine] Keller and Mark [Lewis Taylor] and I represented, most of us, people who were already committed to liberation theology or feminist theology by the time we were in grad school. . . . We were already doing theology from a more political practice perspective. Our teachers had already started talking about revisionist theology and cultural change. We were incorporating that from day one."[42] The Workgroup took a strong swing toward liberation and political change being the core of their message. Even while it brought in new members, however, it had difficulty drawing many theologians of color or liberationists, undercutting its intentions.

Part of the impetus for bringing new theologians into the group had to do with pressure or hostility experienced at their home institutions. Constructive theology, including in liberationist forms, challenges the ways theology has been done in divinity schools and seminaries in the wake of liberalism and Barthianism. Chopp, again, remarked "People were having a hard time at their institutions like Harvard and Princeton. I had the easiest time because Emory was shockingly open to the radical. It's not that we flocked as refugees. When we were together we were really able to engage each other in the thought we wanted rather than having to defend our basic propositions. It was a feeling of moving forward."[43] Put another way, Mark L. Taylor explained in an interview, "The paradigm that was operative, the dominant thematic when I joined [the Workgroup], was still that there was a major paradigm shift underway. We were shifting into a postmodern era, and a conversation around whether this is a shift within modernity or a shift into postmodernity. And what does this shift mean for the tasks of doing theology?"[44] The Workgroup on Constructive Theology provided a place where likeminded theologians were able to develop interdisciplinary connections and social justice oriented theological projects in a way that may not have been embraced in their home departments. The participants in the second instantiation of the Workgroup, which produced the second textbook, brought a concern for liberation, justice, and an acceptance of the cultural move from modernity to postmoder-

42. Rebecca Chopp, in discussion with the author, December 22, 2015.
43. Ibid.
44. Mark L. Taylor, in discussion with the author, February 2, 2016.

nity, from liberalism as a discursive modern project to critiques of the hegemonic discursive projects of modernity.

The question over whether to do theology around the traditional doctrinal loci once again came up and was the center of serious debate. Though the framework isn't as strong as in the first or the third textbook, the group in the end did generally stick to using loci to structure the book, although each locus is expressed by confrontation with a specific contemporary crisis in need of a theological response. For better or worse, in departing from the explicit doctrinal construction, one of the greatest critiques of the book has been that it was difficult to use for the purpose of teaching, which remained the main aim of putting together an introductory theological text. Taylor related that "maybe we departed a bit too much from the doctrinal template and took contemporary problematics as our template, and various problematics paired with a doctrine. That was to give a larger role to the context outside of theology, and a larger role methodologically."[45] Taylor himself would come, in his own individual works, to abandon the doctrinal framework entirely.

Reconstructing Christian Theology has a very different tone from the other three books composed by the Workgroup on Constructive Theology. Published in 1994, its language is that of crisis and the fear of environmental disaster looms over the entire text, as the explicit problem taken up in some chapters and frequently referenced or alluded to in almost every chapter. "Crisis" really defines the entire work. In *Constructive Theology*, published later and which will be discussed more below, the introduction claims that this book sought to deal substantively with liberation theology. In a certain sense this is true, as the chapters each take up a different context and the circumstances of making theology liberative, or at least empowering, in that context. Yet the method never approaches that of liberation, and shockingly little is said about the foundational liberation theology in the United States, namely Black liberation theology. Despite the later claim by the editors of *Constructive Theology, Reconstructing Christian Theology* gestures toward liberation theology while never fully internalizing its methods or polemical rhetoric as constructive theology's own.

Seventeen contributors are listed as well as ten in the preface who were consulted but did not contribute writing, bringing the group to around twenty-seven, more than double than at the time of *Traditions*

45. Ibid.

and Tasks. The introduction to the book once again emphasizes the many different perspectives that contribute to the text. Rather than a method to unite them, this book claims a pedagogy of liberation/activism as the thing that holds the many different chapters together.[46] Every chapter but one employs the structure of history, analysis, then reconstruction. Once again, within the context of pedagogy, the doctrines are emphasized, although this time without the seeming embarrassment with which the first editors foreswore they would not employ such a structure if not beholden to it for expediency. "This book is an invitation for students to delve into Christian theology's deep and rich traditions, to truly engage in analysis and evaluation of those traditions and contemporary social challenges, and then to bring Christianity's chief doctrines, reconfigured or reconstructed as hope-filled responses to . . . 'crises' of suffering."[47] One of constructive theology's dominant concerns is to mediate between history and contemporary challenges. It seems more comfortable this time around with employing the language of doctrine, even while ironically making the logic behind doctrines harder to follow.

The first overriding issue identified is that there has been an important discursive shift. The use of "discursive" is important with respect to constructive theology being a self-conscious participation in discursive construction. At this juncture, the Workgroup starts to name its work as responding to and participating in the discursive shifts it recognizes as demanding a new paradigm for doing theology. Those shifts are:

1. A shift away from the Anglo-Saxon, WASP-y American Dream in recognizing that such a construct has always been oppressive and exclusive of contexts and experiences that are not white middle-class male.[48]
2. A re-emergence of the language of crisis.[49]
3. An increased recognition of ambiguities of postmodern culture and seeing "truth-creating as an ongoing conversation." This is what most defines constructive theology and is likely its most enduring strength.[50]

46. Rebecca S. Chopp and Mark Lewis Taylor, eds., *Reconstructing Christian Theology* (Minneapolis: Augsburg Fortress, 1994), ix.
47. Ibid.
48. Ibid., 3.
49. Ibid., 5.
50. Ibid., 6.

4. Toward a postcolonial sensibility.[51]
5. A move to be in deeper dialogue with world religions.[52]

With these in mind, the editors explain, "The purpose of this book emerges more clearly when viewed in relation to these discursive shifts. The volume aims to address these kinds of current issues from the perspective of Christian doctrine and with the goal of shaping revisioned Christian communal praxis."[53] *Traditions and Tasks* sought to introduce a new, future-oriented agenda for Christian theology. This volume, in the wake of liberationist critiques, instead seeks to propose new forms of praxis in light of discursive shifts that have happened, whether or not Christian theology recognizes it.

While *Traditions and Tasks* exhibited an affinity with liberal theology, *Reconstructing Christian Theology* asserts a marked discomfort with it and somewhat aggressively tries to distance itself from it. Its reasons are related to the defining discursive shifts, and they are:

1. The "presence of African Americans, women, and Latin American scholars [bringing] greater awareness to theology of the importance of community"[54] against the presumed individual, primarily white male perspective brought to liberal theology. Challenges to this conception of liberal theology could obviously be brought, but the main critique, even as a caricature, is important.
2. "Concern for the 'practical' crisis of survival and flourishing."[55] This critique is similar to the first. It argues that theology needs to be rooted in the experience of those most oppressed or marginalized against what is seen as liberalism's overly white, educated, affluent nature.
3. Recognition "within Christianity that it itself was a religion, one living in a global neighborhood with other religions, in one community with other communities."[56] The question of adequately and generously engaging other religious traditions begins to take a much larger role in the idea of what constructive theology can contribute to theology in this volume.

51. Ibid., 8.
52. Ibid., 9.
53. Ibid., 11–12.
54. Ibid., 16.
55. Ibid.
56. Ibid.

4. "A turn in the understanding of knowledge itself . . . increasingly seen as always intersubjective, as always formed through the mediation of communal traditions and through social-symbolic or cultural-political processes as much as through empirical and analytic operations."[57] This once again brings attention to the "constructive" nature of constructive theology. This especially harkens back to the earliest days of proto-constructive theology, as well as Meland's idea of culture and religion/theology in an ongoing symbiosis with one another, and Ten Broeke's constructive basis before that.

Insofar as this book has a method, it is embodied in the structure of the chapters' use of analysis and reconstruction. The unifying aim is worth quoting at length, because it gives the clearest idea of what constructive theology is meant to accomplish as expressed in *Reconstructing Christian Theology:*

> Reconstructing Christian theology thus means both reworking theology's symbols and doctrines in various ways and also a continual re-engaging of the diverse communities that Christians address and with whom they must work today for an emancipative restoration of personal and social flourishing. . . . In this way we hope to introduce readers not only to theological interpretation as disciplined reflection but also to the variety of approaches possible when one explores the whole intricately related web of meanings that constitutes theological reflection.[58]

This middle book, at a moment that the group saw as a crisis, sees Christian theology as in need of *re*construction.

Asked what is important in the term "constructive," Chopp pointed to the departure from methods that had dominated before, remarking,

> there are all sorts of ways to have a system. The modern architectonic version is only one way. . . . I'm a little wary of the systematic thing, if one uses systematic theology to talk about what I call architectonic systems developed in modernity. . . . I think constructive theology was first a move of anti-essentialism. I think there was that notion in the 19th and 20th century assertion that there was a common experience. And it's a rejection of that. We wanted theology to be about changing the world. We liked the mystical-political. The other thing that was constructive is that the very discourse itself was undergoing a real paradigm change. It was

57. Ibid.
58. Ibid., 21.

> going to look a lot more like cultural anthropology and sociology meet religion.[59]

Echoing Kaufman, Taylor remarked, "constructive emphasizes imaginative dynamism in all thinking. They're related because that dynamism comes from people who occupy the world in different contextured ways." With the second convening of the Workgroup on Constructive Theology and the textbook they produced, philosophical and interdisciplinary insights are put toward the purpose of changing the world through theology, and emphasizing the context of theology for the purpose of reconstructing theology in such a way that it changes culture and practice generally. The constructed nature of all theological assertions remains emphasized, the importance of imagination and construction maintained. But construction also enables constructive theology, in a more marked way than in the past, to participate in the critique and reconstruction of the world, itself seen as constructed.

The first book, *Traditions and Tasks*, sought to clear a path for a generally liberal theology to critique the tradition while making space for divergent theological claims to exist alongside one another within the same tradition. The second rejects liberal or classically progressive liberal tradition in response to what it calls "discursive shifts," while still maintaining a zone where agonistic theological voices can dwell together. It contextualizes the doctrines of theology. The third book negotiates between these two, while more thoroughly developing a self-conscious idea of what it means to be "constructive." It also provides a cursory retrospective look at from whence the Workgroup on Constructive Theology has come. It revisits the agenda this new paradigm proposes for theology. It oversees a shift from seeing "crises" as being the marginalization of certain contextual spaces, to the crisis of an economic system that oversees the enforcement of that marginalization, sometimes called neo-liberalism or late capitalism.

Constructive Theology: A Contemporary Approach to Classical Themes

The third iteration of the Workgroup on Constructive Theology saw theologians being brought in who had observed the group throughout its history and sought to be a part of it. Paul F. Lakeland was a doctoral student of Hodgson's and familiar with his Workgroup activity. Serene

59. Rebecca Chopp, in discussion with the author, December 22, 2015.

Jones was a feminist theologian well plugged into that community, which included Chopp, Catherine Keller, Kathryn Tanner, and many others who had participated frequently in the Workgroup. After the group had been dormant for a few years, former group leadership proposed that Jones and Lakeland be inducted into the group, on the stipulation that they would be co-conveners and co-editors of a third textbook.[60] The work of the newly reconvened group would try to recover some of the theological tradition highlighted in the first book combined with the justice sensibility of the second book.

The Workgroup once again took a pedagogical focus as the motivation for producing a text, but they sought a distinctive mode of doing so. Lakeland recounted, "I think our approach was very different, just in the way we structured each section. . . . It wasn't systematic. It was intended to be structured in such a way that you could see the dialogue and difference going on among and between theologians as they worked. And that was very deliberate. So anyone who used that book could see at the end of the process that there's a lot of collaboration here but there's also a lot of space for difference." Lakeland relates how constructive theology resists systematization, opting instead for a dialogic, open-ended theology and, further, one in which the dialogue and disagreement are not glossed over for the sake of simplicity or coherence in presentation.

Jones, in an interview, noted that the Workgroup began by taking up liberal issues, then became a group centered around liberation. With the third cohort, according to Jones, it took a harder turn into the postmodern. Jones also characterized the Workgroup on Constructive Theology, in her experience, as a space for young theologians to network and be supported. "The idea was, and has always been, to create a space for younger theologians to network and be supported who are doing cutting edge work and need to have conversation partners they usually don't have at their home institutions."[61]

The third iteration also assembled the largest group of theologians that had yet been included in the Workgroup. Lakeland explained that, "We wanted people who were ecumenically open as far as theological discussions are concerned. We wanted a mix of races, ethnicities, and genders, and a mix between Protestants and Catholics."[62] It grew, under Jones and Lakeland, from about twelve to fifty. "We wanted to

60. Paul F. Lakeland, in discussion with the author, January 29, 2016.
61. Serene Jones, in discussion with the author, February 12, 2016.
62. Paul F. Lakeland, in discussion with the author, January 29, 2016.

do something different but something people would recognize so we used the classical loci," said Lakeland. There was a sense after the second book that, though it did very important work, especially in terms of making constructive theology thoroughly steeped in liberationism and justice, the discernible connection to the theological tradition had been obscured. Lakeland further explained,

> We were very conscious of the need to have something for seminaries. But the seminaries were changed radically from the way they were during the Workgroup's earlier work. Many more people in the seminaries were not attached to particular traditions and were not studying for ministry in a particular church. . . . Many were ambivalent about their own traditions and other traditions and some were ambivalent about religion in general.[63]

The third group decided that in order to move into the future, constructive theology still needed to look to the past. Firmly reestablishing the doctrinal loci as the anchors of the book, though still ambivalently, recalls both the first book and the overall theological tradition. The overall intended effect is a contextualized, multivocal, open-ended demonstration of how theology can be done in a cooperative fashion with an eye toward the future, especially with respect to changing demographics and new crises.

From the outset, *Constructive Theology* sounds much more like a return to the tone and point of view of *Traditions and Tasks*. Its primary starting point affirms the discursive shift of *Reconstructing Christian Theology*, but largely does so in a voice that sounds more conciliatory and retrospect. As always, it begins with the claim that doing theology today is a fundamentally different task than it has been in the past. Reasons for this include Enlightenment challenges, discursive challenges and the recognition that things that seem innate are in fact "constructed," and a critique of the normative position from which theology is to be done. The group, now grown to fifty, explains, "In the pages of this book we offer you a glimpse of what this task looks like when undertaken by a committed, diverse group of theologians who stand at the beginning of a new millennium and in the center of the world's most powerful empire and ask again: How should the Christian faith be understood today here and now, in this place in time?"[64]

63. Paul F. Lakeland, in discussion with the author, January 29, 2016.
64. Serene Jones and Paul Lakeland, eds., *Constructive Theology: A Contemporary Approach to Classical Themes* (Minneapolis: Augsburg Fortress, 2005), 1.

The emphasis once again emerges as maintaining a tension between the tradition and the current time. The theological conclusions drawn in this book are not meant to be good for all time, but rather to speak, explicitly, to this time and place.

The third book is more self-consciously reflective on what it means to do constructive theology. *Constructive Theology* clearly seeks to breathe new spirit and renewed energy into the project of constructive theology after the second seemed, in some sense, to leave the reader with an incredibly pessimistic and fragmented view of the world and the role of theology in it. In fact, the closest any of the first three books comes to a positive definition of constructive theology is given in the introduction: "We are not interested in merely describing what theology has been; we are trying to understand and construct it in the present, to imagine what life-giving faith can be in today's world. In doing so, as with any construction job, we are attempting to build a viable structure. In our case, that structure is an inhabitable, beautiful, fruitful theology."[65] Constructive theology is perpetually ongoing. Including more and more disparate voices is not a goal of the method of constructive theology, but is instead ingredient in the method itself. The emphasis on praxis and making contemporary theology relevant is maintained in insisting on the structure constructed being "inhabitable."

Constructive Theology sees itself as even a newer version of the "new paradigm" offered in *Traditions and Tasks.* This third phase, the "New Constructive Theology," "continues to be inspired by the liberal theological agenda expressed in the first set of volumes, and we share the political and social concerns of the second volume as well, but we find ourselves living in different times and speaking to a very different generation of students."[66] A few observations can be made about this self-understanding. First, constructive theology "admires" liberal theology, but seeks to distance itself more or less completely from that theological agenda. Further, while it takes the liberationist critiques seriously, it seeks to move beyond the completely contextualized method of *Reconstructing Christian Theology.* Critique of the tradition, as noted in the first two books, has become so ingrained and devastating, that *Constructive Theology* moves instead to emphasize the creative nature of working with the tradition. Constructive theology, then, consists of being "in the exciting but unusual position of being both Christianity's

65. Ibid., 2.
66. Ibid., 4.

wise conservators and its harshest critics, all the while trying to construct bold visions of hope and justice for a world in desperate need of them."[67] The crucial dialectic of critique and construction continues. Constructive theology doesn't take as its task to critique other theologies necessarily, but instead critiques the tradition itself when it has not been "life-giving," inclusive, or emancipative.

The loci this time are conceptualized as landmarks in theological cartography, which emphasizes their role not as normative but as guides for understanding the theological territory one inhabits and where it lies with respects to the other important questions of theology. The number of contributors to each section, intended or unintended, shows where the anxieties or interests of the group were especially concentrated. A large motivation for the way theology is explored in this book is the shrinking of the churches in light of them becoming less relevant to the life of young people. Therefore, questions of church and relevancy are especially important. Likewise, the Holy Spirit, as conceived in *Constructive Theology*, is a primary source of newness in theology as expressed in the classical doctrine of the trinity. Therefore, it is put last, indicating the openness to innovation of the group and stressing the centrality of creativity, ambiguity, and the dynamism of constructive theology. On the other hand, there is no eschatology section at all, though eschatological dimensions of the other doctrines are sometimes brought out. The emphasis is on life in the world and the ongoing creative potential of theology.

For Lakeland, the constructive aspect of constructive theology emphasizes an "inductive" over a "deductive" strategy for doing theology. In conversation, he related that "I think of constructive theology as theology that begins from below, from a particular context, and builds to some level of generalization, while systematic is a term that implies, even if it does not intend, a method abstracting from a particular context and aspiring to formulate universal truths."[68] The third iteration of the Workgroup on Constructive Theology intentionally incorporated a greater number of Catholic theologians. Lakeland confided that, "Catholics even more than the old liberal Protestants recognize systematic theology or foundational theology as the governing areas in the Catholic theological tradition. So when you say constructive theology, or at least when you did some decades ago, people would get nervous. Because constructive sounds like you're beginning from

67. Ibid.
68. Paul F. Lakeland, in discussion with the author, September 24, 2015.

somewhere else than what you've received from the tradition."[69] Nevertheless, constructive theology has had a strong Catholic presence throughout its history, including people like David Tracy, Roger Haight, John Pawlikowski, Michele Saracino, and others. Constructive theology maintains an inherently ecumenical approach. It views conversation that is wide ranging in its context and sources as critical to developing theologies for the present. Catholic theology that privileges context and the rethinking of doctrine finds a home in constructive theology.

Jones emphasized the importance of working with tradition in doing constructive theology, but letting go of the defensive or descriptive qualities of systematic theology. She related how the interests of the Workgroup have changed throughout its history, and yet it has maintained its collaborative ethos, its emphasis on new generations of theologians and theological thinking, and its commitment to the importance of constructive theology informing quotidian life of individual believers and the church.

In terms of theological traditions, the Workgroup tries to live somewhere between liberal theology and liberation, attempting to reconcile the two. Liberation theology contains an inherent critique of liberal theology and its historical complicity and sometimes even underwriting of unjust social systems. Constructive theology's critique of theology's history of complicity highlights its affinity with this concern of liberation theology. Yet, despite *Reconstructing Christian Theology's* effort to assimilate liberation tendencies, its arguments still mostly center around the classic and ongoing proposals and issues of mainstream, mostly white middle class theology. The third book reaffirms this identity. Yet constructive theology isn't simply a reiteration of liberal theology, as defined by Dorrien, either. It can at times have revolutionary leanings as far as doctrines go, and while it is largely open to historical criticism and natural sciences, it isn't preoccupied with their findings. While constructive theology does seek to make Christianity credible and socially relevant, it is largely based on a realization and acceptance that liberal theology has failed to do so, as evidenced by vacating churches and students who have no foundational knowledge whatsoever about theology, or Christianity generally, when entering higher education. The fourth and most recent textbook seeks to make sense of all of these tensions in a self-conscious way.

69. Paul F. Lakeland, in discussion with the author, January 29, 2016.

Awake to the Moment: An Introduction to Theology

The concern for students in higher education lacking previous knowledge about Christianity or theology carries into the fourth textbook by the Workgroup on Constructive Theology, *Awake to the Moment: An Introduction to Theology*. Unlike previous formations of the Workgroup, after the publication of *Constructive Theology*, members decided to continue meetings without a break. Much of the same membership carries over from the group convened by Jones and Lakeland into the fourth cohort, led by Laurel C. Schneider and Stephen G. Ray Jr. Some contributing members to *Awake to the Moment* even stretch back to *Reconstructing Christian Theology*. The Workgroup in its latest form has included voices of constructive theologians who have been involved in three formulations of the Workgroup on Constructive theology and their associated collaborative work. The carryover proved to be both a strength and a challenge for the group. Upon completion of *Awake to the Moment*, the group undertook a rethinking of its structure and a reframing of its ongoing mission. On the one hand, the continuation of the group straight through allowed for important continuity, and for a unifying conceptual understanding of constructive theology to carry through after the previous book began to offer a vision of constructive theology as its own tradition. On the other, because the group had expanded to fifty then sixty-eight under Jones and Lakeland, and brought in two more members in the interim between the third textbook and Ray and Schneider's convening of the group, membership swelled to seventy, testing the limits of the resources the Workgroup had available.

One novel aspect of the fourth textbook that immediately offers some insight into the evolving mentality of the Workgroup is the authorship credit, prominently displayed on the cover: "The Workgroup on Constructive Theology," with Schneider and Ray noted as editors. Previous books briefly describe the Workgroup and its task in preparing textbooks in their introductions. *Awake to the Moment* claims the Workgroup at the point of first contact with the reader. This is a statement on both the visibility of the Workgroup itself, implying the variety of theology inside and the caliber of scholars who have contributed, as well as a clear affirmation of the collaborative nature of the group. *Awake to the Moment* asserts the collaboration that went into the content found inside before the text proper begins.

Awake to the Moment in some way hearkens back to the themes of the second Workgroup textbook, *Reconstructing Christian Theology*, with rhetoric and a prognosis closer to that of the third. It takes "crisis" as its starting point, environmental, racial, international, but adds a small dose of humor to lighten the heavy tone of the second book. The refrain "it's the end of the world as we know it," repeats throughout, citing a sarcastically apocalyptic song from 1988 by R.E.M. that offers a peppy, uptempo narrative of the conclusion of the world, which contains its own ironic response, "and I feel fine."

Awake to the Moment is the most straightforwardly self-reflective of the textbooks on what exactly constructive theology is in relation to theology as a whole. Once again the Workgroup starts with the assertion that Christian theology absolutely must speak to contemporary, embodied experience.[70] It begins from the most basic consideration of not only what theology is and how it should be done, but why theology needs to be done in the first place. The Workgroup claims that decoupled from actual events and the lived experience of Christians and other religious people, theology becomes extraneous and unnecessary.

Part of the change in tone of the book has to do with the intended audience. Attending to the perceived needs of the members of the Workgroup as professors, many teaching outside of graduate school and seminary contexts, the Workgroup decided to make *Awake to the Moment* a textbook that could be used primarily by undergraduates, whereas previous Workgroup textbooks targeted for the most part seminarians and divinity school students. Getting in on the ground floor of theological studies, the book claims constructive theological method while introducing students to the concept of the academic study of theology at all. As a result, the structure is different as well. Rather than taking on specialized theological loci in an explicit way, articulating their pasts, analyzing them, and offering a mini-reconstruction, the book explores what theology is, how it can matter for the contemporary world, and makes an argument for its need in a constructive mode specifically. That is, *Awake to the Moment* revisits the persistent question of the appropriateness or not of constructing around doctrinal loci. It is the first textbook by the Workgroup that seeks to offer a vision of what constructive theology is as such. In a distinctively constructive theological way, however, that vision is constructed recursively and in self-referential conversation throughout

70. Ray and Schneider, eds., *Awake to the Moment*, 5.

the text. The text offers many "constructive theology is" statements that piece together, taken in sum, a dialogical view of the role constructive theology plays in the theological academy as well as the part Christian theology should play in the world at large.

Condensing its many proposals about what constructive theology is, the introduction explains,

> We are theologians who are not afraid to criticize the role our own religious traditions have played in creating the problems in our world today. Out of our anger and protest at Christian abuses and out of love of our Christian traditions, we are inspired to engage those traditions more energetically and constructively. We see in all of our religions—and in our own traditions of Christianity specifically—many seeds of hope and wisdom for the world for which we passionately work, a world of peace and justice, a world where racism, sexism, poverty, ecological degradation, and oppression are overcome.[71]

It continues, "With our feet firmly planted in the present, in all that the sciences, the humanities, and the social sciences offer, we are convinced that what we have to learn from our religious traditions are pathways toward a world of healing, of justice, and of reparation for the wrongs of our past."[72] That is, *Awake to the Moment* brings to light what this book argues, that constructive theology is a critically conscious integration of interdisciplinarity and activism/advocacy. It concludes:

> So constructive theology is a distinctive form of Christian theology that does not separate heavenly concerns from worldly ones. Some theologians see their work to be a careful stewardship and reiteration of sacred doctrines handed down by church authorities, and they strive to keep those doctrines as pure as possible of the messy world of politics and social struggles. But constructive theologians see religious ideas as inseparable from the fabric of human existence. We are theologians because we are convinced of the significance of religious ideas in the *whole* tapestry of human and creaturely life, and we are constructive theologians because we apply a critical lens to the many ways that Christian ideas participate in making the world, both for good and for bad. We recognize that all theology is a blend of human and divine, of imagination and revelation. All theology is constructed out of the best efforts of human beings to understand the ineffable reality and experience of divinity in the world. And so theology always must be treated with a mixture of credibility and criti-

71. Ibid., 10–11.
72. Ibid., 12.

> cism. Like human hearts, theology is always undergoing improvement as long as it remains open.[73]

Constructive theology claims its own space outright in *Awake to the Moment.* It is relevant, ongoing, fallible, interdisciplinary, concerned with tradition, and attuned to the crises and struggles for justice in the world today. *Awake to the Moment* lucidly formulates the results of forty years of constructive theological work, giving brief and tentative looks into what unifies the diverse group of theologians who identify as "constructive." It continues to affirm, assert, and amplify the distinctive characteristics of constructive theology as they have been developed from proto-constructive theologians through the present.

The introduction concludes by boiling constructive theology in its particularity down to five parts: It is critical of tradition while also maintaining the absolute necessity of working with the positive, life-giving strains of it;[74] it engages meaning systems;[75] it is between the heavenly and the earthly;[76] it involves ongoing interpretation, especially of the Bible;[77] and it is "disaffected from . . . religions' abusive complicity in a world of hurt," which necessitates greater commitment on the part of the theologian.[78] As a result of these features, *Awake to the Moment* argues that the "approach" of constructive theology:

1. Starts with "not only with what counts as knowledge in our time but also with how we know what we know," or epistemology.[79]
2. Necessitates "a deep engagement with the many traditions that hold and shape what we know of God."[80]
3. Embraces "both the disaffection and the resonance that characterize contemporary attitudes toward religion."[81]
4. "Stages a kind of intervention—an interruption of business as usual in order to share a vision of the world that is a different version, rooted in life and flourishing."[82]
5. And finally, "Takes up the riches of our traditions, [highlighting]

73. Ibid.
74. Ibid., 17.
75. Ibid., 11.
76. Ibid., 12.
77. Ibid.
78. Ibid., 13.
79. Ibid., 15.
80. Ibid.
81. Ibid., 16.
82. Ibid.

> the concrete *practices* of a life-giving, justice-seeking version of Christianity."[83]

A crucial innovation of the fourth textbook, highlighted in the fifth tenet, is its emphasis on spirituality, contemplative practices, and religious practices, not necessarily only justice praxis, although practice should serve justice ends. Previous Workgroup textbooks, especially *Reconstructing Theology*, emphasized the need for Christian praxis, the linking up of theology with concrete work for justice in the world. *Awake to the Moment* emphasizes traditional Christian practices for their own sake, while highlighting the ways that those practices themselves contribute to work for justice and equality in the world. Not only the theology of Christianity, that is the thinking and understanding of what makes up the religion, its beliefs, and essential characteristics, must be subject to reconstruction and reinterpretation, but also the quotidian practices of Christianity: church, prayer, reading of the Bible, and other such practices from the perspective of both clergy and laity. Practical, lived theology plays a greater role in *Awake to the Moment* than it does in any other Workgroup textbook, where Christian spiritual and contemplative practices as realized in everyday life were implied, but their utmost importance not made explicit.

Awake to the Moment also puts a special emphasis on the outright replacement or reinvention of historical Christian doctrines and beliefs that have caused hurt and suffering.[84] To "reinvent" powerfully evokes the extent to which reconstruction is being undertaken. Retaining the crucial hold on tradition, the Workgroup insists that Christianity must nonetheless be reinvented to counteract its own past complicity and death-dealing. Constructive theology does not only respond to crises, it recognizes, repents, and reprimands its own involvement in those crises. Christianity has compelled and accelerated many of history's most egregious injustices and catastrophes. Constructive theology, rather than looking away and disavowing that participation, dares to acknowledge and claim its own past wrongdoing, while committing to wholesale reinvention, if necessary, of Christianity to start the work of recognizing and correcting those actions. Contemporary constructive theology is not simply revisionist, but actively turning inward to name, confess, and reconstruct around its own gravest mistakes.

In interviews, Ray and Schneider parsed out the role of traditional

83. Ibid., 17.
84. Ibid., 172.

loci in *Awake to the Moment*, going back to the book being intended for an undergraduate audience. Ray commented that, "All of our previous groups reflected on the different categories or different loci. So we decided to introduce the audience to different ways of doing theology and different sources available for doing theology. We thought this would best serve our desire to contribute to the next generation of constructive theologians as well as participate in the construction of theology as such." Because the audience of *Awake to the Moment* is thought to have less familiarity with theological work than even the audience for *Constructive Theology: A Contemporary Approach to Classical Themes*, the book emphasizes plurality in approaches and sources, as well as emphasizing the need for theology at all. Using doctrines as anchors, it is thought, may presume a level of theological knowledge or familiarity with historical issues in Christianity that contemporary undergraduates, and even many seminary students, may not possess.

On reducing the visibility of the doctrines in *Awake to the Moment*, Schneider commented,

> In the process of imagining this book, we started by saying, 'our audience is no longer seminary students who have a pretty good background in Christian teachings or have been schooled in Christian theology. Our audience is those who have no background in this. So how do we say, this is what constructive theology is? Because we can't just say it's what we say about God, what we say about church, and go through the loci. Before we even talk about God and before we even talk about Christ, what are the pieces that play into that?

The fourth textbook steps back to examine just what theology is generally and how constructive theology creates a space for it in the world today. She continued, "In the proofing I realized somebody reading this is going to wonder, 'when are we going to construct something?' And there's a sense in which we don't until the conclusion. It's the beginning of saying, 'if we're going to talk about God,' etc." For Schneider, the doctrines are almost not present at all throughout the book. Ray, however, acknowledged the low-profile presence of the doctrines, suggesting, "one of the reasons we subtly kept the doctrines is that as much as we refer to ourselves as constructive theologians, the majority of us were trained in programs that are systematic theology."

Once again, *Awake to the Moment* echoes *Reconstructing Christian Theology*, which also sought to distance itself from the rigid doctrinal format, yet maintained them in the background, keeping doctrines for the way they reflected contemporary crises, while acknowledging the conflict over keeping them at all that carries throughout the tradition. *Awake to the Moment* concludes, "Throughout this book we have worked to clarify and enlarge the field of inquiry through which traditional theological categories (like God, church, Salvation, and so forth) can be understood, anchoring them in a specific concern for justice and flourishing."[85]

In line with the constructive theological tradition throughout its development within the Workgroup, doctrines are not maintained to be self-evidently necessary or permanently valid. They are important because they connect contemporary theology solidly with the historical Christian theological tradition and, most importantly, because doctrines provide a framework for connecting to questions of justice and flourishing today. Even though the doctrines are not listed as section headings, they make appearances, implied or explicit, throughout the book, including creation,[86] eschatology ("time of endings," and "the end of the world as we know it" throughout), theology proper,[87] Christology,[88] a doctrine of other religious traditions, which was first introduced into the Workgroup's own set of doctrines in the second textbook,[89] ecclesiology,[90] and so on. The doctrines are not named in their specialized theological terms.

But the text takes moments to step back and construct, however briefly, around classical loci throughout. The continued importance of the doctrines for constructive theology, despite the seeming diminutive part they play in this textbook, is summarized, "Our work participates in doctrinal development and the work of justice, two ongoing tasks of the church. Doctrinal development concerns assessing tradition and appropriating it for the sake of current belief and practice as well as for the sake of future generations."[91] In the end, *Awake to the Moment* keeps explicit construction around doctrines subdued because it is intended for an audience that must first be convinced of the relevance of Christian theology at all. It ends with its only *explicit* construction around a doctrine, namely a doctrine of theology proper, or God.

85. Ibid., 177.
86. Ibid., 29.
87. Ibid., 175.
88. Ibid., 100.
89. Ibid., 92.
90. Ibid., 162.
91. Ibid., 91.

To put it in sum, *Awake to the Moment* manifests the Workgroup's ongoing conflicted embrace of doctrinal loci in a dramatic fashion.

Constructive theology has always maintained a conflicted relationship with liberation theology. From its inception the Workgroup sought to account for and incorporate liberationist insights, but it has struggled to bring that desire to fruition. *Reconstructing Christian Theology* made it a priority, yet struggled because the Workgroup had a difficult time making a case to scholars of color and other marginalized and minoritized perspectives to join. By the third textbook, *Constructive Theology*, the Workgroup had become much more diverse, but still had trouble articulating its stance toward liberation. *Awake to the Moment* unapologetically affirms its embrace of liberation theology. As Ray explained, "What the book does in a way that is almost subliminal is that it presumes the liberationist stance's validity. Which is a huge difference from earlier where so much of a chapter was spent explaining the decision to take liberation seriously. Here liberation is placed at the entrance. The questions we try to answer emerge from it." Fulfilling an intention that started to form with the first iteration of the Workgroup, *Awake to the Moment* simply starts with the assumption that liberation is a crucial element of any contemporary Christian theology. As a result, the incorporation of liberation shows up throughout the text. It becomes informative of every point made in the textbook, and a baseline test for the legitimacy of any faithful Christian theology in the context of the contemporary world's crises around race, gender, sexuality, ableism, ageism, and the ever-expanding recognition of marginalized and minoritized communities in a world-system Christian theology is called to indict.

Among the important things *Awake to the Moment* adds to the constructive theological conversation, three stand out. First, the constructive nature of constructive theology is emphasized, especially as it relates to reconstructing around sites of historical hurt and embarrassment on the part of Christianity. In no uncertain terms, the Workgroup writes, "Theologians have the choice of ceding God to these [extremist or oppressive] interpretations or of vigorously accepting the challenge to interpret God otherwise. It is a theological opportunity as much as a dire need."[92] Second, pluralism and diversity in theological propositions and interpretation is necessary, inevitable, and a strength rather than a weakness. Third, the use of contemplative practices, liturgy, and

92. Ibid., 10.

embodied religious experience and expression as primary sources of constructive theological knowledge is proposed. This is a novel addition to the Workgroup's textbooks, and affirms constructive theology's commitment to being theology that can affect and be a part of people's daily lives. Finally, the self-reflective emergence of constructive theology as a distinct category is made clear. *Awake to the Moment* more than any of the previous textbooks, claims constructive theology's status alongside but apart from other historical and contemporary forms of Christian theological work.

When asked what makes constructive theology "constructive," Ray commented,

> From my perspective, it means being very clear that I'm being attentive to these doctrinal issues but doing so in such a way that I have a commitment to contribute to a more life giving faith. If I were going to say it more plainly, when we say systematic theology there is a way in which the assumptions are that we're talking about a project where the form is largely based on either European or certainly white male theologians of the mid-20th century and the debates going on between them. That's the thing I want to watch out for. When I say constructive theology, I very much mean doctrinal, but disrupting the ghettoized way of thinking about these ideas.[93]

Schneider adds, "In one way, there is no non-constructive theology. Because that is what humans do. We construct our image of God from texts. Constructive theology takes systematic theology's presuppositions further, that we are co-creators with God. God relies on our genius for invention and storytelling to bring to understanding what God reveals to us in the world and in the text. For us not to see the construction in theology is to be blind to the human imprint."[94] Both Ray and Schneider note how constructive theology draws out an under recognized quality of all theology. As underscored by the prolegomena to constructive theology above, constructive theology's distinctive contribution to Christian theology is to draw out and make explicit the imaginative construction of theology. To do theology with that firmly in mind, to do constructive theology, changes the shape and outcome of theologizing.

As with the editors of the earlier textbooks, both emphasize the role that the process, the construction itself, plays in setting construc-

93. In conversation with the author, July 15, 2016.
94. In conversation with the author, August 11, 2016.

tive theology apart from other varieties of Christian theology. Further, both commented on the dialogic nature of the book in its final form, as well as the work that went into putting it together. *Awake to the Moment* contains its own internal tensions and disagreements. The text holds together as a unity, but the differing views emerge in a sensitive reading. Like the textbooks before it, this is a valued quality of the final product, that it has the resilience to hold together despite the breadth of perspectives, some of which are at odds, held within.

Again, breaking with tradition, the Workgroup has decided to continue on after the publication of *Awake to the Moment* without taking a break. However, the group underwent important restructuring. After growing from the original fifteen to twenty of the first iteration to approximately seventy in its most recent form, the group decided to refocus on its role in fostering new, cutting edge theology. The cap for membership was lowered with the intention of bringing more new scholars in contact with established scholars in order to keep momentum in the group's conversation as the theological landscape continues to shift. Maintaining its commitment to being a Workgroup that produces publications and tangible outcomes, a more frequently re-envisioned group will receive the task of undergoing projects in shorter cycles, around five years. Each previous textbook has seen a consistent interval of ten to twelve years before the next, with smaller works in between. The Workgroup going forward is looking to produce collaborative works of substance, though not necessarily introductory textbooks in theology, more frequently. Though the Workgroup is undergoing restructuring, the changes in fact reaffirm its past identity and commitments. It will continue to produce works in a collaborative fashion, put junior scholars into conversation with senior scholars for the sake of the development of constructive theology, value internal diversity and conversation, and set the theological agenda for the Workgroup, which itself through the participation of its members and the works they produce, both inside and outside the group, will shape forthcoming progressive Christian theology across the United States. In some cases, constructive theology has begun to find advocates for its spread around the world.

Conclusion

Reduced to its simplest elements, constructive theology, as developed by the Workgroup on Constructive Theology, is exactly what it claims in its name: the acknowledgment that ultimately theology is a constructive, discourse building discipline with real life ramifications for people living in the present. It calls theologians to be self-reflective and self-critical when doing so. Culture affects theology and theology affects culture, and ultimately human beings are the ones trying to make inhabitable social structures in the first place.

Nevertheless, constructive theology is a radically humble variety of theology; it categorically rejects propositional statements that limit the interpretive possibilities concerning God, except to affirm that the ones that participate in marginalization or the historical complicity of Christianity in injustice cannot be tolerated. It accepts essential diversity of theological claims and opinions as a strength rather than as a fatal flaw or heresy. And, as abandoning the adjective "systematic" implies, it refuses any pretense that suggests theology can be completely systematized, and every doctrine logically cohered into one grand system.

Going forward, the Workgroup will likely need even more variety, more diversity, and perhaps most importantly, a more rigorous yet radically hospitable approach to outside religious traditions as well as atheist and non-affiliated perspectives. Many of these issues and questions are dealt with by individual constructive theologians outside of the context of these very few texts put together by the Workgroup. It remains, then, to turn to the major guiding themes of constructive theology that have led the work of constructive theologians, both inside and outside the Workgroup, the first of which is an overriding and persistent concern with producing theology that is authentically interdisciplinary.

3

Constructive Theology as Interdisciplinary Theology

The Workgroup on Constructive Theology gave constructive theology a sense of legitimacy within the theological academy. Yet the conversation for constructive theology doesn't end within the sphere of theology. Starting with its emphasis on philosophy, social sciences, and culture, constructive theology has been in conversation with other academic disciplines throughout its history. That is to say constructive theology is inherently interdisciplinary. In its effort to be an actionable, relevant form of theology, it has always, from the proto-constructive theologies of Ten Broeke and Meland, through the Workgroup's textbooks and today, maintained the importance of incorporating insights from other disciplines into its corpus.

Identifying the two central motivations for constructive theology as a need for conversation with other academic disciplines, especially religious studies, and the need for a thoroughly progressive, activist theology points to important realities but is also a false division. Constructive theology, often, is not one or the other. The activism of constructive theology comes to be based on the insights drawn from other disciplines as a corrective to the theological tradition. Nonetheless, there is a question of emphasis throughout constructive theology's history, and different theologians, at different times, under different circumstances, tend to emphasize one or the other more. And though constructive theology did tend to lift up its interdisciplinarity in its early history more than its activism, the chronology doesn't hold fast. Elements of both emerge almost from the beginning, though with Ten Broeke and early Meland, the activism aspect hadn't yet arrived. Both themes are legitimate, and work symbiotically. The two reflect different guiding methodological concerns, both of which are crucial to constructive theology's project.

Religious studies as an independent department in the academy emerged in the 1960s, around the same time, in fact, that constructive theology coalesced as an interdisciplinary theology. Clearly studies of religion existed before religious studies proper came into being. However these were done in various specific methodological ways, like the history of religions, philosophy of religion, comparative religion, sociology of religion, anthropology of religion, and of course, theology. The uniqueness of religious studies is that it incorporates all of these different methods, with theology sometimes considered an exception, under one umbrella term. Because of its perceived objective standpoint, religious studies has found a home in colleges and universities throughout the United States regardless of religious affiliation or lack thereof. Theology holds a conflicted place within religious studies. On the one hand, religious studies has not been able simply to eliminate theology altogether from its circle because so much of the history of religious thinking has been done from a theological standpoint. However, because historically theology has overwhelmingly been done from the standpoint of religious adherents, and most often within Christianity been defined using Anselm's famous "faith seeking understanding," religious studies has often seen theology as violating its goal of being disinterested and objective. As a result, it is common for universities to offer graduate level study in both theological disciplines, for the most part in divinity schools, and in religious studies, usually housed in schools of arts and sciences.

Religious studies includes methods as diverse as historiography, classics, philosophy, economics, sociology, anthropology, psychology, neuroscience, hermeneutics and literary studies, cultural studies, and many others. In reality, religious studies is not so much one discipline, but the gathering of many different disciplines all around one subject. Almost any discipline could feasibly be considered legitimate within religious studies as long as it offered a perspective on religion as an important phenomenon within human experience. And, indeed, throughout its history the conversation of religious studies has alternately been dominated by influential proposals from these different viewpoints and disciplines. Basic courses in the theories and methods of religious studies tend to include canonical works by important thinkers from before the advent of religious studies whose ideas are incorporated into the analysis of religion, as well as specific applications of those insights with respect to religion. Religious studies doesn't have its own endemic canon. It is an interdisciplinary endeavor par excellence, having no central theoretical texts exclusively its own, instead importing its foundational thinking from other disciplines in a grand amalgamation of scholarly techniques.

Over the question of confession or commitment, as well as in the competition for attention and resources, theology and religious studies are inherently suspicious of one another. This creates an odd tension when considering faculty is so often shared between the two. When departmental resources are scarce, religious studies and theology both face existential dilemmas at the institutional level. On the one hand, religions are often seen as philosophies with God included, and so integrated uncomfortably into philosophy departments. In the case of stand alone religious studies departments, because of the pretense to being objective, the appropriateness of theology in the curriculum at all is often raised.

Historically, theology is a self-contained discipline, neither drawing extensively on others or being held responsible to them. Again, a classic quote, this time from Tertullian, "What has Athens to do with Jerusalem, or the Academy with the church?" summarizes the propensity for theology to remain distinct from other disciplines historically. Theology has used outside thinking frequently, especially the exact ancient Greek philosophy that Tertullian speaks out against. But Christian theology has never been held accountable to outside disciplines, instead finding its methods and norms from within its own two-millennia old tradition.

Religious studies and constructive theology came to fruition at about the same time. As religious studies has in some cases displaced theology as the primary academic discipline that engages religion, theology has found itself uncomfortably trying to legitimize itself within a religious studies framework. Religious studies, in its interdisciplinary project, has sought to systematize an objective understanding of religion, yet as contemporary critiques of the category of "religion" itself have shown, its success has been limited at best. "Religion" is notoriously difficult to define with any sort of precision. Constructive theology, however, resists the systematizing impulse of religious studies. While religious studies as a whole has tried to integrate many different perspectives in order to give a comprehensive view of the phenomenon of religion, constructive theology has used a similarly interdisciplinary method to create an impression of Christianity that rejects singularity. Along the same lines, Chopp notes that constructive theologians may be the first significant theological movement that is not primarily made up of clergy and ordained Christians, but rather academics.[1] Constructive theology, in reflecting religious studies' own interdisciplinary nature and often appropriating its same theorists and trends, makes for the possibility of religious studies and theology being in authentic conversation after drifting apart for nearly half a century. Further, it puts theology in a position to participate on an equal footing with religious studies within the academy, and even serve as a corrective in some respects to the impasse of theory with which religious studies has found itself confronted.

The interdisciplinarity of constructive theology goes both ways. As Corey D.B. Walker notes in a review of Catherine Keller's *Face of the Deep*,

> "When you see influential critics publishing major books with titles like *The Genesis of Secrecy, The Great Code, Kabalah and Criticism, Violence and the Sacred, Deconstruction and Theology*, you know you are in the presence of a significant trend." When the late Edward Said penned these words over two decades ago in his influential collection of essays *The World, the Text, and the Critic*, he perceptively took note of an intriguing intellectual trend. For Said, the turn to religion, particularly within the fields of literary theory and criticism, raised new questions regarding the role of the critic and the function of criticism.[2]

The flow between other disciplines and theology is bidirectional. The conversation has been initiated on both sides, though the two in many respects still seem to be talking past one another rather than to one another. Religious studies has often imported insights from these other disciplines, and from time to time exports its own insights back. Theology has been more reticent. Constructive theology, however, has

1. Rebecca Chopp, in discussion with the author, November 30, 2015.
2. Cory D.B. Walker, review of *Face of the Deep: A Theology of Becoming*, by Catherine Keller, *Journal of the American Academy of Religion* 75, no. 3 (September, 2007): 733–34.

positioned itself to be the best conversation partner for other disciplines, and their synthesis within religious studies. Its interdisciplinarity, once controversial, has become a mainstay for any type of theology that wants to be taken seriously in the contemporary intellectual landscape. In order to prove viable in the current and forthcoming academy, theology must in good faith and seriously confront other disciplines and offer insights back. Constructive theology does this in a way like no other theological movement has ever done in the past.

The importance of interdisciplinarity for theology is twofold, and constructive theology has become the best expression to date for this need. First, theology has, fairly or not, struggled to justify its presence in the modern academy, specifically because of its history of being confessional and provincially concerned with Christian belief. Second, theology has nonetheless developed in important ways that deserve to be heard throughout the wider university. Christian theology—as well as theologies of other religious traditions—has new things to offer philosophy, the social sciences, literary studies, and even the sciences at this moment in history. Constructive theology presents an entry into a conversation between theology and any number of other disciplines on an equal footing. It forms the basis of a two-way conversation, or better yet, multiply oriented discussion, that reintegrates theology as an intellectually credible, viable, and vigorous tradition in the twentieth and now twenty-first century.

The interdisciplinary engagements of constructive theology are limitless. As many other disciplines as exist present themselves as potential conversation partners. Because constructive theology's primary interlocutor is religious studies, it has most often anchored its interdisciplinarity in the same insights and theories that have been important in religious studies. These include hermeneutics and literary studies, the social sciences and psychology, philosophy, and cultural studies. The examples below are not exhaustive of the interdisciplinary work of constructive theologians. Rather, they represent the most influential versions of interdisciplinarity, and, for this chapter, the ones that are most strictly interdisciplinary (rather than activist, or also activist, which is the subject of chapter four). They have been chosen because they are the most widely known and regarded within the constructive theological tradition in terms of creating an external conversation, and those working in their same interdisciplinary streams tend to draw on their foundational work. Many began in the '60s and '70s, at the time the Workgroup on Constructive Theology formed. But the trajectory of their careers, in conversation with the constructive tradition at large, best reveals their importance. Within the works of the theologians read and interpreted below, the primary methodological works of each will be prioritized and analyzed in an effort to show the unifying methodological commitments of constructive theology done in an interdisciplinary mode.

Sallie McFague: Hermeneutics, Literary Theory, and Meaning in Language

The interest in language and meaning in constructive theology emerges at the very beginning, even in proto-constructive theologians like Ten Broeke. The turn from trying to describe the tradition to trying to make sense of it, historically and in the present, makes a discussion of the discursive function of language crucial. Ultimately, if theologians create something rather than describe it, the foundational realization and break from systematic theology for constructive theology, that creative work is done through language. In many ways, the realization that language forms the structures of theology, that human meaning and the interpretation of life, including religious life, is a function of language, the modern into postmodern argument that human beings are beings of language through and through, is the most basic starting place for formalized constructive theology. Constructive theology doesn't come to this conclusion itself, but imports it from philosophy, religious studies, and literary studies, especially Hans Georg Gadamer, Paul Ricoeur, and other mid-century theorists of religious hermeneutics. Peter C. Hodgson and Sallie McFague, colleagues at Vanderbilt University, are two of the most important figures in the early Workgroup and represent the centrality of literary concerns and hermeneutics to constructive theology.

Literature and the Christian Life by Sallie McFague (then TeSelle),[3] published in 1966, *Jesus—Word and Presence* by Peter C. Hodgson in 1971, and *The Meaning of God* by Robert H. King in 1974, the first books published by each, point to the cruciality of language and literary interpretation in constructive theology. The titles alone all indicate that language has become central. These three theologians ultimately have different claims to make, but they all enter into a reconstruction of some part of Christian theology, or the whole method of doing theol-

3. For simplicity's sake, only McFague will be used, even though McFague's earliest works included her married name, TeSelle.

ogy, through the power of language and the recognition that language and interpretation are central to recovering Christian faith and practice in a world where meaning has become destabilized. Central for all is the question of "meaning." After the perceived failure of liberalism and the emptiness of supernaturalism, whether Christianity, or indeed the word "God" itself, has any meaning looms large. McFague, as a central figure in constructive theology who embodies the literary-hermeneutical variety of constructive theology and later serves as a paradigmatic activist constructive theologian, provides an archetype to be analyzed.

Constructive theologies that take the literary critical, hermeneutical route arise from interdisciplinary reformulations of the ways purpose and meaning are given to human existence after metanarratives and supposedly objective, metaphysically based interpretations are dispensed with. The move toward literary ways of reconstructing theology centers on two interdisciplinary engagements: first, with literary critical methodologies emerging in literary studies and employed in religious studies as well; and, second, with non-scriptural texts. Foundationally, because Christianity is after all a book-based religion, literary constructive theologies incorporate reading and hermeneutical techniques to confront the Bible anew, and to explore the ways the Bible and the Christian religion relate to outside literary sources. This relationship can be mutually constructive or antagonistic. Ultimately, constructive theologies that start from an interdisciplinary literary critical standpoint build on the constructedness of Christianity by acknowledging that the metaphysical claims about the existence of God and the primacy of Christianity are not, and perhaps cannot be, broadly accepted as normative in contemporary culture. Human beings' relationship with God is fundamentally one of words, both in terms of encountering the tradition through its foundational scriptural and theological texts, or in terms of the word "God" itself, which faces a crisis of potential non-meaning as an empty linguistic container.

Sallie McFague taught for most of her career at Vanderbilt University. McFague is broadly acknowledged as one of the earliest proponents of constructive theology and she was a founder of the Workgroup on Constructive Theology. Dorrien argues that "The liberal tradition had a good number of creative theologians in the 1980s and 1990s, but except for the process school, they were strictly individual performers. Three of them taught at Vanderbilt Divinity School—Peter Hodgson, Edward Farley, and Sallie McFague—making Vanderbilt a leading outpost of liberal theology. . . . All of them argued that liberal theology had to develop new ways of relating to philosophy, culture, and/or the natural world."[4] These varieties of theology found themselves, as Dorrien points out, without an institutional home. The Workgroup on Constructive theology became a pan-institutional home for theologians working in this vein. And, while in the 1970s through '90s these theologians may have identified themselves with the liberal tradition, their theologies, by engaging with other disciplines, acknowledging the flagging nature of liberalism, and reconstructing theology, have formed a methodological movement that shares certain liberal theological characteristics but departs from it as a method for doing theology.

Proposing Connections between Literary Theory and Theology

Literature and the Christian Life is McFague's earliest work, and proposes methodological overlaps between theology and literary theory. She also edited *Soundings*, a journal that tellingly describes itself as "interdisciplinary." McFague's central early programmatic works, *Speaking in Parables* and *Metaphorical Theology*, expand on the literary aspect of the claims she makes about theology and lay the foundation for the literary-focused theologies and ecotheologies she is most well known for. Throughout, her theologies rely on literary criticism as an important, even necessary, conversation partner with Christian theology. Especially given Christianity's historically conflicted relationship with the arts, McFague thinks that a clear delineation of the appropriateness of using texts other than the Bible to expound Christian theology as well as claiming the usefulness of theologizing nonreligious narratives strengthens Christian theology in a way that has become indispensible.[5] Likewise, with the breakdown of inherent meanings in postmodern theology, dispensing with what has often been called "metanarrative," McFague's theology develops into a project that identifies problematic models and metaphors and proposes new ones in their places. The overarching concern throughout is with bringing together literature and Christian beliefs and practices, enhancing and rethinking Christian theology for McFague's contemporary world that renews theology's relevance and starts to undermine the marginalizing aspects of classical theological models.

4. Dorrien, *The Making of American Liberal Theology*, vol. 3, 325.
5. Sallie McFague TeSelle, *Literature and the Christian Life* (New Haven: Yale University Press, 1966), 7.

Literature and the Christian Life carefully outlines that interdisciplinarity does not mean conflation.[6] In order to ensure the strengths of both theology and literary studies, she maintains the importance of highlighting the distinctiveness of each. That is to say, interdisciplinarity in theology doesn't intend to simply absorb other disciplinary assertions, but rather to remain in conversation and be enhanced by the connection. Most basically, McFague rejects four ways that she thinks Christianity and the arts have been problematically related historically: "religious amiability," "Christian discrimination," "Christian aesthetics," and "theological criticism." The problem with each lies in its unfair privileging either of the literary texts themselves or of Christianity. Each flattens the distinctiveness of the two disciplines in a way that doesn't serve either. Literary studies is wary to be associated with theology while Christian theology is cautious to overly integrate Christianity into worldly expressions.

Speaking in Parables brings the techniques of literary studies to the Bible itself. She argues that, for Christianity to renew its vitality in the present, the parables of Jesus as found in the New Testament should be mined as primary theological language. "If a person is a Christian and by vocation a theologian, then the task at hand is to help this society hear the good news. The assumption of the present book is that theology could better fulfill this function were it to attend to Jesus' parables as models of theological reflection, for the parables keep 'in solution' the language, belief, and life we are called to, and hence they address people totally."[7]

Casting parables as metaphors emphasizes their literary character. If parables are read primarily as creative narrative material for interpretation, the authenticity of the parables as words of the historical Jesus is minimized, if not rendered irrelevant. Parables as metaphor express religious truths in irreducible ways. The point of the parables is not to reveal an eternally existent divine system that can be described by theologians, but rather to be the primary theological speech itself. Jesus, for McFague, essentially does theology in the New Testament. Truths about God cannot be expressed in neat, comprehensive ways. Literary expression, going back to the New Testament writers and Jesus, is the means of capturing what human beings need to know about the divine, about God, and about the Christian life.

6. Ibid., 3.
7. Sallie McFague, *Speaking in Parables: A Study in Metaphor and Theology* (Philadelphia: Fortress, 1975), 2.

McFague takes the insights of linguistic and literary analysis and brings them to the biblical text, not to rewrite theology, but to interpret it for the present historical and cultural situation. In an early footnote, she points to the hermeneutical work of Erich Auerbach, Owen Barfield, Max Black, Martin Heidegger, Susanne Langer, Elizabeth Sewell, and Philip Wheelwright.[8] Glancing at the index shows that the authors and works discussed in the book are equally theological and literary. *Talking in Parables* is truly interdisciplinary in a novel way for theology. It is in an ongoing reciprocal conversation with hermeneutical strategies that are foreign to the discipline of theology historically.

A key reason for doing theology in conversation with literary and hermeneutical theory is the open-endedness of these other disciplines with respect to the meaning that can be found in the Bible specifically, and in Christian theology more broadly. McFague writes,

> A theology that is informed by parables is necessarily a risky and open-ended kind of reflection. It recognizes not only the inconclusiveness of all conceptualizations when dealing with matters between God and human beings (an insight as old as religion itself), but also the pain and skepticism – the dis-ease – of such reflection. Theology of this sort is not neat and comfortable; but neither is the life with and under God of which it attempts to speak. The parables accept the complexity and ambiguity of life as lived here in this world and insist that it is in *this* world that God makes his gracious presence known.[9]

This is a persistent characteristic of constructive theology, the insistence that theology cannot be completed. Because parabolic language is accessible to a nonspecialized audience, in fact is derived from the everyday experiences of people who encountered Jesus, it is also accessible today.

Literature and creative narrative expression are ongoing human projects, which call for new reading strategies and new interpretations. Hermeneutics in literary theory change so quickly because the evolving nature of meaning in literature is acknowledged in a way that it hasn't been in theology. Yet McFague says, "Theology is, then, always hermeneutical, always concerned with how the gospel can be 'translated' or understood—grasped—by people."[10] Theology is not a

8. Ibid., 2.
9. Ibid., 7.
10. Ibid.

descriptive task, but a task of engagement and creativity. Presuming an objective reality to what theology evokes means that what each new reader or interpreter brings is essentially irrelevant because it interferes with capturing the system objectively. As McFague notes,

> What is attempted in this essay is what theology always tried to do—to serve the hearing of the word of God in a particular time and place. The assumption is that theology could better fulfill this function were it to attend to Jesus' parables as models of theological reflection, for the parables keep the language, belief, and life we are called to in solution and hence address people totally. If theology becomes overly abstract, conceptual, and *systematic*, it separates thought and life, belief and practice, words and their embodiment.[11]

Literary, hermeneutical encounters reject this conceit outright. Interpreters are active agents in the construction of theology.

Reconstructing Theology through Metaphor

McFague's most programmatic work, and the one that represents her theological method, even after her turn to activist theology, is *Metaphorical Theology*. Building on the hermeneutical project established in *Speaking in Parables*, McFague goes deeply into theories about the function and purpose of metaphor in theology. She argues that certain historical models for God have dominated in such a way as to become destructive. Models are naturalized metaphors, ways of talking about something, in this case theological things, that are sufficiently representative and repeated so often that people have forgotten that they are only symbolic. The classic example of this process is the model of "God the father." Comparing God to a father was in fact a very apropos metaphor and still is, when held alongside other metaphors. However, the Christian church has used the metaphor so frequently and so seriously that fatherhood, as metaphor, has become conflated with the actual being of God.[12] If examined critically, "father" as a model for God has become both "irrelevant" and "idolatrous." McFague proposes the solution of intentionally offering other metaphors for God that represent other qualities, characteristics, or actions of God, including those that are feminine, non-gendered, or drawn from the natural world. She

11. Sallie McFague, "Parable, Metaphor, and Theology," *Journal of the American Academy of Religion* 42, no. 4 (December, 1974): 630.
12. Sallie McFague, *Metaphorical Theology: Models of God in Religious Language* (Philadelphia: Fortress, 1982), 145.

finds precedent for this procedure in the Bible itself. This metaphorical method is especially illustrative of the break McFague, in constructive theology, makes from systematic or dogmatic theology. Systematic theology tries to describe the reality of God's character, while failing to realize that what we see as God's character is actually a construction based on human language. In Christian theology, God can be no more a father than a mother or a brother or a sister or any other number of relational human categories. All speak of qualities of God that are irreducible to the metaphor, nor can be adequately captured in other language. This is the function of metaphor. Constructive theology in McFague's stream recognizes this constructedness of our language about God, and takes up the task of constructing more sufficient and timely metaphors and models for God.

McFague stresses the importance not only of interpreting literature, but also for Christian theology to participate in theologizing through literary creation itself. She goes so far as to say that the next step in this variety of theology won't resemble a typical theological work at all, but rather that, "The present work suggests a method and resources toward such a theology; another book of another sort is called for eventually, because if metaphor is the method, the result will be more like a parable than a system."[13] Parables are narratives. They are not fundamentally intellectually critical works. Verisimilitude is key for a parable. It must be clear, recognizable, relatable, and have a succinct force of message. Notably, this envisioned parabolic theology rejects "system." Parables for McFague are primary theological language because their interpretation is always ongoing. Each new encounter with the simple narrative of a parable invites new interpretation, a new back and forth of offering personal experience to the simplicity of the text, and receiving a new interpretation back. Hermeneutical-literary constructive theologies fall outside the bounds of systematic theologies because they intentionally create an open-ended, ongoing theological project. By its very nature, the variety of hermeneutics applied in this case emphasizes encounters with primary theological language. The text means nothing in itself, but needs a reader, historically and contextually situated, to have any meaning at all. Therefore, constructive theologies reject permanent, persistently and objectively true theological systems for theologies that emerge

13. McFague, *Speaking in Parables*, 8.

from readers in ever new situations, facing ever new problems, crises, and challenges to the relevance of Christianity.

David J. Bromell, in the *Journal of the American Academy of Religion*, recognizes two key conceits that he sees as being contradictory in McFague's theological method. On the one hand, "It is frankly acknowledged that the concept of God, and our imaginative construction—and reconstruction—of it, represents a heuristic fiction or projection of possibilities which may or may not be true, but can never be known to be so. . . . The claim implicit in the theistic witness of faith that God exists is made explicit and validated by means of a natural theology for our time, which takes its criteria common human experience and reason."[14] Yet McFague never claims to be writing "natural theology." Her later career focuses on theology about nature, yet it does not suppose, as natural theology does, that evidence of God or God's character can be found by human reason in the natural world. Rather, even her ecotheologies, which make an argument for viewing "the earth as God's body," do so because the image is constructively viable and important, not because of any metaphysical suppositions about the actual correspondence between God's being and the world. That is to say, it is a metaphor, as her method suggests. And as such, it suggests something true about God that cannot be expressed otherwise, yet doesn't correspond with the actual being of God. Bromell believes McFague leans toward the second of the two poles he identifies, when from a constructive point of view, the first is more true. McFague doesn't concern herself with the question of whether there is an objective existence to God at all, but instead makes imaginative construction and reconstruction the work of her theology through and through. She works with the already established tradition of Christianity in order to reconstruct using the interdisciplinary insights of linguistics, hermeneutics, and literary criticism.

Encountering the Bible to Reconstruct Theology

Constructive theology in this vein introduces the abandonment of historical criticism of the Bible as the privileged way to interpret the text, which is a key characteristic of liberal theology before it. What matters in the biblical text, as a literary text with theological content, is not necessarily Jesus' original intention, the particular situation in which

14. David J. Bromell, "Sallie McFague's 'Metaphorical Theology,'" *Journal of the American Academy of Religion* 61, no. 3 (Autumn, 1993): 499–500.

a parable was spoken, or the historical development of the New Testament texts themselves including writers, redactions, and approximate times. Instead, the way the text is encountered today serves as the source of theology for the present. It doesn't abandon historical criticism's findings as unimportant. Many constructive theologians employ the findings of historical criticism, or from the hermeneutic-literary standpoint, utilize historicist or new historicist modes of reading. Instead, it assumes that such findings are less important for contemporary interpretation and employment of the gospel than has been assumed by liberal theology. The truth or relevance of Christianity cannot be equated with the historical life of Jesus of Nazareth or the historical facts of the life of Jesus as the Christ as accepted by Christians. Such findings—tentative though they are—may be useful from an interdisciplinary point of view, or for melding interpretation with history. But historical critical analysis of the Bible loses its place as the final word on legitimate reading of the Bible, specifically for the task of constructing theology. This aspect of constructive theology is heavily indebted to the induction of feminism into theology. Because of the patriarchal core of the Bible, feminist theologies—many of which are in fact constructive theologies—prioritize these sorts of creative, often counter-textual readings.[15]

This overall literary hermeneutical method becomes typical for a whole class of constructive theology. Some of these, especially the earlier ones, maintain the importance of historical criticism of the Bible or aspects of the quests for the historical Jesus. All prioritize the recovery of the meaning of Christian faith through close readings of the received text.[16] The distinction between these hermeneutical/literary motivations and philosophical ones is subtle. There is significant crossover between the two. But the interdisciplinary nature of constructive theology is what makes it so adaptable to these approaches that have both overlap and divergence. The hermeneutical/literary figures take reconceptualizing and reengaging language itself as its primary task. Theologians must better understand the language they use about the divine in order to more successfully construct around theological loci. This can mean the expansion of the canon or openness to outside

15. Phyllis Trible, especially in *Texts of Terror*, is an example of a feminist biblical scholar who shares this strategy.
16. For other key examples of this interdisciplinary approach to constructive theology, see Peter C. Hodgson, *Jesus—Word and Presence: An Essay in Christology* (Philadelphia: Fortress, 1971), and Robert H. King, *The Meaning of God* (London: SCM Press, 1974), Hodgson focuses on a hermeneutical turn in theology while King focuses on the loss of meaning for "God" and the need for its recovery.

sources, renewed engagement with the Bible itself, greater sensitivity to the literary devices used throughout Christian history, or delving into the insights of analytical philosophy as to the way human beings are creatures of language through and through. The reimagination and reconstruction of theology from this point of view means replacing old, outdated models, plumbing theory around language, and initiating a conversation with noncanonical, contemporary literary works.

Turning to philosophically interdisciplinary theologians, it's important to keep in mind the lack of a hard break between hermeneutics and proposals for new philosophical frameworks for theology—a fact rooted in hermeneutics' and literary theory's turn to these philosophies. Just as both analytical and continental philosophy have blurred the lines, or have been blurred by their incorporation into literary theoretical projects, so the border between what I've identified as hermeneutical-literary constructive theologies and philosophical constructive theologies is porous. Both take narrative, imagery, and metaphor as central. But there's an important difference in emphasis, mainly in relationship to sources.

Catherine Keller: New Philosophical Frameworks and Inherited Process

Harkening back to proto-constructive theology, in particular Ten Broeke, philosophically interdisciplinary constructive theologies implicitly take the tack that contemporary philosophies may well serve as better foundations for Christian theology than the philosophies that have been used classically. Many different philosophies have been incorporated into constructive theology throughout its history as it takes seriously the plurality of approaches needed to enable a theology broad enough and diverse enough to do justice to the Christian tradition reconceived constructively. Far and away the most thoroughly explored, however, is that of process theology in the spirit of Alfred North Whitehead. Of course, process philosophy is its own stream of philosophy and constructive theology doesn't have a monopoly on process versions of theology. Process theologies predate constructive theology, and as Dorrien notes, process is perhaps the most persistent and most well developed living strand of liberal theology today.[17] Not all process theologies are constructive theologies, and for sure not all

17. Dorrien, *The Making of American Liberal Theology*, vol. 3, 190.

constructive theologies are process in nature. Again, there is overlap between liberal process theologies and constructive process theologies on account of their shared philosophical underpinnings. Dorrien explains the broadness of process theology, "'Process' thought includes all theologies and philosophies that conceptualize becoming, event, and relatedness as fundamental categories of understanding. Identified more narrowly, one might identify process thought with the school of organic realist cosmology."[18] And it is not surprising that process should be such an endemic tradition in constructive theology considering the prevalence of process in the Chicago School of Theology, including Bernard Eugene Meland.

There are many reasons for the rise of process theology as such a dominant tradition of liberal and progressive theology. Perhaps the most prevalent and most oft cited, however, is that of theodicy and the problem of evil. By emphasizing becoming, process theology casts God as in process alongside creation. Whitehead's philosophy is known for its comprehensiveness, its sophistication, and its creativity in offering a new metaphysics easily adapted to theological ends. It lends itself especially well to ecologically bent theologies. John Cobb, being the most famous and most influential process theologian, employed it in exactly this way, as do many constructive theologians. Confronted with crises of violence, which made the simultaneous benevolence and omnipotence of God untenable, as well as the burgeoning environmental crisis, process provides a means of revisiting views of God that allows for theologies that appeal to the circumstances of the latter half of the twentieth century into the twenty-first century and its accompanying crises.

For the purpose of this history of constructive theology, Catherine Keller serves as a representative figure of process put to constructive ends. It must be emphasized, though, that process is not the only modern philosophical system that has been employed for the purposes of constructive theology. Much of the incorporation of contemporary philosophy has served the ends of the next chapter, that is, serving as justification for activist theologies, including critical theories and philosophies around identity, power, and discourse. Catherine Keller in fact embodies both of these drives, and will emerge again in the next chapter with respect to activist feminist theology as well as ecologically sensitive theology. The process metaphysics of Whitehead, in

18. Dorrien, *The Making of American Liberal Theology*, 191.

any case, provides a comprehensive philosophical scheme that many constructive theologians have adopted as more appropriate to Christian theology as Christian experience is encountered today. The subtle difference between constructive process theologies and other process theologies is the difference between intentional, directed *construction* of theology contrasted with a theology that attempts to describe a system that most closely resembles process philosophy. The role of human agency in the construction of Christianity rather than in the uncovering of it is a key difference. This distinction holds going back to Meland, and before him, Ten Broeke (though not in a process vein). Philosophy provides a basis on which to construct Christian theology, not to which it can be adapted and conformed.

Creation, Apocalypse, and Interdisciplinary Process

Catherine Keller's theological work is undeniably interdisciplinary. It spans biblical studies, literary studies, critical theory, and most thoroughly, philosophy. Her work can be described as process, feminist, ecofeminist, postmodern, and sometimes radical or political, amongst other things. Starting in the second generation of constructive theologians, hers has been a consistent presence that pushes the boundaries of theological method in countless ways. She inhabits one of the few positions explicitly named as a professorship of constructive theology, at Drew University.

Her process theology magnum opus, *Face of the Deep: A Theology of Becoming*, introduces the *tohu va bohu* as a refutation of the classical doctrine of *creatio ex nihilo*. She instead proposes a doctrine of *creatio ex profundis*, creation from the deep, as a reconstructive redefinition within the classical doctrine of creation. Relating to the theologians analyzed above, she likens her theology to "hermeneutics."[19] Situating herself within the constructive theological tradition, she explains,

> While critically engaging history and scripture, my argument remains a project of *constructive theology*. Offering like most theologies an account of 'the creation,' this one (unlike most) lets creation itself emerge from the *topos of the Deep*. . . . So this becoming theology continues a *deconstruction* of the paradigm and presumption of linear time: the bottom line of origin, the straight line of salvation history, the violent end of the line of time

19. Catherine Keller, *Face of the Deep: A Theology of Becoming* (New York: Routledge, 2003), xvii.

> itself I mark 'the beginning' instead as a beginning in process, an unoriginated and endless process of becoming: *genesis.*[20]

This offers Keller's shorthand definition of constructive theology from her vantage point. It deals with traditional doctrine, yet differentiates itself by not situating that doctrine within a greater systematic structure. It deconstructs the historical formulation of the doctrine, taking stock of what the doctrine has become, how, and whom it serves, yet then turns toward redefinition and reformulation. "This theology continues an attempt, necessarily from the inside of the biblical tradition, to heal that desiccating hope. As constructive work, therefore, the present archeology of the deep becomes *ipso facto* a tehomic theology."[21] Tehomic theology, "tehom" being the transliteration of the Hebrew word for the "deep" or the "abyss," is open-ended, pluralist, unoriginated but creative and in flux. That is, constructive theology in Keller's view is not created *ex nihilo* but *ex profundis* from the Christian tradition, yet in a way that continuously evolves and becomes.

The technical vocabulary of *Face of the Deep* comes by way of process theology. Process philosophy is an ontology of becoming, a metaphysical description of being in the midst of change and flux. The watery imagery of the Hebrew creation myth found in Genesis lends itself to this sort of fluidity, possibility, and potential.

Keller introduces process ideas by analyzing the "tehom" encountered in the account of creation in Genesis 1. It serves as the backdrop and orienting model for the type of creative, poetic theology she seeks to propose:

> *Face of the Deep* labors to reclaim for theological reflection the tehom inscribed 'in the beginning' itself. I do not pretend to construct its opening as it ever was, but as it might yet be: as it unblocks possibilities within, at least, a particular postmillennial context. I read these possibilities as divine gifts and graces. A tehomic theology will reflect in style the flows and eddies of its content. Its language crosses media, genres, disciplines, sexualities, economies, spiritualities, as theology always has. But a tehomic theology does so openly and affirmingly.[22]

Constructive theology, as Keller points out, is honest in its engagement with other disciplines. As an interdisciplinary theology, it lays bare

20. Ibid.
21. Ibid.
22. Ibid., xviii.

its indebtedness to other disciplines, rejecting the appearance of self-containment characteristic of earlier varieties of theology. It is open-ended and incomplete. Unlike process theologies that seek to explain a complete system that adheres to process philosophy as developed by Whitehead and others, it suggests intentional openness and future revision. Even though it uses the language and concepts of process philosophy, it is not a simple one-to-one insertion of Christian theological concepts into a framework of process thinking. Of course, liberal process theologies aren't simple correspondences either, but they presume a process philosophical system, itself not inherently Christian but which creates a space for the divine, to which Christian theology can be adapted. And finally, Keller emphasizes the importance of tehomic theology being situated in its contemporary setting. The sources drawn upon and the questions answered will reflect the "post-millennial context" in a way that exhibits its undeniable situatedness. The constructive process theology Keller asserts is not a once-and-for-all theology based on a static philosophical system. Instead, it admits its limitedness, incompleteness, and need to be situated within the theological tradition, in conversation with the present, and open to future expansion and revision.

Keller, before *Face of the Deep*, used similar process rooted concepts to explore and revise the doctrine of eschatology. In *Apocalypse Now and Then*, she issues a "call to coalition, to revision, to confrontation," which "echoes the urgent tones and tropes of the apocalypse. . . . A counter-apocalypse will not demonize the demonizers but offer its critique in a self-critical spirit. I hope it converts emergency into emergence, 'second coming' into a sustainable be-coming. I hope it lets a playful spirit displace the dooming demons of every determinism. I hope above all that it releases an energy of—hope."[23] Again, using categories of process, within the doctrinal locus of eschatology, Keller summarizes the constructive theological project at large. It confronts crisis from categories endemic to Christian theology, stresses reconception and revision, and rejects the outright rejection of the rich tradition of Christianity. She argues that only through the tradition, through the classical loci, can Christian theology navigate the impasse left by liberal and supernaturalist theologies. Once again, her constructive theology is based on process categories of flux, becoming, and rejection of the traditional view of a static God of divine perfections. Instead, the impe-

23. Catherine Keller, *Apocalypse Now and Then: A Feminist Guide to the End of the World* (Minneapolis: Fortress, 1996), xi.

tus has fallen on human beings, theologians, to recast Christian theology in a way that opens new possibilities for the future, for the renewal of Christianity on terms that are relevant to the present, speaking to crises, and in line with a philosophical system that more closely fits the experience of modern human beings as well as the perceived purpose of Christianity as a religious worldview.

Relationality, Plurality, and Polydoxy

Working with Laurel C. Schneider, co-convener for the fourth iteration of the Workgroup on Constructive Theology, Keller continues her constructive project in *Polydoxy*, where the philosophical insights of process serve as a basis for proposing a pluralistic, multiplicitious theology that emphasizes not the uniformity of theological insight, but its absolute ambiguity and plurality. "Polydoxy" itself is an apt term for the way constructive theology works to propose theological coherence. It is the assertion of multiple words on the doctrines of Christianity, an openness to many voices. *Polydoxy* reflects the ongoing collaborative nature of constructive theology, bringing in scholars from a number of different theological fields, engaging across disciplinary lines. In the introduction, Keller and Schneider argue,

> In recent years, a discernible movement within theology has emerged around a triune intuition: the daunting differences of multiplicity, the evolutionary uncertainty it unfolds, and the relationality that it implies are not problems to be overcome in religious thought. They are the starting points for it. Divinity understood in terms of multiplicity, openendedness, and relationality now forms a matrix of revelation rather than a distortion, or evidence of its lack. The challenges and passions of theological creativity blossoming at the edges of tradition and at the margins of power have shown themselves, far from being distractions from doctrinal or doxological integrity, to be indispensable to its life.[24]

Thus, *Polydoxy* exhibits in its form the tenets of constructive theology. In a way, it stands as an intermediate installment of the textbooks created by the Workgroup on Constructive Theology, including many theologians involved in the group, challenging and expanding inherited tradition, and emphasizing reconstruction through collaboration. "It refuses, in fact, the false dichotomy of nihilistic dissolution of mean-

24. Catherine Keller and Laurel C. Schneider, eds., *Polydoxy: Theology of Multiplicity and Relation* (New York: Routledge, 2011), 1.

ing on the one hand and unification by self-appointed orthodoxy on the other. It seeks instead an evolving coherence in the midst of actual, lived complexity. It remains mindful of the toxic by-products of any doxic certainty. It appreciates the semantics of *doxa* as 'mere opinion,' 'appearance,' 'illusion,' and 'glory' inflecting the doxologies of Christian confession."[25]

Not all of *Polydoxy* is process, or even primarily philosophical in nature. Keller's introduction itself is process oriented, but shows the inherently open nature of constructive theology. No single constructive theology—even those based on different contemporary philosophical projects—can encapsulate the entire "orthodoxy" of Christianity. Christian theology is inherently, and truthfully always has been, polydox in that it expresses many truths not only at different points in time but simultaneously. No single philosophical framework or theological work, no matter how systematic, can capture the entirety of the Christian tradition or the legitimate things that can be said about God, Christ, the work of salvation, or who it affects. Instead, a variety of philosophical projects can and must be wedded to traditional Christian speech to bring to fruition the complexity of contemporary Christian experience.

A significant part of this speech, for Keller, consists of the importance of theopoetics. Theopoetics asserts that humans are co-creators with God, or further, in some sense are makers of God. It is an embrace of interdisciplinarity that emphasizes fluidity, openness, and mystery. One of the defining features of her writing since the beginning of her career has been the pervasive use of linguistic flourishes and evocative imagery. Dorrien characterizes Keller's writing as "dense, expansive, multivocal, richly evocative, sometimes poetic prose."[26] Writing theology is an imaginatively creative work. Indeed, the inability to objectively substantiate the claims of theology about the divine make it an inherently theopoetical enterprise, even when its nature as a creative constructive work, rather than a descriptive one, is not acknowledged.

Constructive theology, as a creative work, admits that no image is final or comprehensive. Like a literary canon, theology needs many creative works and perspectives to offer any sort of useful, justified conception of God. Keller's engagement with biblical narratives like creation and apocalypse affirms the same. The witness of the Bible is so widely varied that to be honest to the tradition means to hold in tension seemingly contradictory or paradoxical images of God found

25. Ibid., 3.
26. Dorrien, *The Making of American Liberal Theology*, 502.

within the Bible with our own ongoing experience of the divine and the Christian life. For Keller, this all ties back to a God conceived within the context of a constructive process philosophical project. Neither theology, nor God Godself, is a finished product, and never could be.

Keller has been a proponent of constructive theology for decades. In fact, she holds one of the few positions specifically in "constructive theology" in theology today—though more are appearing, and most constructive theologians hold positions in systematic theology despite the methodological dissonance. The provisionality of constructive theology, its openness to change and becoming is what has made it a home for her. Kathryn Tanner, on the other hand, has oscillated between "systematic" and "constructive" theology. Keller and Tanner have both been key figures in constructive theology's interdisciplinary mode. Their resonances and dissonances in method serve to show different aspects of constructive theology within its wide net.

Kathryn Tanner: Social Sciences and Cultural Studies, Economy, and Politics

Kathryn Tanner's theology spans widely throughout the social sciences. The social sciences are brought to bear in different ways in many different constructive theologies, but hers put contemporary social scientific theories that challenge the status quo front and center. Tanner is an especially interesting case because she bridges systematic theology and constructive theology in an ambivalent way. Her work has never shown a clear preference for one or the other, and she is currently the Marquand Professor of Systematic Theology at Yale Divinity School. In 2001 she published *Jesus, Humanity, and the Trinity: A Brief Systematic Theology*. Yet she has participated extensively in the Workgroup on Constructive Theology and identifies as a constructive theologian. This may at first seem to contradict the assertion that constructive theology and systematic theology are different things. Yet, more so, it reveals that one can do work in each of these modes, embracing different methods at different times, pending the appropriateness of the project at hand. Further, the differences between her constructive work and her systematic work help to clarify the distinctions between working in a constructive and systematic mode. And most fundamentally, constructive theology and systematic theology are two different but related methods with the same aim of providing a compelling account of Christianity.

Engaging Anthropology, Engaging Culture

Tanner has written books that take their theological starting point from cultural studies, politics, and economics. In her influential and programmatic *Theories of Culture*, Tanner views Christians not as ascribing to some objective system out there to be clearly defined and committed to. Rather, she identifies Christianity in the context of theories of culture that propose that the religious truths of Christianity are up for debate amongst commonly interested and committed Christians, regardless of creed. In her introduction, she offers,

> I contend that the anthropological notion of culture can be profitably employed in theology. As it does in other humanistic disciplines in the academy, an anthropological notion of culture sets new questions and directions for theological research. Indeed, such a notion has already infiltrated contemporary theology by way of common sense. . . . This influence on theology often, however, remains implicit and unselfconscious, thereby blunting the capacity of such a notion to establish fruitful new avenues for theological study, and hiding from the theologian's purview a decisive shift in the anthropological understanding of culture within the academy.[27]

Engagement with other academic disciplines is the foundation of her long-term theological project. By making her commitment to interdisciplinarity and her incorporation of anthropological and cultural studies insights explicit, she hopes to open new directions for constructive theology to go and to open a new dialogue about what exactly Christian identity means in the context of a new orientation toward culture and Christianity's relationship to it.

Tanner specifically makes use of culture as it's defined within anthropology. That is to say, it's not a generically or ambiguously defined term invented for use within theology, but rather a specialized definition drawn specifically from another discipline. She offers a nine part definition of culture, the crux of which is that "*culture is understood to constitute or construct human nature . . . cultures are conventions in the sense that they are human constructions* . . . the plastic character of human biological equipment, the fact of cultural diversity, and the purported origin of the diversity in the vagaries of human history, combine to suggest strongly the *contingency of cultures*."[28] Likewise, if theology

27. Kathryn Tanner, *Theories of Culture: A New Agenda for Theology* (Minneapolis: Augsburg Fortress, 1997), x.

works in conversation with and alongside contingent cultures, it itself must also be contingent and constructed. The assumptions imported from interdisciplinary engagement with cultural anthropology underscore the constructed nature of her theology. The anthropological category of culture is especially useful to constructive theology because it makes the same assertions about culture that constructive theology does about Christianity. In an important way, Tanner argues that Christianity is a culture within a culture, or perhaps a highly constitutive part of Western culture. The working out of culture is circular—involving description, construction, evaluation, and subsequent repetition of this process. Christianity, specifically through the task of theology, does the same thing.

Part two of *Theories of Culture* makes specific claims about the tasks of theology, contextualized within an interdisciplinary conversation with anthropological definitions of culture. Tanner writes that,

> The anthropological understanding of culture bridges, then, a surprising range of theological schools of thought, as well as theological topics. The idea of culture as a human construct not only bridges the neo-orthodox and liberal wings of contemporary Christian theology; it is also the basis upon which Gordon Kaufman and his followers argue for their understanding of theology as a creative enterprise. Moreover, theologians who make it their mission to reinterpret the Christian tradition in light of the contemporary situation, or to correlate situation and Christian message, often understand the situation at issue in explicitly cultural terms. Finally, the distinction between theory and practice commonly employed in liberation theology has a history tightly interwoven with the modern—and now postmodern—development of ideas of culture found in the social sciences.[29]

Anthropological definitions of culture work for theology because they make explicit a concept theology has already been working with. Interdisciplinarity, as employed by Tanner, helps theology to be less ambiguous about its own categories, clearer in its aims, and more responsible to the overall climate of intellectual work being done across the academic spectrum, recalling Farley's insistence on the ethical imperative upon contemporary theologians to be honest within contemporary academic discourse. This call for accountability and transparency didn't land without resistance at the time it came, though

28. Ibid., 28.
29. Ibid.

it has very broadly been incorporated into contemporary progressive theologies, particularly those that identify as constructive.

Challenging Hegemonic Economics

Besides cultural anthropology, Tanner also delves into economics. In *Economy of Grace,* Tanner states from the very start, "The primary burden of my method is to . . . allow one to see the way that every theological category and topic is of direct economic import, how every Christian idea about God and the world is directly and from the first an economic doctrine."[30] Economics provides a useful basis for theology because, as Tanner claims, economics is a discipline that pervades every area of life. Human beings—including within the bounds of Christianity—are thoroughly economic creatures, always exchanging goods and services with one another for survival or enjoyment. *Economy of Grace* is largely a prescriptive book, however, developing an economic model Tanner sees as a critique and response to current global capitalism from the perspective of Christianity's inherent tension with prevailing structures. Her primary focus is, as the title suggests, "grace," the quality that expresses God's free and abundant giving as juxtaposed with capitalism's emphasis on accumulation over and against the neighbor. Drawing on the Bible, Christian tradition, culture, and economic models, Tanner offers a constructive reimagining of both Christian theology and economics.

This latter point is especially important for constructive theology, while also being an element of the project that has struggled to come to fruition in the context of interdisciplinary conversation. Constructive theology not only seeks to incorporate the insights of other disciplines but to offer its insights to the broader academy. Tanner doesn't have a fantastical belief that current capitalist structures will simply recognize the power of the Christian economy of grace argument that stresses noncompetitiveness as an antidote to capitalism's fierce version of self-interest. Rather, she claims that "By setting Christian ideas of the production and circulation of goods into a comparative economy, by making that comparative framing an economic one, my intent is just to suggest that a Christian economy has everything to do with the material dimensions of life—with the economic more narrowly construed."[31] Further, she argues, "The discipline of theology in a time

30. Kathryn Tanner, *Economy of Grace* (Minneapolis: Augsburg Fortress, 2005), 1.
31. Ibid., 30.

of economic dead ends can work to open up the economic imagination in much the way the disciplines of history and anthropology can; it can fund socio-cultural criticism in the way that histories of political and economic ideas, and cultural anthropology do."[32]

Politics and the Interdisciplinary Turn to Activism

Finally, looking slightly earlier, Tanner turns to one other arena within the social sciences, that is, politics. Published in 1992, *The Politics of God: Christian Theologies and Social Justice* coincides with the release of *Reconstructing Christian Theology*, the second book by the Workgroup on Constructive Theology, of which she was a part at that time. Like the Workgroup generally at that moment, Tanner's work swings toward a concern with justice and activism. In the preface, she writes, "I hope to show how Christian beliefs about God and the world may be disentangled from a history of use in support of a status quo of injustice and reconstituted as a resource for commitment to progressive social change."[33] Like many, indeed most, other constructive theologians, Tanner's work is not finally interdisciplinary for interdisciplinarity's own sake. As constructive theology at large took an explicit turn toward working for justice and "progressive social change," Tanner's work takes up specifically how to enlist Christianity in political action for such change. She continues, "One could say the constructive project of the book explores the possibility of an 'internal' rather than 'totalistic' critique of traditional Christian beliefs. Instead of being rejected outright, Christian traditions that lend support to a status quo of injustice are turned against themselves."[34] *Theories of Culture* and *Economy of Grace* embody the interdisciplinary aspect of constructive theology. But like other constructive theologians, her work often spans both defining characteristics of constructive theology, interdisciplinarity and activism. She deepens the understanding of constructive to reflect the project of engaging and reimagining Christian doctrines with a special concern for changing those historical beliefs that have caused harm. Her explicitly activist political project in *The Politics of God* clearly resonates with *Awake to the Moment*, the most recent collaborative book by the Workgroup. Constructive theology, in its fully realized combination of interdisciplinarity and activism, which *The Politics*

32. Ibid., 32.
33. Kathryn Tanner, *The Politics of God: Christian Theologies and Social Justice* (Minneapolis: Fortress, 1992), vii.
34. Ibid., viii.

of God manifests, enlists tradition to make the traditions of Christianity more just and equitable. That is, the constructed nature of theology allows for the "turning against themselves" that is needed in undercutting problematic historical doctrines, beliefs, practices, and actions within Christianity.

For the interdisciplinary analysis in *The Politics of God*, Tanner introduces what she calls a "sociocultural perspective." She clarifies that "In short, religious beliefs are a form of culture, inextricably implicated in the material practices of daily social living on the part of those who hold them."[35] In order to understand the political actions and understandings of Christians, it is necessary to understand the connections among beliefs, judgments, and actions. Contrary to what may be seen as a cordoning off of the religious from political selves, Tanner argues that "religious beliefs tend to be already at work, therefore, when and wherever judgments of proper attitude and action are necessary."[36] Ultimately, using the sociocultural perspective, Tanner attempts to show that Christianity can be conceived as a "self-critical culture," that is, one in which "self-reflection is created by a structure of belief that encourages a 'view from a distance' on a society's own forms of life."[37] Drawing as above from the well of cultural anthropology, Tanner encourages Christians to examine the constructedness of Christianity as a part of contingent culture. As a part of culture, Christianity, and the theology that underwrites it, may be turned toward progressive political ends by fostering self-awareness and self-critique.

The conclusion of Tanner's sociocultural analysis of Christianity is that activism is necessary. She specifies that "Not everyone is called to make agitating for justice the explicit focus of their life's work, for example, by become a community organizer or political lobbyist for minority rights. One can do all manner of things with one's own life, but in the process one should be attentive to furthering a respect for the basic value and rights of all persons as creatures of God." The explication offered here of "activism" reflects the activism of the theologies analyzed in the next chapter of this book. Tanner's own application of her interdisciplinary work, which she would bring to greater realization in *Theories of Culture*, leads her to promote engaged, self-critical, reconstructed theology in the service of creating greater justice and equality in the world. Whether this is done through direct means or in

35. Ibid., 9.
36. Ibid.
37. Ibid., 36.

the resistance to and redefinition of classically oppressive theological constructions, the point is that Christian theology is a site open to just such analysis, critique, and reconstruction. In Tanner's view, Christianity and religion in general, as a part of culture, emphasizes its contingency and need for reconstruction. Her work at times demonstrates constructive theology's interdisciplinarity in its clearest form. *The Politics of God* anticipates the turn to advocacy and activism taken up more fully in chapter four.

Expanding Constructive Theology's Conversation Partners

Interdisciplinary constructive theology, in Tanner's model, starts by incorporating insights and ideas from other disciplines. She uses the social sciences to expand the conversation of Christian theology outside its provincial bounds, noting that theology has been impinging on other disciplines without confessing to anyway. Upon engaging historical theology and Christian witness with the findings of other disciplines, however, the crucial step of theological construction happens. Christian theology can creatively incorporate, expand, and create anew from the foundations other disciplines offer. Finally, constructive Christian theology must seek to reengage the disciplines from which it draws in order to offer its own Christian inflected, socially and culturally progressive critiques and insights. The conversation of interdisciplinary theology is circular, not a vector. Kathryn Tanner's theology and its ongoing engagement with a range of social sciences and academic disciplines is an especially clear example of this aspect of constructive theology.

With this expansion, the potential interlocutors for constructive theology become innumerable. The social sciences have split into so many different fields and subfields that theology's interdisciplinary engagement with them creates an opportunity for a nearly infinite expansion of the creative potentials for doing meaningful intellectually rigorous contemporary theology. In order to be meaningful within this context constructive theology has had to embrace plurality. If engagements with all of the different social sciences—and beyond—is important and necessary, then different theologies will emerge from the concepts imported from each discipline. Given that the disciplines themselves are often in conversation and disagreement over fundamental aspects of human life and behavior, Christian theology itself becomes steeped in these very arguments. The social sciences are friendly territory for interdisciplinary engagement from the perspective of Christian theology because Christianity is fundamentally a social enterprise made up of communities and cultures that are disparate throughout history, yet it claims some sort of unity despite all of its diversity. This problem of ecumenism is given a fresh look through the social sciences. They provide powerful new tools for making sense of the faith and behavioral claims of Christian theology historically and in the present.

Juxtaposing Construction and Systematics

Tanner embodies in her work the tension between constructive theology and systematic theology. She played a central role in the Workgroup on Constructive Theology, and the works analyzed above clearly show their investment in the tasks of constructive theology. They are focused on particular doctrines, interdisciplinary, intentionally provisional, and incorporate activism at the same moment constructive theology generally was turning toward more culturally and politically engaged work that seeks to cast Christianity as a force to work for change. Chronologically, from *The Politics of God* to *Theories of Culture*, Tanner moves from emphasizing activism to emphasizing interdisciplinarity. Neither is completely absent in either work. In *Jesus, Humanity and the Trinity: A Brief Systematic Theology*, published in 2001, however, she writes of the text at hand, "systematic theology offers a vision of the whole, a sense of how to bring together all the elements of Christian involvement into unity around an organizing center or centers."[38] She concludes, "figuring out what Christianity is all about requires, therefore, intellectual effort, and intellectual effort of a primarily systematic sort: one must put together, unite into some interconnected whole, the disparate and often logically disjointed variety of things that Christians tend to think, feel, and do in and out of church."[39] Moving into systematic territory, Tanner looks to create a unity, something that coheres the "logically disjointed" experiences of Christians. It looks for a complete work that finds an essence to Christianity, despite the fact that she acknowledges that Christian theologies are historically and contextually bound. The book itself acknowledges its own limitations as a short and self-consciously light systematization.

38. Kathryn Tanner, *Jesus, Humanity and the Trinity: A Brief Systematic Theology* (Edinburgh: T&T Clark, 2001), xiii.
39. Ibid., xv.

Nonetheless, it points to future, longer works that will flesh out a complete systematization, which will try to make sense of the whole of Christianity from a theological perspective.

Christ the Key is the "promised sequel" to *Jesus, Humanity and the Trinity*. Its own relationship to systematization is conflicted. Tanner writes, "The first book developed the basic import of this Christ-centered theological vision by showing how it could be productively used to talk about almost anything of Christian interest in an integrated way. . . . The present book takes the heart of that theological vision—Christ—and shows in less systematic fashion how this understanding of Christ throws fresh light on otherwise tired theological topics and opens up new avenues for approaching them."[40] The book treads a fine line between constructive theology and systematic theology. It takes up doctrines almost in a systematic fashion, develops each doctrine essentially as a version of Christology. It echoes Gordon Kaufman's reduction of all doctrines to theology proper, but instead reducing all doctrines to Christology. Yet *Christ the Key* still attempts to be a type of less systematic systematic theology.

In its ambiguity in the constructive theological tradition, Tanner's work helps to bring into clearer view the distinction between constructive and systematic theology. In any case, Tanner takes interdisciplinary constructive theology into many new terrains: anthropology, economics, and politics, amongst others. *The Politics of God* gestures toward the next chapter, where activism becomes central, and chapter five where ultimately interdisciplinarity and activism cannot be separated. The arc of Tanner's career shows the emergence, contraction, and contours of constructive theology in relation to other theological approaches in the contemporary academy. Throughout its entirety, however, it is through and through interdisciplinary.

Conclusion

It's not an exaggeration to say that constructive theology began fundamentally from an effort to make Christian theology, which has long been a project conflicted over its relationship with the world and other intellectual modes, thoroughly interdisciplinary. As Ten Broeke's *A Constructive Basis for Theology* shows, not only does the contemporary world offer many rich resources for connecting the long history of Christian theology with current modes of thinking and ways of viewing

40. Kathryn Tanner, *Christ the Key* (New York: Cambridge University Press, 2010), vii.

the world, some theologians view contemporary thought systems to be an even better foundation than historical ones for Christian theology altogether. This claim, that new philosophies and discourses can be radically better than classical ones, seems at least a little suspect, or at least damaging for the Christian tradition. Nonetheless, the point is an important one. Theology, in order to remain relevant, absolutely must learn to dialogue with other disciplines, not only receiving but giving back. Reaffirming that this isn't a superseded way of doing constructive theology is also important. Though it arose first, interdisciplinarity remains a primary concern of constructive theology. Activism and social justice concerns have become a complement, not a replacement of, constructive theology's role as an interlocutor with other academic disciplines.

A number of key ideas for understanding constructive theology emerge from analyzing its interdisciplinary nature:

1. The importance of "models," simultaneously identifying the constructed quality of Christian theological assertions and recognizing the possibility of incorporating more appropriate, or at least different, ones.
2. Breaking out of the mold of doing theology as an internally coherent discipline responsible primarily to itself for the validity of its claims and the rigor of its arguments; perhaps ironically, constructive theology finds new rigor in abandoning sytematization as an ideal and instead holding itself accountable to the standards of external academic disciplines.
3. The centrality of proposing insights that could be useful for other disciplines alongside absorbing insights from those disciplines.
4. A new emphasis on plurality, both internally for Christianity as well as with respect to other religious and social systems, proposed through construction.
5. Holistically engaging ideas that have emerged both as a result of the Enlightenment as well as in response to it; from the interdisciplinary perspective, this is constructive theology's break from liberal theology in that it doesn't seek to reconcile itself to the Enlightenment—something liberal theology has already done—but to assimilate and critique, when necessary, the fallout from the Enlightenment. This abandons the historiographic obsession of liberal theologies that concern themselves with recovering some objective, usually historical, truth in Christian

texts for theology, instead finding truths in its very flexibility and ongoing development.

Models

Models, from Robert H. King and Sallie McFague on, provide a way of talking about the overarching worldviews that Christian theology has to work with and to creatively shape. Yet the idea of a model is not peculiar to the literary/linguistic territory of McFague and King. Models are found throughout the sciences, social sciences, literature, and in a certain sense, philosophy. Constructive theology in its interdisciplinary mode often uses the language of model explicitly, or uses models implicitly, in order to critique what exists and offer something new. The idea of a model emerges from insights that reject essentialized versions of what human beings are and how they behave. Culture, religion, nationality, economics, customs and proper behavior, almost everything about the way that humans act is in some profound way influenced, which is not to say completely determined, by the models accepted within their contexts. Models across communities differ. Constructive theology recognizes that Christianity works on this model basis as well. Indeed, the very internal diversity of Christianity itself betrays the mind-blowing number of different models employed within a Christian community that makes a claim to be unified in some way. All of the theologians in this chapter have used the language of "models" when relating theology to an outside discipline. Models in any discipline provide a worldview, suggestions for behavior and goals, implied beliefs about the world both from an objective and subjective standpoint. Fundamentally, the recognition of the centrality of models in constructive theology reveals the constructed nature of theology itself. If theology relies on models that are not essential, irreplaceable, or monopolistic—despite their contention to be—then the constructed, open, flexible nature of Christian theology must at least be entertained, if not accepted as a criterion for doing theology that will continue to matter in the contemporary world. Put simply, old theological models have been and continue to be important, but new models are nonetheless needed.

Accountable to Outside Disciplines

The bibliographies of constructive theologies are wildly interdisciplinary. The sources for any individual theologian or theological work can be as revealing about the primary perspective and purpose of the work as the introduction. Constructive theology, when taken as a whole, makes a sincere attempt to be on the cutting edge of the full range of disciplines within the contemporary academy. This means drawing on influential works in those fields as well as being open to criticism from interlocutors in them. Being accountable to other disciplines is how constructive theology comes to reflect religious studies and provides the foundation for constructive theology's conversation with religious studies. Religious studies as well is not one technique or method, but rather an aggregate of a vast diversity of methods and approaches to understanding one phenomenon, which itself is not well defined. Just as religious studies has struggled to offer a convincing single definition of its primary subject matter, constructive theology has wrestled with the fact that Christianity is very difficult to define as any single thing. For King, this raises the question of the loss of "meaning" of the word "God" entirely, since it seems, for many, that the word has lost the "game" in which it functions. For McFague a number of models all point to worldviews in which interpreters understand themselves to be part of the same interpretive community. Keller's process inflected theology not only eschews single monolithic definitions of Christianity as a whole, but suggests that God and Christian witness to God are themselves developing alongside the world. Tanner posits the ways that Christian diversity is in flux amongst a wider social conversation, namely around the sites of culture and economics. The credibility of each of these approaches hinges on an evaluation of their understanding of another field. If the underlying claims of hermeneutics/literary studies, philosophy, or social sciences—anthropology and economics in this case—are misunderstood, then the theology built upon it is surely faulty as well. Constructive theology done in this way must be in an ongoing conversation with its interdisciplinary interlocutors or else risk seeming hopelessly out of date and founded on false and easily dismissed premises.

Providing Insights That Are Compelling for Other Disciplines

Though this is an important feature of constructive theology in its interdisciplinary mode, the extent to which other disciplines have taken notice of constructive theology's advances is debatable. Despite Said's recognition mentioned above that religion had come to play a large part in the theory of a wide range of fields, theology itself hasn't broken through in the same way. The study of religion in other academic disciplines, especially from the perspective of religious studies and its claims to objectivity, has seen a surge of interest in recent decades. Theology, on the other hand, is still finding the right tone and subjects to make itself appealing to other disciplines. Some theologians have made significant crossovers. It seems likely that constructive theology will break into greater relevance across the humanities and social sciences at some point, though by whom and how will likely be unexpected. In any case, it is crucial that theology does make that leap at some point for its own ongoing rigor, relevance, and existence within the intellectual landscape of the academy. This isn't to say that theology must wholesale accommodate itself to the methods and assertions of other disciplines. Rather, it means that theology must find a way to offer insights back in a fashion that other disciplines find compelling and impossible to ignore. Proving relevant both to theology and interlocutor disciplines is inherently difficult. Constructive theology has set an immensely high bar for itself in trying to be relevant and intellectually rigorous both within the theological tradition, leaving itself open to criticism based on 2000 years of continuous theological development—a pressure any theology must confront at this point—and criticism on the part of specialists in other fields. But to be successful in this task, truly becoming a conversation partner in the broader academy built on the interdisciplinary methodology of constructive theology, could invigorate Christian theology in innumerable important ways, and encourage a greater place for progressive Christianities within the contemporary United States.

Recognition and Embrace of Plurality

The above tenets have forced constructive theology not only to accept, but to embrace as a strength, a plurality within Christian theology. The plurality of constructive theology from this perspective is twofold. First, it is to recognize that the many possible starting points for theology, when other disciplines are taken seriously, inherently create diversity within the conclusions of constructive theology generally. This diversity must be viewed as a whole, across methods and theologians, in order to produce a coherent account of Christianity generally. No single theologian or method will touch on all elements of the historical Christian tradition. Not all interdisciplinary methods lend themselves to all of the doctrines traditionally encountered in theology. Constructive theology, therefore, must be polyphonic in order to account for Christianity as a whole, as a worldview that can be adopted, rejected, or reimagined for contemporary people. The second aspect is that, through recognizing the constructedness of parts of life that seem innate and unchangeable by way of other disciplines, the internal diversity of Christianity itself becomes apparent. This internal diversity comes to be seen as one of Christianity's most important and strongest features rather than as one of its greatest liabilities, as it has been viewed since the church began splitting nearly from the beginning.

Further, in aligning itself more closely with the interdisciplinary methods of religious studies, constructive theology is inherently open to religious pluralism. Constructive theology does not concede that Christianity doesn't make truth claims that may be contradictory to other religions' truth claims. In coping with its own historically constructed nature, however, it must at least respect and engage the ways other religious systems have elaborated upon similar questions as Christianity has. This is not to say constructive theology is inherently interfaith or interreligious. Rather, the interdisciplinary nature of constructive theology suggests the possession of resources that could be especially strong for such an engagement, contrasted with a theology that might seek to explain a supposedly objective structure or system that is Christianity itself as it might exist apart from human discursive projects.

Both Engaging and Moving beyond Questions Raised by the Enlightenment

Finally, the question of constructive theology and theological liberalism is once again raised. Liberal theology responded to the challenges posed by the lessening of the authority of traditional theological wellsprings, most specifically scripture and the church. Reason, a scientific worldview, and an individualistic mindset, coupled with advances in technology and the rise of capitalism and new political systems lessened the role scripture and tradition played in the lives of Christians. The liberal theological tradition accommodates itself to these challenges through historical criticism of the Bible, yielding to scientific discovery—most notably in the case of evolution—and an emphasis on ethics in a modern context.[41] For sure early constructive theology took these same questions as its starting point, especially the problem of religious doubt. The credibility of the Christian faith prompted proto-constructive theologians and early constructive theologians to write semi-apologetic works that sought to rehabilitate Christianity in the light of other disciplines, especially science and to a certain extent psychology. Later constructive theology, however, acknowledges these hang-ups but most often points to them as something to be moved past or rejected. Modernism and liberalism go hand in hand. Constructive theology, especially in its post-structuralist and postmodern forms, which is most of the tradition, explicitly critiques objective, modernist, metanarrative, structuralist type theologies. The "constructive" of constructive theology is more often than not better described as "reconstructing." The reconstruction is aimed at the materials left behind after modernist, liberal projects have been confronted with critiques like those of Karl Barth's, Paul Tillich's, and Reinhold Niebuhr's, as well as the creeping realization that Christian theology itself is best viewed as a human construct, capable of, and in great need of, reconstruction.

These interdisciplinary endeavors, especially into the social sciences, enabled the type of analysis and offered the tools that served to launch the second key quality of constructive theology, to be a justice oriented, activist type of contemporary theology. Critical analyses of race, class, sexuality, gender, war and violence, amongst other things, brought about constructive theology's orientation toward a liberationist ethic anchored in doctrinal theologizing. Constructive theology is still wholly interdisciplinary. As noted by Rebecca Chopp, it may be the first theological movement spearheaded primarily by non-clergy. As a result, it has a strong investment in the academy. That's not to say constructive theology turns away from the church. Rather, it sees the greatest promise for continuing to grow the church as a relevant entity in the contemporary world through a wholesale engagement with cutting edge intellectual developments of the present. Constructive theology faced scrutiny and criticism for turning so heavily toward disciplines outside itself. And yet as time has shown, within the university structure, theology needs to engage with more enthusiasm and honesty with other disciplines. The time for theology to be its own evaluator and to set its own criteria for relevance and rigor has passed.

41. Dorrien, *The Making of American Liberal Theology*, vol. 3, 3.

4

Constructive Theology as Activist Theology

Constructive theology took a decided turn with the publication of *Reconstructing Christian Theology* in 1994. Intent on taking account of liberation theologies, the Workgroup on Constructive Theology decided once again to try to reimagine theology for the contemporary world. Once again, the traditional formulation of doctrinal loci was favored despite its seeming obsolescence.[1] The method of constructive theology didn't change. Instead, the apparent need amidst world crises for a theology that acts for the mission of justice was incorporated into a project that had already distinguished itself.

Of course, constructive theologians had been working in a progressive, justice-oriented mode before the second textbook. A sense of activism can be found well before 1994 in many constructive theologies, even going back to its beginnings. However, activism becomes a central concern only gradually within the greater trend of constructive theology. Especially with the liberation ethos that emerged as a result of Latin American liberation theology, Black liberation theology, and Jürgen Moltmann's theology of hope, constructive theology found itself compelled, as a movement bent on confronting ongoing contemporary problems, to take up social causes wholeheartedly.

In a certain way it is strange that constructive theology, as embodied

1. Chopp and Taylor, eds., *Reconstructing Christian Theology*, 14.

by the Workgroup, took as long as it did to make liberation and activism a central concern. Liberation theologies emerged in the '60s and '70s, at the same time the Workgroup on Constructive Theology formed and started working on its first book. The theologians who took part in that first project were already socially engaged, progressive thinkers. The distinctive variety of engaged, activist theology that constructive theology embraces is always based in critical insights derived from other fields expanded into a theological zone, and put toward causes for justice.

The definition of "activism" used here needs to be defined. Within this book it is a compromise word. It's easier to say what it isn't. An activist theology isn't necessarily liberal, though many liberal theologies have been activist. At the same time, it isn't necessarily liberationist, although liberation theologies often call for activism. The term doesn't fit perfectly with the variety of theology described here.

At the same time, there is no current word that fully captures the phenomenon being described. "Liberal" is too politically fraught, especially in the current context of a twenty-four hour news cycle that often reduces politics to "conservative" and "liberal." Besides that, an intentional distinction has been drawn throughout this book between constructive theology and liberal theology. "Progressive" is also too thoroughly linked up with liberalism, and also carries with it an unwelcome evolutionary aspect, in the sense of the state of things progressing from some inferior state to a better one. While the theologies here do fight for better circumstances and conditions for various communities as well as all human beings and creatures, they tend to be ambivalent about the "progress" human beings have wrought historically as well as the potential for progress today, including in the projects they champion. They are rooted in postmodernism and its suspicion of progress and essentialisms.

The term "activist" is used because, for lack of a better word, it highlights the work these theologies do to call Christian communities to work for justice. They enable Christian justice work by providing a framework within the Christian tradition, in light of current circumstances, for those communities to carry out this work *as Christians*. This isn't an exclusivist claim about religion. Rather, it says that Christians are called especially to work for these causes because of the scriptural and traditional promises of Christianity. These special calls are registered in the language of Christianity, through the doctrinal, or symbolic, framework of the religion. These constructive theologies attempt to link up Christian communities with activist work in the world across religious—and nonreligious—lines, based on the particular call to Christians through the Bible and through the Christian tradition to work for justice.

One notable outlier in terms of social engagement in constructive theology is that of feminism. Feminism emerges much earlier within constructive theology than the liberation theologies situated around other contexts and experiential starting points. Indeed, much of the interdisciplinary material in the last chapter aimed at reconfiguring models of Christianity and God, with one explicit aim being the rejection of oppressive patriarchal conceptions of God. Feminism has been such a philosophically based movement that it was adopted early in constructive theology as part and parcel of philosophy and hermeneutics. There is no period of constructive theology, from its formalization with the Workgroup on Constructive Theology, in which feminism is not a constitutive part. Sallie McFague, as one of the earliest adopters of a constructive mode of doing theology, embodies feminism's place within constructive theology from the start. At the same time, in a book with fifteen authors, *Christian Theology: An Introduction to Its Traditions and Tasks* only has one woman writer.

Sallie McFague and Constructive Theology's Early Engagement with Earth Crises

Sallie McFague evocatively illustrates the insertion of activism and justice work into constructive theology, serving as an example both of constructive theology done with an emphasis on interdisciplinarity as well as activism. In an essay titled "An Earthly Theological Agenda," McFague details an important experience she underwent as a theologian:

> In the closing years of the 20th century we are being called to do something unprecedented: to think wholistically, to think about 'everything that is,' because everything on this planet is interrelated and interdependent and hence the fate of each is tied to the fate of the whole. This state of affairs brought about a major 'conversion' in my own theological journey. . . . After years of work on the poetic, metaphorical nature of religious language, (and hence its relative, constructive, and necessarily changing character), and in view of feminism's critique of the hierarchical, dualistic nature of the language of the Jewish and Christian traditions, my bonds to Biblicism and the Barthian God loosened. Those years were

> the 'deconstructive' phase of my development as a theologian. My constructive phase began upon reading Gordon Kaufman's 1983 Presidential Address to the American Academy of Religion. Kaufman called for a paradigm shift, given the exigencies of our time. . . . I answered this call, and my subsequent work has been concerned with contributing to that task.[2]

Though this story is told in brief and in passing, it's easy to overlook how much McFague packs into it. She sees two distinct phases in her theological career. The first she identifies as her interdisciplinary, Barthian influenced theology centered on metaphor, models, and what was identified in chapter three as literary-hermeneutical constructive theological approaches. The second is her response to the ecological crisis and the call to take seriously contemporary crises as the motivation for doing theology. Strangely, McFague argues that these two phases are made up of an initial derivative phase, a second phase of 'deconstruction,' and finally the third stage, that is the activist, ecologically focused one, as her constructive phase.

Yet her participation in the Workgroup on Constructive theology predates this conversion. Kaufman's stirring address occurred in 1983, but McFague contributed an important piece to *Christian Theology: An Introduction to Its Traditions and Tasks*, the first textbook composed by the Workgroup on Constructive Theology in 1982. Her narrative raises the subtleties between "construction," "deconstruction," and "reconstruction" once again. Her earliest work predates the Workgroup on Constructive Theology, but the form it takes is decidedly constructive in the sense of constructive theology. Her contribution to *Christian Theology: An Introduction to Its Traditions and Tasks* affirms her earlier work and its emphasis on metaphor, model, literature, and hermeneutics. In fact, both phases are constructive in the sense that constructive theology implies. The break, between "deconstruction" and "construction" as she narrates it, is in fact her own leap within constructive theology, from a focus on interdisciplinarity to a focus on activism.

A key part of McFague's "conversion" is the rejection of the idea that social ethics or theology that is engaged with the real world and seeks to change unjust circumstances is somehow less intellectual and should have less of a place in the academy. She writes,

> Until the rise of liberation theologies, theology was more concerned with having intellectual respectability in the academy than with forging an

2. Carol J. Adams, ed., *Ecofeminism and the Sacred* (New York: Continuum, 1993), 85–86.

> alliance with the oppressed or particular political and social attitudes and practices. There was a convenient division between theology (concerned with the knowledge of God) and ethics (a lesser enterprise for action-oriented types). Theologians were also usually 'solo' players, each concerned to write his (the 'hers' were in short supply) magnum opus, a complete systematic theology. As the deconstructionists have underscored, these theologians also strove to assert, against different voices, the *one* voice (their own—or at least the voice of their own kind), as the truth, the 'universal' truth.[3]

Again, McFague captures the tension between the two motivating concerns for constructive theology. Early constructive theology, when done primarily with an interest in interdisciplinarity for the sake of intellectual respectability, resembled more closely liberal theology. With the irruption of liberation theology and the confrontation with numerous crises that emerged in the world between the 1970s when the Workgroup on Constructive Theology was first formed and the 1990s when the second textbook was published, constructive theology felt compelled to address both. This started with a hard swing toward activism—though as a matter of emphasis, as it also never abandoned interdisciplinary endeavors. McFague also points out the key difference in method that distinguishes constructive theology from systematic theology.

Employing Models for Earth Activism

McFague's first book-length work in this new direction is *The Body of God: An Ecological Theology*, published in 1993, right after her decision to heed the call of Kaufman. She writes, "The model of the body of God is only one model, but one that is neglected, essential, illuminating, and helpful both to Christian doctrinal reformulation and to planetary well-being. It represents one square in the quilt, one voice in the conversation, one angle of vision on the unbelievably difficult and complex issue of planetary health and the contribution Christianity might make to it."[4] The heart of the methodological characteristics of constructive theology are identified by McFague here. It includes "doctrinal reformulation," that is, rethinking Christian theology through its endemic categories rather than abandoning theological convention entirely. It precludes comprehensiveness—"one square

3. Ibid., 86.
4. Sallie McFague, *The Body of God: An Ecological Theology* (Minneapolis: Fortress, 1993), viii.

in the quilt"—or to being sufficient on its own—"one voice in the conversation."

Where it differs from the constructive theology in chapter three, including McFague's own earlier constructive theology, is specifically in its aim to support "planetary health and the contribution Christianity might make to it." In this theology, Christianity's need to speak within the academy has become a distant second player to that of being apropos of the crisis the earth faces. The conversation partner for constructive theology as McFague casts it here is not other academic disciplines, but rather activists and activisms. Work to combat human caused crises with respect to the environment and the earth as a whole doesn't start with McFague, or even Kaufman, or any other theologian. The fight starts in the realm of activism, informed by research in the sciences.

The relationship to other disciplines, in this case specifically the (earth) sciences, is made explicit in her introduction:

> This book is not about science, although it uses science as a resource for theology. The model of the world or universe as God's body is, I will argue, in keeping with the view of reality coming to us from contemporary science. It is a plausible theological response to that view of reality, a response that ought to make Christian interpretations of the relations between God and the world more credible than interpretations based on outmoded views of reality. This essay is not, however, about shaping theology to science, finding a tight fit between the two areas. Rather, it is interested in a loose fit between the contemporary scientific picture and theological construction.[5]

When thinking about earth crises, this concession comes across as especially interesting. So much of the raw intellectual work concerning catastrophes the earth faces relates statistics, figures, and scientific findings as if these facts should compel people to change their behavior. McFague's approach takes a different route. It assumes the findings of science and decides to reshape theological models to empower Christians to act proactively against the apparent coming crisis. Most basically, it seeks to organize and direct the Christian community toward just ends. Christianity in this constructive theological form rejects the status as an objective set of beliefs that demand assent, and calls for Christians to be a community that works to resist the creeping catastrophes human actions reap on the environment and on the

5. Ibid., ix.

earth. It does so by calling Christians back to Christian theology itself, albeit in a changed and focused form. The alternative discipline, in this case science, has become a presumed support of the theology to be proposed rather than central to the theology itself. It takes the activism, the organizing of Christians, to confront and change the earth's circumstances, as its central mission.

Calling Christians to Action on the Earth

Life Abundant represents McFague's more fully realized ecological theology. "The thesis of this one is that we North American middle-class Christians need to *live differently* in order to love nature, and in order to live differently, we need to think differently—especially about ourselves and who we are in the scheme of things. . . . I believe that all Christians must have a *working theology,* one that can actually function in their personal, professional, and public lives."[6] McFague's ecotheology becomes not about discerning objective truths about God and the structure of Christianity as a system that describes human beings' relationship to God, but rather about an active, actionable theology that reflects the ways Christians both do live and should live. In light of an ecological crisis that threatens God's creation as well as human beings' existence on the earth, a new type of theology is called for that orients Christians toward working to end that crisis. McFague, building on her earlier work, suggests a new model for God, specifically the panentheistic conception of the "world as God's body." She draws the image from the early church, claiming it's a model of the person of God that has been forgotten for centuries but that could act as a crucial corrective to the models used for God that encourage human beings to behave selfishly, individualistically, and greedily.

Life Abundant also departs from *The Body of God* by delving into economics. She sees the lack of economic analysis in *The Body of God* as its greatest weakness. Fundamentally, as a problem of consumption driven by capitalist Western appetites, the crises the earth faces are economic ones. In order to change the behavior of the community to which she speaks, McFague argues an entirely new economic model must be put in place. She moves from a primarily interdisciplinary literary-hermeneutic approach to an almost entirely activist one, then turns slightly to merge the two.

6. Sallie McFague, *Life Abundant: Rethinking Theology and Economy for a Planet in Peril* (Minneapolis: Fortress, 2001), xi–xii.

McFague has not been alone in this endeavor: Kathryn Tanner—from the perspective of the doctrine of creation—and Catherine Keller—from the perspective of the doctrine of eschatology—have also taken up ecological and environmental issues within the context of constructive theology. John Cobb and Gordon Kaufman have as well—Cobb from a process perspective and Kaufman, of course, inspired McFague's own turn to ecological theology. Constructive theology was early to embrace ecological and environmental justice oriented activism. It incorporates the language of crisis and the realization that human beings are destroying the very conditions for survival on the earth from the moment these things came to be acknowledged in general cultural discourse. Constructive theology, against the typical image of theology being reactionary and always behind the times, was and is out in the front when it comes to fighting the destruction human beings reap on the earth as a whole. Using doctrines of the nature of God and of creation, as well as of theological anthropology, the urgency of the global ecological and environmental crisis finds sufficient expression in Christian religious theological language. Constructive theology has intended to engage just as earnestly with race, but has found it to be much harder terrain to negotiate.

Constructive Theology and Race: Dwight Hopkins and James H. Evans Jr.

Race presents one of the greatest challenges to constructive theology's striving to be theology that works for justice. Constructive theology is, to this point, a distinctively United States phenomenon. And race presents particularly difficult issues, most especially for the academic establishment, to deal with in any sort of adequate way. Two chapters appear in *Reconstructing Christian Theology* that are explicitly about race. Only one is written by a person of color. Overall, the book is painfully short on contributions from people of color, despite the explicit claim to be primarily about liberation.

The third book by the Workgroup includes many more contributors of color, and theologians writing on race worked with the group throughout its second and third instantiations. The fourth book presumes the legitimacy and necessity of liberationism, especially in regard to race issues. It is telling that against the backdrop of liberal Black theologies that were available to constructive theology that the Black theologians who took part in the Workgroup or identify as constructive theologians identify as liberation theologians. Dorrien writes, "Black theologians Dwight Hopkins, James H. Evans Jr., Kelly Brown Douglas, and Jacquelyn Grant did not regard themselves as participants in the liberal struggle with religion's cultured critics; to them black liberation theology was primarily about the religious experiences and struggles for justice of oppressed people of color."[7] Hopkins and Evans have both contributed to the works produced by the Workgroup. M. Shawn Copeland and Sheila Briggs were the earliest Black members of the Workgroup, but didn't contribute to the textbooks it produced. Other constructive theologians, like Sharon Welch, Robert H. King, and Peter C. Hodgson have also explicitly taken up questions of race. And others who did not contribute to previous Workgroup textbooks have worked in a constructive vein, like Stephen Ray and Victor Anderson. Ray edited, with Laurel Schneider, the most recent Workgroup textbook, *Awake to the Moment.* Regardless of the race of the contributor, constructive theologians, starting with the incorporation of activism into constructive theology, privilege a liberationist perspective over a liberal perspective when it comes to questions of race.

Black Liberation Theology Done Constructively

Dwight Hopkins did his doctorate at Union Theological Seminary with James Cone. Cone was purportedly invited to participate in the Workgroup on Constructive Theology and contribute to their works, but declined. Yet he does, softly, claim to be a liberation theologian who works constructively. Hopkins, on the other hand, solidly claims to be a constructive theologian, though he does, in his foundational methodological work *Shoes That Fit Our Feet: Sources for a Constructive Black Theology*, refer often to constructing a systematic theology. This, in my opinion, can be attributed to constructive theology's ambivalence, to this point, about splitting with systematic theology as the right method for doing theology. Liberation theology is, of course, inherently activist in nature. Across the spectrum of liberation theologies a foundational claim is that theology comes after right action. That is, theology reflects on the activism and action that reveal the will of God in the world through liberation. *Shoes That Fit Our Feet* uses traditional theological doctrinal loci, but only those that specifically pertain to the crisis being engaged. These loci are theology proper, Christology, and theological anthropology.[8] The books also tries to align theology with

7. Dorrien, *The Making of American Liberal Theology*, 173.

Black experience, but specifically with the Black experience of today, another central tenet of constructive theology: "Thus theology continually questions the identity and purpose of a specific people in new situations and for new generations. Because today's African American community and church have the unique experience of God both in their *political* resistance against white racism and in their positive assertions of black *culture*, there is a need to understand and present clearly the particular witness of this black-God union."[9] The term "shoes that fit our feet" specifically points to the need for Black theology to have a mode that is appropriate to the Black church's historical and ongoing work for justice on the part of the Black community in the United States. It is based in Black sources and geared toward making explicit the "instinctive" theological work that is peculiar to the Black community's historical faith.

Constructive theology is an especially apropos method for doing Black theology, particularly in an activist mode, because a key argument of liberation theology has been that white theology, and the system it is based on, is both morally and intellectually bankrupt. It simply doesn't work, and much of the justification for the system as we know it comes from the Enlightenment, which informed the liberal theological tradition. Insofar as the system of systematic theology reflects the intellectual well from which it's drawn, it also reflects the white supremacism that is an inextricable part of it. Experiences of liberation for the Black community don't tend to be accounted for in the systematic theology that comes before Black liberation theology and constructive Black theology. An adequate systematic theology would preclude racial prejudice, white hegemony, and white supremacy entirely as not being the will of God. Yet the pervasiveness of white supremacism and racism in historical dogmatic and systematic theologies, even amongst the most forward thinking and progressive theologians of each period, is well documented. It doesn't seem coincidental to me that the language of rebelling against the "system" or "systemic" injustices brought about by white supremacy and the white intellectual tradition echoes the rebellion against systematic theology. Of course, this isn't without tension because Christianity has been such a driving force in the work for liberation of the Black community. Constructive theology allows Black theology to choose and emphasize the doctrines that

8. Dwight N. Hopkins, *Shoes That Fit Our Feet: Sources for a Constructive Black Theology* (Maryknoll: Orbis, 1993), 4.
9. Ibid., 5.

have most served the task of liberation both historically and in the present.

Honoring Black Diversity in Constructive Theology

Black constructive theology revolves around how to interpret the varieties of Black experience within Christianity and how to build a sound theology on that experience without flattening it. Because there are diverse experiences of being Black, constructive theology lends itself especially well to this task because it refuses to see any single theology as being self-sufficient. Describing Evans' key work, *We Have Been Believers*, Stephen Ray writes,

> In my estimation, what Evans accomplished with his book was to bridge . . . chasms that existed in the scholarship and ecclesial practice of African American Christian theological discourse. . . . While many attributed these fissures primarily to the shifting poles of communal and religious identity, Evans demonstrates that it was also substantially the case that emerging differences in theological methodology in relation to sources, their uses, and the norms by which they are integrated into a theological vision were at play.[10]

A systematic approach to Black theology insists that one system—with sources and norms properly identified and evaluated—could account for Black theology at large. Constructive theology allows that a number of different theologies, from different perspectives, with different conceptions of sources and norms, are needed to provide a sufficient basis for understanding Christian witness with respect to the Black community.

Ray continues, "The issue which made these differences a chasm was that academic theology, and the philosophical systems from which much of it drew, had no way of making sense of the experience of black persons or their communities. Thus Black Theology, as an academic discipline, used categories and frames that made no sense to members of the Black Church because they drew on abstract systems which, ironically, privileged hegemonic normativity."[11] Once again, though the terminology of "systematic" theology isn't thrown out outright, Evans voices his suspicion as to the ability of systematic theology to

10. James H. Evans Jr., *We Have Been Believers: An African American Systematic Theology* (Minneapolis: Fortress, 2012), xiii.
11. Ibid.

account for Black theology. He also raises the persistent question of constructive theology whether an entirely new philosophical system may be needed to replace the traditional philosophical underpinnings of Christianity. Drawing from the constructive theological tradition all the way back to Ten Broeke and Meland, constructive Black theology continues to ponder whether new philosophies would serve as a better basis entirely for Christian theology, with conflicting and mixed responses. And once again the mixed response is exactly the point.

We Have Been Believers identifies two key characteristics of a black constructive theology, the "praxiological" and "hermeneutical" aspects. Black constructive theology with liberation as its focus must hold these two aspects "in perfect balance," "responding to the needs of both the head and the heart." The praxiological aspect is the introduction of activism into the constructive task already established by a focus on the hermeneutical. The wedding of orthopraxis and orthodoxy is a classic mainstay of liberation theologies. Evans's constructive spin on this combination changes orthodoxy, the right confession or doctrine, to hermeneutics. Though Evans's work is liberationist in nature, it argues that understanding theology correctly is a matter of hermeneutics, not simply correctly describing the shape of a liberative Christianity. Especially given the historical forms of Christianity developed by white people, which have supported slavery, Jim Crow, and formulations of doctrine that serve to oppress and dehumanize people of color, Christianity in Black constructive theology must be seen as a construct that can be changed. This happens through analysis, deconstruction, and ultimately reconstruction, the typical methodological steps of constructive theology.

Evans identifies the central tasks of Black theology as confronted in the present as "to clarify the contexts—historical, sociopolitical, cultural, and intellectual—in which African American Christian faith is affirmed," "to articulate, interpret, and assess the essential doctrinal affirmations of African American faith for the contemporary African American community of faith," and "to examine the moral implications of that faith for Christian witness in the world."[12] The focus of Evans' work in *We Have Been Believers* is the second. That is, it is to understand the contemporary context and propose a method that is appropriate for the African American or Black community in light of the present. Evans specifically, in the constructive mode, takes up the

12. Ibid., 6.

doctrine of revelation. Further, he rejects liberalism as a fruitful direction for contemporary Black theology: "The history of revelation and the history of liberation are the same history. God's self-disclosure is not meant to increase humanity's storehouse of cognitive merchandise or to intensify one's inward feeling of piety, but to demonstrate that God's presence and power are limited by neither geographical boundaries nor political structures."[13] The line between constructive theology and liberation theology, in the context of the conversation about race, is often blurred. Ultimately the question becomes one of self-identification. Evans identifies, at least implicitly, as a constructive theologian by his involvement in the Workgroup on Constructive Theology. Others, like Cone, sense the affinity between constructive theology and liberation theology.

Relating and Separating Systematic and Constructive Black Theologies

Liberation theologies often retain "systematic" language, and theologians of color who write about race are more likely to identify as "Black" or "liberation" theologians. Hopkins and Evans both name their theologies "systematic" despite working as constructive theologians. Evans's *We Have Been Believers*, especially, takes on a systematic form in discussing doctrinal loci from theology proper through eschatology. Liberation theology shares with constructive theology the investment in speaking to the present, the recognition that Christianity is a structure developed by human beings—in this case, historically white supremacist ones—and the insight that the structure needs reconstruction and reimagination. Liberation theology is ambivalent about construction because it rests so heavily on the claim that Christianity does have an objective core, that is, the work for liberation on the part of God as evidenced in the Bible and history.

Victor Anderson emerges as a constructive theologian who begins to outline the departure of Black theology from systematic methods of doing theology. In *Creative Exchange: A Constructive Theology of African American Religious Experience*, Anderson writes that he had to reconceive the shape the book would take while working on it because "I found myself greatly dissatisfied with the approach that I was taking—an approach I had learned from my studies in Western philosophy and of

13. Ibid., 12–13.

religion. I initially thought that I would write a philosophical theology more in line with traditional modes of argument on problems: the problem of religious knowledge, the problem of evil and suffering, the problem of God, and the problem of human meaning—the usual line-up."[14] Because of its basis in Black experience, which exceeds philosophical systems usually used in the past, that is, predominately white philosophical systems, Anderson rejects the "usual line-up." His deconstructions and rejections are of people he knows, that is, fundamentally contemporary. The activism of the book arises because

> In writing this book, I could not easily put on the mask of the disinterested critic who enjoys nothing more than carving up concepts and figures for intellectual consumption. I found myself deeply interested in and affected by the materials making up this book's content. This is a critical book insofar as it takes seriously the ways that African American religious thinkers conceptually frame the meaning of race and religious experience; however, it is also constructive insofar as I put my own thinking into the hermeneutics of African American religious experience. This book is a constructive theology. It is not historical research on black religion.[15]

Black constructive theology confronts but ultimately rejects historical theology that is systematic and dogmatic theology or outlining what theology has been in the past, as sufficient to account for contemporary Black experience. This is the reason constructive theology is so important for activist theologies that seek to change current constructed systems, including from the perspective of race. Anderson's description of *Creative Exchange*—including the title itself, "creative" pointing to the ongoing creative constructive work being done in theology and "exchange" indicating the ongoing, open-ended, collaborative nature of constructive theology—makes it a constructive theological project through and through, though he undersells the distinction between constructive theology and other theologies. *Creative Exchange* is not best contrasted with theologies that describe and analyze historical theologies, but rather with theologies that recapitulate and reconstitute theologies on old philosophies, inherit white perspectives as objective descriptions of an existing system, and resist dipping into work that tries to effect real contemporary societal change. The fact that Anderson converses with living scholars, his mentors and peers,

14. Victor Anderson, *Creative Exchange: A Constructive Theology of African American Experience* (Minneapolis: Fortress, 2008), 1.
15. Ibid., 2.

brings this activist, constructive aspect to the fore. He can neither dismiss the work of other scholars as an academic exercise, as he believes typically happens in academic work, nor affirm the sufficiency of their historical, disinterested pretense to objectivity.

Coping with a Lack of Black Voices in Early Constructive Theology[16]

Constructive theology's attempts to deal with justice issues around race are not limited to theologians of color. As mentioned above, both Sharon Welch and Peter C. Hodgson have written works explicitly about racial injustice in the United States. Hodgson, in a short book titled *Children of Freedom: Black Liberation in Christian Perspective,* writes that "non-blacks can only welcome the effort by black theologians to preserve and reinterpret the Christian symbols—to hold together the theological heritage of the Christian West, the distinctive religious experience of the black community, and the sense of outrage and self-discovery that so characterizes black consciousness today. It is not an easy thing to do and of late has been frequently challenged."[17] Hodgson raises the question of redefining traditional Christian symbols—a foundational task of constructive theology. He holds out hope that a white man might be able to participate genuinely in a theological conversation about race because "true understanding, in the final analysis, is possible because the horizons of human experience are not static; rather they are open and constantly merge into each other. Access to Black literature and Black consciousness is open to those prepared for a reshaping and fusing of horizons, and increasingly that is happening as a new America comes to birth."[18] The changing intellectual and cultural circumstances in the United States demand an entirely new approach to doing theology. Like other constructive theologies, Hodgson's entrance into an adequate, unfinished account of theology is premised on an openness to artistic expressions like literature and everyday Black experience.

Of course, ultimately, a white perspective on race must be limited.

16. For a fuller account of the often ironic historical relationship between constructive theology and Black liberation theology and the tensions and agreements between the two, see "Constructive Theology, Black Liberation Theology, and Black Constructive Theology: A History of Irony and Resonance," *Black Theology: An International Journal* 15, no. 3 (Winter 2017).
17. Peter C. Hodgson, *Children of Freedom: Black Liberation in Christian Perspective* (Philadelphia: Fortress, 1974), 1.
18. Ibid., 3.

Hodgson's approach may still be criticized for being too categorically and intellectually driven. Though he intends to take up James Cone's call for a white theologian to take Black experience and Black oppression as the starting point for theology, he problematically makes the distinction that "It should be clear at the outset that what follows is a *theological* essay, not a phenomenology of black religion. The interpretive categories and structural divisions of the essay do not follow directly from the black experience itself but reflect the biblical and doctrinal tradition, as well as modern philosophical discussion, although I have attempted a basic reinterpretation of traditional views of freedom on many points."[19] This essay was still early in the formalized constructive theological tradition, coming only two years after the publication of the first Workgroup textbook. Nonetheless, it shows both the potential for an activist constructive theology geared toward race as well as the limitations that still pervade today with respect to constructive theology's success in fully accounting for and internalizing liberation theology. Traditional doctrines are used, but only as they are needed to make the greater point that oppressive symbols must be redefined. It demands the use of modern philosophical thinking rather than maintaining traditional philosophical systems for theology. Nevertheless, it denies the Black experience as being sufficient unto itself, without white theological categories for constructing Christian theology that support white supremacism. He states further, "Whether black religion in America will ultimately even support something like a 'theology' as its mode of reflective articulation is a difficult and as yet unanswered question."[20] This may indicate either that Black religion requires some other type of reflection than what has historically been considered "theology" at all, itself an interestingly (re)constructive statement. At the same time, it seems more likely to indicate that Hodgson, in 1974, isn't sure whether Black experience alone can support a theological project. This latter hesitation reflects constructive theology's greatest failing with respect to taking liberation theology as seriously as it proposes. It is critical, nonetheless, to recognize that Hodgson was an early adopter and tried to engage with Black liberation theology in good faith. While the book may have ultimately come up short, it speaks to the central intention of constructive theology to lift up liberation theology. He, and constructive theology, must be credited with genuinely trying to embrace Black and other liberation

19. Ibid., 4.
20. Ibid.

theologies. It would take several decades for that intention to come to fruition.

Sharon Welch comes at race from the starting point of feminism. Challenges from womanist and Black feminist thinkers forced feminism, frequently critiqued for its overwhelmingly white middle-class nature, to remain cognizant of intersectionality, that is, the overlap between marginalized identity markers for the last several decades. Welch is also predominately an ethicist. Constructive theology blurs the line between theology and ethics, especially when it comes to activist theologies. More importantly, as critiques of marginalizing structures and institutions become more sophisticated, constructive theologies develop accordingly more sophisticated analyses, critiques, and reconstructions of key theological ideas. Intersectionality cannot be ignored as constructive theology develops and increases its activist stance. It allows constructive theology to build upon its growing tradition as an open-ended, critically informed, dialogical theology that insists Christianity cannot be monolithic. Constructive theology rejects single strands of comprehensive systematic theology as adequate for understanding God, Christianity, and the ways in which the world works. Feminist and sexuality/gender oriented activist constructive theologies illustrate this development.

Feminism, Gender, and Sexuality: Rebecca Chopp and Laurel Schneider

Gender and sexuality are historically fraught topics for Christian theology that have risen to prominence in recent years in culture generally. More often than not, "Christian" views about women, gender, and sexuality are conflated with religious right views, that is, conservative, reactionary ones that tend to use the Bible as a proof text and resist expansive, inclusive notions at all costs. Yet, Christianity has a multivocal history on these issues. Constructive theology's engagement with feminism, gender, and sexuality both reinvigorates forgotten liberatory strands in the Christian tradition and, more apropos, works to criticize the historically oppressive structures that have been built in the guise of Christianity and reconstruct in a more inclusive, just, affirmative way.

Feminism, gender studies, and sexuality/queer studies are not the same thing. They are, however, all historically and theoretically related. Queer studies couldn't have emerged without earlier LGBT and sexuality critiques, and also relies on destabilizing gender critiques. Likewise, these movements arise out of the insights of the multiple waves of feminism that preceded them. Feminism takes up the empowerment and fully realized humanity of women against the backdrop of historical misogyny and almost universal privileging of men's voices. Gender critique and analysis, especially since Judith Butler famously problematized the category of gender as performative, confronts the existence and affirmation of a much wider array of gender expressions than have traditionally been recognized in a dichotomous system of male and female, buttressed by views anchored in Christian theology. Sexuality critique has to do with sexual expression specifically—rather than performative gender expression—although sexuality is informed by one's gender. Finally, queer studies blends gender and sexuality, insisting on the blurring of boundaries between fixed gender and sexual expressions. All of these areas are entrenched in ongoing battles in the United States as women continue to struggle for rights and privileges equal to that of men, LGBTQ folks continue to fight for rights and equality both culturally and legally—notwithstanding the recent victory of same sex marriage—and queerness seeks to disrupt historical categorization and advance fluid, expansive, ever-changing conceptions of identity.

Feminism and Constructive Theology: Early Conversation Partners

Rebecca Chopp published *The Power to Speak* in 1989. Feminist theology, of course, has a long history before then, including within constructive theology. "Women will be forever strangers unless their words and their voices revise the social and symbolic rules of language, in subjectivity, and in politics into a grace of rich plenitude for human flourishing. . . . In this fashion women may not so much balance or equalize the hierarchy as change its monotheistic ordering of the 'one' as opposed to the 'other' into a multiplicity, allowing differences and connections instead of constantly guaranteeing identities and oppositions."[21] In many ways this parallels McFague's mission to offer new metaphors and models for God. It differs in its greater emphasis on changing the world at large. For McFague the task is mostly a theological one, while for Chopp in this instance the theology supports the activism. She continues,

21. Rebecca S. Chopp, *The Power to Speak: Feminism, Language, God* (New York: Crossroad, 1989), 2.

> My discourse attempts, in its own strategies, to criticize and move toward transforming the social-symbolic order. I do not think that women can opt out of this order to make up new discourses, nor do I think correcting the order is enough. . . . Until we change the values and hidden rules that run through present linguistic practices, social codes, and psychic ordering, women, persons of color, and other oppressed groups will be forced—by the language, discourses, and practices available to them—into conforming to ongoing practices, to babbling nonsense, or to not speaking at all.[22]

For Chopp, theology is a matter of politics and power, not solely reconstructing theology from the inside or enlarging theological conversation to include metaphors that represent women. At the same time, she still remains very much in theological discourse. Her primary prescription for empowering women from the standpoint of constructive theology is "proclamation." In a constructive theological move, Chopp identifies proclamation, the activity of ministry as proclaiming the word, as the theological site to be analyzed and reconstructed in *The Power to Speak.* Drawing on postmodern critical theorists like Jacques Derrida and Michel Foucault, Chopp writes: "Language, subjectivity, and politics: these three realms, dimensions, common places, form today the structuring of the dominant social-symbolic order and provide the problems and possibilities of transformation."[23]

At this stage in constructive theology, language about power, dominance, oppression, and social transformation becomes important. Feminist constructive theology moves beyond reconstructing only Christian theological categories, seeking to influence society as well. Chopp does this through an analysis of language and symbols, not only within theology but in culture at large. The point of constructive theology becomes to change the world, not just Christianity. Proclamation, in this sense, is not only for the Christian community, but about ways Christianity can help to reform and revolutionize an oppressive system that it has helped to create. The "power to speak" refers to the potential for Christian theology to empower women, as well as other oppressed groups, to have their voices heard by everyone, not simply within the context of Christian theology or the Christian church. The church itself, and Christian praxis then, come to be named as agents for social change.

22. Ibid., 7.
23. Ibid., 103.

Incorporating Critical Theories of Gender and Sexuality

Feminism brings the destabilization of hegemonic identities based on binaries into the theological conversation. Laurel Schneider, building on this work, expands this thinking into realms of sexuality and gender, simultaneously incorporating other insights from nascent queer studies. She begins by, as she calls it, "confronting the backlash against feminism" in Christian theology, which leads to her new multiplicity in unity. She describes this unity as monism, a critique and expansion of the trinity—indeed, naming monotheism as a problematic construction itself[24]: "Monotheism is a theological construction that affirms divine greatness by seeing the existence of other divine realities as competition or denying the existence of other divine realities altogether. . . . Feminist theologies have begun over the years to entertain the possibility that monotheism itself, the doctrinal heart of the religious traditions of the West, is part of the problem."[25] In the 2000s, Schneider's work expands from feminist concerns to those around gender and sexuality.

Feminism is incorporated heavily into constructive theology nearly from the beginning. Theologies around sexuality, gender, and queerness have still not been as thoroughly incorporated, at least in a sustained way by any single constructive theologian. Influential queer, feminist, and womanist theologians still often identify as systematic theologians, or instead as ethicists and entirely outside the theological discipline. Patrick Cheng, a leading queer theologian known for his books *Radical Love* and *Rainbow Theology*, considers his writings to be both systematic and constructive, respectively. The distinction between the two in his work is useful because *Radical Love*, his accessible introduction to queer systematic theology, develops every doctrine of traditional Christianity in a systematic way. *Rainbow Theology*, on the other hand, stresses multiplicity and open-endedness, and especially the importance of affirming the full humanity of all persons despite gender or sexuality. That is, it goes beyond description or apologetic for why Christianity can tolerate or embrace queerness into advocating for Christian theology's role in furthering the important work of queering gender and sexuality norms.

Feminism and queer theory stand as excellent conversation partners

24. Laurel C. Schneider, *Re-Imagining the Divine: Confronting the Backlash against Feminist Theology* (Cleveland: Pilgrim Press, 1998), 157.
25. Ibid., 155.

for constructive theology. As critical discourses they fundamentally affirm constructive theology's basic tenet that social identity, power, and knowledge are constructed in ongoing social negotiations. Like constructive theology rejects the objective reality of a structure that is Christianity, so feminism rejects the essentialisms imbued in the idea of "woman" and gender/queer critique rejects simple binaries between male-female and heterosexual-homosexual. Christianity, regardless of the objective existence of God or other tenets of belief, is a discursive project. Much as in the case of sex, gender, and sexuality, that realization profoundly transforms how the conversation should proceed. Beyond this change in thinking and discourse building, feminist, LGBTQ, and queer theologies participate in changing policy, culture, and societal attitudes that dehumanize and marginalize non-male and non-heterosexual people. As such, a powerful force for the shaping of attitudes, ethics, and behavior, Christianity presents itself as potentially one of the most useful tools available for expanding inclusivity with respect to people that fall anywhere along and outside traditional feminine, gender, and sexual norms. In recent fights for things like marriage equality the participation of churches, informed by emerging theologies that are constructive in nature, was palpable. Constructive theology enables churches to get involved in this work, while also providing important discursive re-imagining for those outside the church as well.

Action in constructive theology, its activist nature, can be expressed in different ways. Constructive theology around race emphasizes working to lift up and construct discursively from Black experience, history, and tradition. Feminist, LGBTQ, and queer theologies do this as well from their own vantage points, also adding specific pragmatic agendas such as marriage equality. Constructive theology also has a stream of explicitly political theologies, with the goal of mobilizing activism for all of these issues, as well as specific political and economic ones. Turning to these types of constructive theologies will reflect on the above as well as introduce another brand of constructive theology that continues to build on its activist tradition.

Politics, Class, and Constructive Theology: Mark L. Taylor and Joerg Rieger

Activist constructive theology that confronts politics and economic injustices isn't exactly the same as political theology, though some political theologies are constructive theologies. Political theology is a variety of theology that has arisen over the last century or so, to a large extent in response to Carl Schmitt and his aptly named book, *Political Theology*, published in 1922. Political theology takes as its mission to analyze politics and political systems and to analyze their relationship to theology. This may include questions like how a political system is supported by a certain type of theology, what a political system means theologically, or how theology and politics relate. Constructive theology, when done with politics in mind, attempts to change political systems. The point of engaging politics within constructive theology is to interrogate current hegemonic political systems and structures and mobilize Christians to work for politics with greater justice and inclusiveness. Similarly, as economic justice and politics are so closely related, constructive theologies can take up a critique of economic systems as well as proposals for ways Christianity can help to change those systems to be more just and more equitable for all people living today. Mark Lewis Taylor provides an example of activist constructive theology with a political twist, while Joerg Rieger stands as a leading example of a constructive theologian intent on mobilizing Christianity to change the current economic system that oppresses so many by introducing class critiques that have been latent for some time.

Rethinking "Theology" and the "Theological"

Mark Lewis Taylor's reconstruction of Christian theology starts with the word "Theology" (intentionally capitalized) itself. He intends to introduce the "theological," which he considers being something distinct from "Theology" as promulgated in the academy. To the point above he writes, "This book's argument for the theological is not so much a political theology as it is a political theorization of the theological. The latter is already ongoing."[26] The theological is a "distinctive discourse, issuing from [the] agonistic dimension of political and social life." The theological, then, emerges from the lived experiences of those "under the weight of the world," found on the bottom of society's power structures. As contrasted with the Theological, it is meant to emerge from the bottom up, a capitulation of the actions, hopes, fears, and theological insights of the oppressed and subjugated. These groups are called to agonism in the public and political spheres,

26. Mark L. Taylor, *The Theological and the Political: On the Weight of the World* (Minneapolis: Fortress, 2011), xiv.

to passionately oppose constituencies that enforce dehumanizing and degrading social structures. Taylor calls for the theological to correct not only Christian theology, but to fight against all oppressive social structures in the contemporary world. He radicalizes the constructive theological call for activism, making changing society from the top down—or perhaps better put, from the bottom up—the imperative of his variety of political constructive theology.

Taylor's constructive theology presents somewhat of a challenge to the typology of constructive theology being laid out in this book. Because of his opposition to the capital-T "Theological," he departs from the constructive theological tradition of maintaining the use of doctrinal loci for specific activist purposes. In fact, this harkens back to an early intra-methodological dilemma for the Workgroup on Constructive Theology. Gordon Kaufman, as one of the best examples of early formalized constructive theology, also protested against the use of traditional loci for constructing theology.[27] Kaufman called for the termination of the use of loci for the sake of radical creativity in theology. Taylor does it here to propose radical agonistic politics that reject the political system as it stands. And despite the book's structural departure from doctrinal loci as its guides, it is nonetheless about theology itself, that is, the project of doing theology. In a sense, he offers a later prolegomenon, an excursion into considering what theology is, as Kaufman did as well. Constructive theology always walks this line. Taylor—and Kaufman before him—are outliers in rejecting the loci as orienting tropes for constructing theology. They nevertheless participate in the reconstruction of theology based on its, as they would come to be called, traditions and tasks. Taylor's theologizing also participates in theology that precludes an ending and embraces the fundamental ongoing nature of theological discourse, specifically in continuing conversation with those who bear the weight of the world. Taylor's work is an outlier in format, not in central concerns or ideas. And in any case, if Taylor did propose to work within doctrinal loci, he would be within the spheres of theology proper and ecclesiology.

Fundamentally, in terms of construction, Taylor rejects onto-theology as well as the inherent nature of political structures. He draws on philosophers and critical theorists who reject essentialism and expose the discursively constructed nature of the world at large like Michel Foucault and Pierre Bourdieu in order to link up the theological

27. Peter C. Hodgson, in discussion with the author, December 12, 2015.

with the political and demonstrate the role the theological has to play in transforming the world so that it works for everyone rather than a powerful few. He claims that the theological "haunts" the political, provoking the agonism and radical practices necessary to "challenge sovereign power and discourse."[28] Drawing on interdisciplinarity, especially from continental philosophy and critical theory, Taylor attempts to show how the theological exists in the world apart from the academy. Theology, with a capital "T," is systematic, that is, part of the very system that subjugates and disenfranchises.[29] Taylor's constructive theology deconstructs theology entirely in order to put the work of theology and the goals it seeks to attain in the secular world. The theological has never properly found its home in the academy at all. It is meant to be a tool, or rather a "specter" that refuses to allow the status quo to rest easy. "The ghostly and the spectral are what the poststructuralist traces as fault lines, fissures, infiltrations operating in the colonizer's centralizing cultural and political apparatus. To trace them is to find the vestiges of the vanquished, often to highlight and strengthen long-colonized peoples, aiming to eviscerate the strength of colonizing and imperial projects."[30] Taylor makes the surprising but powerful claim that the theological haunts oppressive powers. It is a potential specter for power, perhaps the greatest specter available to break the oppressive chains of current political systems that function on a logic of marginalization. Reinterpreting and reimagining theology, taking theology out of Theology as a tamed discipline within the inherited elitist power structure, reveals and releases its power to be a motivating, empowering, actionable force for positive change.

Confronting Capitalism with Constructive Theological Conviction

Joerg Rieger similarly calls for politically motivated change, but he centers his activism around economic issues, specifically ones around class and empire. He raises class in the context of liberation theology, pointing out alongside other theologians that class, despite being perhaps the first subject of critical theory, has remained mostly unspoken of generally in the academy for several decades, no less in theology. Liberation theologies, especially those out of Latin America, faced harsh criticism for their use of Marxist class analysis and critique. Yet

28. Ibid., xviii.
29. Ibid., 25.
30. Ibid., 32.

theologies in the United States, aside from engagements with Latin American liberation theologies, have seldom used class as a starting point for theological reflection (including in other liberation theologies in the United States context). Rieger uses the method of constructive theology to reintroduce and centralize questions of class as a topic in need of reexamination and activist engagement. He deepens class critique by introducing post- and anti-colonial critique as well as empire critical analyses.

In *No Rising Tide* Rieger writes, "There are powerful reminders in the Judeo-Christian traditions that faith does not have to mean blind acceptance or a promise of pie in the sky that would not be subject to testing and questioning. Faith is tied to reality and the transformation of it. More specifically, Christian faith has to do with the transformation of the reality of the least of its followers, as Jesus' response to John the Baptist demonstrates. Without that particular transformation, faith does not make sense, and neither does economics."[31] Rieger points out that people accept both Christian beliefs and economic systems on "blind faith," offering a provocative turn on the usual stigmatization of religion as being the only object of blind faith for human beings. He argues that economic principles, specifically free market ideologies and the winner-loser economy, do not have to be the way that they are.

Indeed, neither Christian faith as it commonly appears in the contemporary United States nor the capitalist market economy that finds its greatest expression in the United States are static, inherent qualities of Christianity or economics respectively. In order to confront both, that is, to propose the ways in which Christians, informed by constructive theology, can help to change the world to make it more just for all, he theologizes around the doctrine of God. He argues that "once both our implicit and explicit images of God are uncovered and brought out into the open . . . theology can engage them, debate them, and propose alternatives."[32]

Rieger offers the specific alternative of bottom up re-theologizing, and proposes an examination and redefinition of justice that takes into account theorization around power. Revisiting the crossover with liberation theology, Rieger promotes solidarity with those most affected by the fallout from economic downturns and predatory market economics.[33] Therefore, "the image of the divine emerging here is

31. Joerg Rieger, *No Rising Tide: Theology, Economics, Future* (Minneapolis: Fortress, 2009), ix.
32. Ibid., 123.

dynamic. A God who favors those whose relationships have been violated can never be pinned down in terms of an abstract notion of fairness. God takes sides for the benefit of all."[34] Our image of God as a community buttresses the economic system we inhabit. If God represents our deepest values and holds human beings accountable for the systems in which they live, then our image of God and the characteristics we associate with God are crucial. Biblical tradition, according to Rieger, doesn't support the conception of God as one who supports zero-sum capitalist economics where some must lose in order for others to win. Nor, more apropos of recent events, does it sync with an image of a God who would think that the poor and marginalized bearing the brunt of economic downturns triggered by the rich and powerful is acceptable. God's justice, according to Rieger, insists that an economic system must support the well-being of the whole community. Our constructed image of God should reflect that.[35]

Rejecting Empire and Christianity's Historical Complicity

In *Christ and Empire: From Paul to Postcolonial Times*, Rieger takes up questions of Christology and offers a critique more specifically aimed at empire. Many recent works across theology and its related disciplines, including ethics, church history, and especially the Bible, have interrogated the often overlooked context of the Roman Empire in which Jesus lived. Interestingly, from a constructive perspective, the subtitle of Rieger's book reveals that the question of Christ for him starts with Paul. Introducing the many "Christs" throughout history complicates the idea that Christ is one thing for all time. Paul's Christ is very different from a postcolonial Christ, yet within Christian theology both exist. "Christ," then, doesn't point to one being or thing, but rather the constructed idea within Christianity and developed within Christian theology. This doesn't, however, deny the actual efficacy or importance of Christ within Christianity. In fact, the redefinitions and constant re-interrogation of "Christ" as a concept throughout the history of Christianity affirms its importance. It affirms why the doctrinal centrality of Christology is so important. Regardless of any objective quality or character of "Christ" outside of human construction, reconstructions

33. Ibid., 136.
34. Ibid., 139.
35. Ibid., 150.

of the doctrine of Christ are fundamental to Christianity in its work for justice and relevance.

Postcolonial theory emerges primarily out of literary studies, with Edward Said usually identified as the founder and most important theorist. Said's arguments concerning "Orientalism" are deeply rooted in historical power relations between the "Western" world—that is Europe and the United States—and the "Orient," which in this case mostly means the Middle East. These power relations and the discursive production of the "Orient" as a foil to the West are strongly intertwined with the privileged place of Christianity in European history. Reflecting this line of argument, Rieger writes, "The primary context in which we think about Christ—whether we realize it or not—is shaped by large and ever-changing conglomerates of power that are aimed at controlling all aspects of our lives, from macropolitics to our innermost desires: this is what I call 'empire.'"[36] Christology needs to be rethought and reconstructed because it has been co-opted by empire. In so doing, Christ can be enlisted in the resistance of empire. Christ has historically served as a tool of empire and colonization, yet a "surplus," as Rieger calls it, has always remained that denied empire's ability to entirely tame it. The task of Rieger's theology is not to describe Christ or Christology simply as they exist, as if they existed apart from empire and human constructions. Rather it is to harness the surplus meaning and symbolism contained within Christ in order to fight empire. Christ, as one of the empire's most enduring weapons, when reconstructed, can serve as one of the greatest tools for fighting and denying empire. Christ through Rieger's imaginative constructive work calls Christians to active dismantling of empire.

Taylor and Rieger, along with many other constructive theologians, address the systemic political and economic realities that lead to marginalization and subjugation in the contemporary Western world. This task is both so important and so tricky because Christianity itself—whether through co-option or by the essence attributed to it in the past—has contributed so massively to the oppressive societal structures we live in today. Many of the "crises" confronted by constructive theology have arisen in part because of Christianity, specifically theological justifications for them based on all sorts of foundations. Constructive theology asserts that these oppressive structures are not Christianity's essence. Models that hurt people are not fundamentally

36. Joerg Rieger, *Christ and Empire: From Paul to Postcolonial Times* (Minneapolis: Fortress, 2007), vii.

part of Christianity as God wills it and which can never be changed because they are part of God's will. Rather, Christianity, regardless of metaphysical realities of God and God's character, is an imaginative construction, and therefore the responsibility to reform and revolutionize the conditions that devastate human beings created by Christian structures and theology falls on Christian theology itself.

Conclusion

For all of the theologians in this chapter, and many others in the constructive theological tradition, changing the way Christian theology participates in discursive constructions that have been historically damaging for large swaths of humanity is a central work for theology. Ecology, race, feminism, and politics/class are only a few of the realms into which constructive theology has infiltrated to do work that employs Christianity to change social structures and end dehumanizing discourses based in Christian theological history. But they are also the biggest and most persistent, and in many ways these basic critiques, around human beings' relationships with the earth, each other, and with power, serve as the basis for the others that have emerged throughout constructive theology's history. With the realization that Christianity is both implicated in all of these structures of domination as well as capable of helping to change them, constructive theology takes up the challenge to support and theorize activism on the part of every marginalized community imaginable.

Methodologically, several key components to activist constructive theologies can be gleaned from the above:

1. Activist constructive theology emerges from the encounter between the mood of constructive theology, that is one that privileges open-endedness and imaginative construction, with the challenge of liberation theology. Further, some liberation theologies are constructive theologies—while not all activist constructive theologies, even those that claim to be—are liberationist.
2. Activist constructive theologies are informed by critical discourses in other disciplines, especially those that reveal the constructedness of social life and power structures in the contemporary world.
3. Like interdisciplinary constructive theologies, activist constructive theology is rooted in the foundational conceit that theology

is a creative endeavor of construction, not a project of revealing objective truths about God or the workings of Christianity.

4. Because Christianity, through Christian theology, is constructed, the responsibility of Christianity to change its own oppressive structures and to undo the oppression it has contributed to in the world through its historical theology falls on Christianity itself. As a rule, with occasional exceptions, this means reconstructing traditional Christian doctrines, but in a focused way rather than in a comprehensive sprawling one.
5. The point of Christian theology is to change oppressive structures in the world, and therefore its realm of influence doesn't end within theology. Activist constructive theology is meant to motivate people in the world to act for greater justice, using a theological basis for the motivation to work for change. The theologies in this chapter argue that Christian theologizing is essentially meaningless unless it effects, or at least seeks to, change in the world on account of a refigured, reconstructed theological understanding of Christianity.

Constructive Theology and Liberation

Although constructive theology makes its turn toward activism because of liberation, it never fully commits to liberation. Its most recent work, building on the engagement of multiple generations of constructive theology, presumes the legitimacy and importance of liberation theology. Some liberation theologies are constructive, but ultimately most constructive theologies, even activist ones, fall short of the revolutionary nature of liberation theology. Further, some liberation theologies are still primarily systematic. And finally, within the context of the United States, constructive theologies from a white perspective, even those that seek to be liberationist, maintain a discomfort with liberation theologies done from the perspective of the most profoundly marginalized groups in the United States.

Nevertheless, taking the conviction of liberation theology seriously provides constructive theology the necessary impetus to turn from a theology concerned mostly with reconstructing Christian doctrines in light of the insights of other disciplines to being primarily a theology aimed at changing the world in which Christianity plays a constitutive part, eradicating injustice and oppression through activist means. The point of these theologies changes from intending to give the reader a better idea of who or what God is, especially against the backdrop of modernist and postmodernist challenges, to giving human beings a better idea of what they need to do. This, again, is not a matter of changing the method of constructive theology, but rather changing the focus. The interdisciplinarity that emerged early on is still presumed, but that use of other disciplines is homed in on critical analyses that reveal the oppressive power structures of culture and society in the United States. Constructive theology, inspired by liberation theology, turns that incisive analysis toward reconstructing doctrine in such a way that Christianity, and the Christians who considers themselves within it, are compelled by the reimagined models of God to change society.

Against liberal theology, this is not seen as a mission of Christianizing the world. Quite the opposite, multiplicity, including religious pluralism, is inherent in constructive theology. Constructive theology does not advocate a closer alliance between culture and Christianity, even though cultural analysis is crucial. Despite its activist tendencies, constructive theology remains very suspicious of too close a link between culture and Christianity, instead arguing the ways these things are intertwined must be interrogated, and the oppressive aspects of Christianity eradicated. Christianity must realize its role in creating injustices and sustaining them theologically, and in turn reconstruct in a way that rejects those injustices and works along with other worldviews and religions to create a more just world.

Christianity as Developed in Christian Theology Is a Construct amongst Other Constructs

The realization of the constructed nature of human experience runs both ways in activist constructive theology. On the one hand, the cultural and societal systems in which people live are neither static nor essential, but are systems that have been constructed and are always in a process of construction. Likewise, Christian theology has long held the view that the role of theology is to seek an essence of Christianity that conforms to God's will or design. But constructive theology instead recognizes that Christian theology actively constructs our images of God and God's work. With the acknowledgment that constructed categories and power discourses are responsible for much of the suffering in the world, both from the perspective of non-Christian and Christian hermeneutics, then the most obvious course of action is to reconstruct those discourses. Christianity has contributed to the social constructs of sexism, racism, classism, Christocentrism, Eurocentrism, and many others. Whether Christianity has simply been used by those in power to justify these marginalizations or whether Christianity has been a primary driver of them, constructive theology calls for the end of Christianity's participation in building up discourses that bestow disproportionate amounts of power to a very few based on things like race, class, sex, gender, and especially Christianity. Christianity, despite being a powerful tool for constructive theologians, and regardless of the metaphysical reality of Christianity's spiritual content, must participate actively in the necessary deconstructive and constructive work that needs to be done to enact greater justice and inclusion. Constructive theology has emerged as *the* method of progressively minded, change-seeking theology in the wake of postmodern critiques of the Enlightenment and modernity.

Acknowledging Past Complicity, Reconstructing Traditional Loci

Despite the very different starting points for all of these constructive theologians, they all take as their starting point the imaginative constructions of Christian theological doctrine. Taylor may be one minor counterexample as far as the doctrinal structure goes, but he is a methodological exception within constructive theology. Constructive theology constructs along lines delineated in the Christian tradition. It has over and over shown its ambivalence about the traditional framework of Christianity, and yet it continues to employ doctrinal loci because they help to situate the activist work within the tradition and provide guideposts for developing a Christianity that is both intellectually sophisticated and socially engaged. Like any intellectual movement, constructive theology has its exceptions, but usually just on one or two points. The exceptions still affirm the majority of the methodological tenets of constructive theology. These activist constructive theologies show the ongoing tensions between systematic theology and constructive theology.

I believe the retention of doctrinal loci is so important for constructive theology because of the very recognition of the constructed nature of all Christian theology. The loci have been crucial because they are a powerful and clear structure that relates Christianity to both everyday experience and religious experience. A powerful argument can be made for abandoning traditional loci, and some have been, such as Kaufman's and Taylor's in rejecting capital-T "Theology" as overly academic and detached from the world and justice work. But realizing that the doctrinal loci are available for deconstruction and reconstruction gives constructive theology a starting point and an ongoing conversation in which to participate. What needs to be rejected and reworked is made evident by participating in longstanding doctrinal debates. Activist constructive theology finds a powerful starting point and justification for its being a Christian theological endeavor in being able to name that its assertions belong in the tradition of theological anthropology, or creation, or theology proper, and so on. An inherent indictment of the oppressiveness of classical formulations comes along with reconstructing the doctrinal loci, as well as a refusal to shirk the responsibility of Christianity both for aiding injustice in the past and for needing to do better in the future.

Employing Sophisticated Analysis to Resist Oppressive Structures

This quality reflects two related conversation partners for constructive theology: liberation theology as discussed above, and critical theory and analysis as informed by Marxism. Liberation theology, especially from Latin America, was criticized early on for its use of Marx. But constructive theology also encounters Marxism through critical theory, Marxism and materialist critique often being viewed as the wellspring of postmodern critical theories. Constructive theology, done in an activist way, agrees strongly with Marx's famous declaration that "philosophers have only interpreted the world, in various ways; the point is to change it." Activist constructive theology sees Christianity as a catalyst for change. Doctrines that have historically oppressed, when analyzed and reconstructed, can provide the raw material for creating a more just, more equitable world, in ongoing dynamic conversation. Further, because constructive theology precludes a final theology, it accepts that its own insights may end up needing revision.

The work of reconstruction and justice-making may move as culture and society change for the better or worse. By recognizing that readings of God and the creation story have created an attitude in which human beings degrade and destroy the earth, not only dishonoring God's creation but threatening their own and every creature's existence, constructive theology can call on human beings to change their understanding of these theological assertions in order to change behavior for the better. By admitting Christianity's often complacence or even contribution to racial disparagement throughout history, a new accounting of the Black church and of theological anthropology reconstructs Christianity to be on the avant-garde of asserting the injustice of racial discrimination. New models for God that reject the sole model of God as "father," "son," and masculine or at best neuter "spirit," asserts the importance of both feminine and non-binary gender and sexual expressions of the divine. Condemning the use of Christianity in justifying unequal political and economic systems and asserting new interpretations of the kinds of systems Christianity supports seeks to mobilize Christians to work alongside everyone to build structures that would ensure equality and justice. Looking back, analyzing, and reconstructing convicts Christianity to do the ambiguous, difficult, dynamic work of building a more just world.

Once again there is a call to send something back from theology to a venue not typically considered to have much of an interest in what theology has to say. In the contemporary world Christianity is not often associated with progressive justice movements. Conservative and fundamentalist Christianities have given rise to the popular image of Christianity as a religion obsessed with other-worldly, posthumous rewards and punishments. Liberal theologies too closely linked nationality and culture *with* Christianity, rather than seeing Christianity as a participant in the ongoing cultural dialogue about who we are as a people. "Progress" and "Christianization" were often seen as synonyms throughout much of the liberal tradition. Constructive theology seeks to offer a prophetic, creative, vital voice to justice movements across religious spectrums, including nonreligious ones.

All of these independent works by constructive theologians that serve as the basis for socially engaged, activist constructive theologies emerge in the mid to early '90s, just before and after *Reconstructing Christian Theology* was published. The acknowledgments in each frequently refer to other constructive theologians past and present. That is to say, the conversation around constructive theologies that are activist in nature had a very definite shape and group of people who participated in it. Although these theologians and their theologies don't make a claim to be developing a method as such, the sources and techniques for building theologies around certain pertinent doctrines are common amongst all of these theologians in a way that distinguishes them from other varieties of theology. Building upon constructive theology's embrace of interdisciplinary work, at this time a method emerges built upon a foundation of social engagement and activism. The methodological similarities between these theologians were never formalized, but essentially what emerges is in fact a method, or more accurately, an expansion of a method that had been in the works since 1975 and even earlier. In the twenty years since the initial wave of activist constructive theology caused a reorientation of what constructive theology sought to do, innumerable constructive theologies have been published that strike very different balances of interdisciplinarity and activism, but always through the same basic method and techniques.

5

Constructive Theology as a Method and a Tradition

As a genre, constructive theologies come in staggering variety. To this point in its history no attempts have been made to define constructive theology as one movement or method in theology. Some encyclopedia entries and cursory descriptions of constructive theology have appeared in various places, but never in a comprehensive way. In one of the most extensive descriptions of constructive theology, found in the *Encyclopedia of Sciences and Religion*, Joerg Rieger writes:

> [Systematic theology] seeks to develop a system, based on philosophical approaches or particular themes or insights, which provides a comprehensive framework for theological topics. Constructive theology, on the other hand, rejects closed systematic frameworks in favor of more open ended reflections. One of the differences between constructive theology and dogmatic theologies is that the latter focuses on doctrines and concepts with little attention to matters of everyday life and experience. Constructive theology, in contrast, links doctrines and concepts with particular expressions of life.[1]

This suggests a good starting place for thinking about what construc-

1. Rieger, *Encyclopedia of Sciences and Religion*, 483–86.

tive theology is. It emphasizes its open-endedness, which is crucial, and contrasts constructive theology with systematic and dogmatic theologies. It also mentions the alternative uses of doctrinal loci that characterizes constructive theology's format. The entry also notes that "constructive theology is, therefore, a discourse that is always in process and open to interaction with other forms of knowledge, including knowledge produced in the social and natural sciences." This understates constructive theology's engagement with other disciplines, because interdisciplinarity is in fact an imperative quality of constructive theology. Rieger also claims the term "constructive theology" began to be used in the 1980s, which vastly undersells the history of the movement—after all, the Workgroup on Constructive Theology itself formed in 1975—especially if one considers the proto-constructive theologians, who reach all the way back to the earliest years of the 1900s. In any case, Rieger's short description of constructive theology helpfully opens the conversation about what constructive theology is, and asserts its distinctiveness from other varieties and methods of doing theology. It engages with other disciplines, takes for granted the constructed nature of Christian theology, and emphasizes the "life-and-death endeavor" that is theology.

A less sympathetic, though just as revealing, description of constructive theology can be found in *The Evangelical Dictionary* in an entry by R. G. Gruenler. Rieger mentions it in his own description. Gruenler writes that, "[The Workgroup on Constructive Theology] adopted as its agenda the task of clarifying how the church can meet and shape the actual world with a Christian message freed from bondage to arcane models of vertical transcendence. Their theme is that the traditional package of classical orthodox faith is discredited and must be reshaped to meet the needs of the modern world."[2] Coming from an antagonistic point of view, this description has both some truth and some misinformation. On the one hand, it is true that constructive theology, as developed by the Workgroup, believes theology must "meet and shape the actual world." On the other, "freed from the bondage of arcane models" is a little dramatic, and also ignores that many constructive theologians still maintain a very high view, that is a vertically transcendent one, of God. "The large question the work group (sic) wrestled with," Gruenler avers, "is the problem of theological method. The pattern that has emerged is Hegelian. Basic Christian doctrines have

2. R. G. Gruenler, "Constructive Theology," in *Evangelical Dictionary of Theology*, ed. Walter A. Elwell (Grand Rapids: Baker Academic, 2001), 293.

been assigned to various members who will follow a common format . . . the constructive work of the group will proceed to reformulate the traditional doctrine in terms acceptable to the mood of modernity."[3] Again, Gruenler correctly identifies that constructive theology is a method, something even many constructive theologians have not adequately grasped. At the same time, his reading of Hegelianism into constructive theology misses the mark, both regarding what Hegelianism asserts in terms of dialectics and what constructive theology tries to do. Constructive theology, in particular, rejects the Hegelian conceit of progress as the revelation of *geist*. Simply identifying *geist* through theology would still be a descriptive rather than a constructive process. Further, critiques of past formulations of doctrines are not antitheses, but rather reconsiderations and expansions of the original theses.

Perhaps most basically, Gruenler casts constructive theology as a relativistic expansion of liberal theology, which "orthodox" theology also characterized as destructive of Christianity: "Primary concerns include the epistemological assumption of the work group that modern pluralism is normative over Scripture, that classical Christianity is arcane, discredited, and addresses the problem of evil less well in our time than constructive theology, and whether the adjective 'constructive' properly describes an enterprise that promotes the deconstruction and demolition of biblical faith as a central task in the reconstruction of theology for our time."[4] In fact, constructive theology does not privilege modern pluralism or normative Christian statements, but rather recognizes that normative Christian statements are, and always have been, issued in a context of pluralism. Constructive theology simply acknowledges pluralist reality, and contrary to what Gruenler claims, reformulating Christian doctrine in a context of plurality rather than denying plurality's existence strengthens Christianity's ethical and theological claims in a situation in which people in the United States have real competing options.

Further, against Gruenler's claim that constructive theology demolishes biblical faith, constructive theology, generally, holds a very high regard for the Bible. Again, Gruenler has in mind liberalism's link with biblical criticism and finding theological truths in biblical historicism. Some constructive theologians still employ historical critical methods in order to assert theological norms, but historical criticism of the

3. Ibid., 293.
4. Ibid., 294.

Bible is less normative and less prevalent in constructive theology than liberal theology. For the most part constructive theology privileges generous creative engagements with the biblical text, once again privileging the biblical text, in Sallie McFague's terms, as "primary theological language." Most fundamentally, Gruenler misses constructive theology's heavy investment in scripture and tradition, albeit mixed with the insights of other disciplines and a strong passion for equality and social justice. This commitment is evidenced by constructive theology's investment in doctrine, high regard for scripture, and consistent concern for a theology that preaches.

Currently working constructive theologians, Rieger among them, have wildly divergent views of what, if anything, constructive theology is. All agree that the project of the Workgroup on Constructive Theology has been important. Constructive theologians, however, differ on whether they see constructive theology as being an expansion or redefinition of systematic theology, a subset of systematic theology, or an entirely new method. Further, systematic theology has continued to try to keep constructive theology within its umbrella. Changes in terminology have come faster than the analysis of what constructive theology actually is. The perception of the term also tracks its development by the Workgroup through its multiple stages. The terminology used by constructive theologians in their individual works betrays the lack of consistency, even within a single author, concerning whether constructive theology is a form of systematic theology or a new type of theology altogether. And the development to a great extent can be followed through the testimonies of the Workgroup conveners and textbook editors in chapter two. These issues suggest a need for an agreed upon, multi-faceted, unified but not systematized approach for constructing theology. Constructive theology, in any case, remains in need of a programmatic statement about what exactly it means to do it. How does Christian theology answer these important questions in light of them being raised in our pressing time?

As a method, to use a structural image, constructive theology very often serves as a bridge between ambivalent pulls in contemporary Christianity and theology. Exploring some of the most important will help to clarify the method that has emerged in constructive theology.

Constructive Theology as a Bridge between Liberal and Liberation Theologies

Proto-constructive theology and early constructive theology have one foot firmly planted in liberal theology, and certain constructive theologians continue to tackle liberal theological questions throughout their work. Likewise, many constructive theologians consider themselves to be liberation theologians, and as a whole constructive theology felt a responsibility to engage fully the liberationist tradition that emerged from the '60s on.

When asked whether constructive theology is simply an expansion of the liberal theological tradition, constructive theologians are split. The debt owed by constructive theology to liberal theology is undeniable.

At the same time, I believe the difference in method is too drastic to be ignored. Though anxieties about the intellectual respectability of the Christian theological tradition (sometimes) remain, the aim of constructive theology is not to demonstrate Christian theology's ongoing viability in the wake of the Enlightenment. Constructive theology eschews the judgment of "cultured despisers" as Schleiermacher would put it, and focuses on reasserting Christianity as a tradition worth listening to in its own right, properly contextualized and situated in an environment of embraced multiplicity. Further, constructive theology rejects systematization, a drive in systematic theology that arises as a result of the Enlightenment emphasis on rationality and coherence in reasoning. Constructive theology opts instead for a multivocal, dispersive, in-flux approach.

Many liberation theologians are constructive theologians. But, liberation theology does not necessarily need to be constructive theology. Some liberation theologies are actually systematic, in that they offer systematized accounts of every doctrine in a coherent whole from a liberationist perspective. But more fundamentally, the claim that liberation theology makes with respect to the critical need to begin from the experience and suffering of marginalized people, is so important that self-naming is more important than categorization. I believe it is crucial, especially given the continued majority whiteness and, in the beginning, maleness of constructive theology, to refrain from impinging on liberation theology's self-situating, self-authenticating mission. At the same time, I also believe most liberation theologies, and most liberation theologians, do identify as constructive theologians, especially more recent iterations of liberation theology. Second generation Black liberation theologians—especially those who rely on interdisciplinary analysis to substantiate their condemnation of white supremacy—by and large identify as constructive theologians.

Conversely, not all, or even most, constructive theology is liberation theology. The activism of constructive theology doesn't always start from the perspective of the oppressed, and it also doesn't always base itself in the idea that radical liberation is the best way to create meaningful social change, that revelation of God in the world takes the shape of liberation in history. That's not to say that most constructive theologians wouldn't agree with those principles of liberation theology. But many constructive theologies nonetheless, for better or worse, start from other places than the experience and suffering of the oppressed and marginalized, the hallmarks of liberation theology. However, as a movement, constructive theology absolutely affirms that Christianity, through doctrinal reconstruction, must actively work to enact greater equality and justice.

Constructive Theology as a Bridge between the Church and the Academy

Constructive theology creates a bridge between the church and the academy in a paradoxical way. On the one hand, it finds its home in the academy, developed and written largely by people who are academics first and clergy second, if at all. On the other hand, especially with its activist turn, it is fundamentally concerned with what the church can do in the world today.

Constructive theology doesn't tend to have the heady, dense style of dogmatic or systematic theology, nor does it require huge amounts of historical knowledge in theology in order to understand what it argues about God and Christianity. It is sophisticated, both religiously and intellectually, but it also prioritizes accessibility. Of course, some constructive theologians are clearer and more concise than others. But by and large, constructive theology takes Christian doctrine and academic insights and makes them accessible to laypeople, churches, and especially students of theology in divinity schools or undergraduate institutions. After all, the problem of promulgating theology to generations of students who lacked the same background in theology as their predecessors is repeatedly named as one of the main motivators for constructive theology since its beginning.

Even though constructive theology has a greater cohort of nonclergy theologians than any theological movement before it, perhaps even because of this, it has a greater and much clearer call for contemporary churches than many other historical theologies. Perhaps because of the emphasis on reconstruction, that is historical analysis followed by rethinking and new proposals, constructive theology leaves bare its thought processes—an aim repeatedly recognized by the Workgroup's conveners—not presuming the specialized knowledge of church elites. Furthermore, because constructive theology takes conversations with other disciplines seriously while also being responsible to the church, it must prioritize being mutually and interchangeably intelligible to theologians, laypeople, and specialists in other disciplines.

Constructive theology's vision of the church, however, is innately ecumenical. Contrasted with dogmatic theology, constructive theology neither invites confessional affirmation nor is written from any specific denominational standpoint, notwithstanding that some constructive theologians identify with specific denominations. Though Protestant theologians produce most constructive theology, a sizeable Catholic contingent works in a constructive mode and has since the beginning of constructive theology.

Systematic theologies in the modern or liberal theological tradition from Europe tend to take a particular denominational perspective as its starting point. Constructive theologians in the beginning of the Workgroup on Constructive Theology pointed to Karl Barth as a needed corrective to liberal theology. Yet constructive theology does not take up the Reformed church as its denominational basis, either from Barth or other dogmatic theologians who influenced its earliest work.

Constructive theology's departure from being confessional or denominational rejects the dogmatic project as bound by denominational limitations. Of course, specific constructive theologians do confess within specific churches. But constructive theologies, as such, don't confess to specific denominational or sectarian divisions. Ultimately, constructive theology contends to be faithfully useful theology for churches of any persuasion or history, based in the common history of constructing theological reflection. If anything, the existence of denominations is a strength, not a liability, because it expresses pluralism and dialogue within Christianity.

Constructive Theology as a Bridge between Four Major Schools of Progressive Theology

Because of the home institutions of many of the Workgroup on Constructive Theology's members as well as the theological movements that originated at those schools, constructive theology has also been characterized as an attempt to blend four major influential progressive theological schools' methods: Vanderbilt Divinity, University of Chicago Divinity, Yale Divinity, and Union Theological Seminary. Constructive theology, both within and outside of the Workgroup, has always included theologians outside those four schools, one of the most prominent and important being Harvard Divinity, which included Gordon Kaufman who was so important in establishing the intellectual framework and vocabulary for constructive theology.

Despite many limitations, this model points to an important aspect of twentieth and twenty-first century progressive theology that constructive theology in some way answers. Liberal, progressive, or socially engaged theologies had no dominant method or institutional home after the dissolution of the hegemony of liberalism following neo-orthodox and realist critiques. As Gary Dorrien points out, the only persistent liberal theological school has been process based, and that has found no permanent home.[5] Vanderbilt housed a hermeneutics oriented version of liberal or progressive theology; the University of Chicago was the historical origin of process theology as well as liberal versions of theological naturalism, both of which play important parts in the history of constructive theology, especially through Meland; Yale is known for post-liberal theology, which interprets Christianity culturally and linguistically in the wake of liberalism's dominance; and Union Theological Seminary for a long time has consistently produced social justice oriented, socially engaged theology. These four approaches have been heralded, mutually respected, but often considered incommensurable.

All of these lines of thinking play important roles in constructive theology. Without a unified progressive voice in theology, lacking institutional anchoring or support, constructive theology has served as a place for these various conversations to inform, support, and expand one another. Those four institutions remain the most prominently constructive theological homes. At the same time, constructive theology

5. Dorrien, *The Making of American Liberal Theology*, vol. 3, 190.

is far from limited to those institutions, and never has been. The first iteration of the Workgroup on Constructive Theology included members from Claremont to Boston, Chicago to Atlanta and Nashville, and anywhere in between. The Workgroup only grew, in both membership size and geographic representation, from there. It is nonetheless true that Vanderbilt, especially, played a huge role in the Workgroup's origin, and the theological concerns of the other schools named have been disproportionately influential throughout constructive theology's history. Constructive theology has developed a trans-institutional method, and the Workgroup on Constructive Theology has served as a trans-institutional home for the most influential members of progressive theology. Constructive theology, through the Workgroup or otherwise, propagates a polyphonic body of theological work that is nonetheless unified by methodology.

Other important metaphors for constructive theology have included theology as cartography and theology as induction. Each is worth discussing on its own.

Constructive Theology as Cartography

Cartographic metaphors for constructive theology pervade the tradition. But Serene Jones makes it her controlling metaphor for understanding what her constructive theology, as a whole, is, and how it works. *Feminist Theory and Christian Theology*, published in 2000, provides a vivid example of the format constructive theology evolves into and the method that emerges, largely queuing on Jones' use of cartography as a primary framework. She writes,

> I undertake the task of 'mapping' in the pages ahead. Picking up the cartographer's tools, I sketch for the reader maps of two worlds of reflection, feminist theory and Christian theology. I like the image of mapping because it captures well my intention to lay out central concepts that structure these two worlds and to draw lines that show the interconnections between them. At their best, maps help us figure out the 'lay of the land' in areas where we might otherwise be lost.[6]

Jones explains that maps, as a metaphor for theology, have both strengths and shortcomings. Maps both reveal and obscure. Importantly, maps should never be confused with the real thing. Or, in other

6. Serene Jones, *Feminist Theory and Christian Theology: Cartographies of Grace* (Minneapolis: Fortress, 2000), viii.

words, Christian theology provides a visualization of Christianity that isn't a substitute for Christianity itself.

Constructive theology doesn't pretend to be a one hundred percent faithful reproduction of Christianity. Instead, constructive theology allows a person to figure out where he or she stands, what landmarks are worthy of visiting, what pitfalls to watch out for. Maps carry with them inherent oversights and distortions because a two-dimensional representation of a three-dimensional reality must flatten the landscape. Likewise, Christian theology, because of context or perspective or simply expediency necessarily distorts aspects of Christianity in order to provide a usable representation of something that can't possibly be completely captured on paper.

Finally, maps must remain open to revision based on a shifting landscape or the realization that something wasn't as it appeared. Maps from centuries ago worked for the people that used them and were necessary to get to where we are today, yet if someone tried to use a map created by explorers in ships for air travel, disaster would happen. Likewise, as Christianity comes into a different focus because of contemporary knowledge or in light of contemporary crises, the changes in the landscape of Christianity must be accounted for in theology.

In *Feminist Theory and Christian Theology*, Jones uses the cartographic metaphor to map both theology and feminism. This two-step cartographic process reflects constructive theology's development into theology that employs both interdisciplinary insights and activist motivations. In an early autobiographical note she relates,

> My faculty colleagues in Women and Gender Studies make me appreciate feminist theory and its social environment. The folks in my Tuesday-night [church] group force me to think about the applicability of feminist theory to the lives of ordinary women and to struggle honestly with the theological issues it raises. . . . Students of theology have much to learn from feminist theory, I believe. It deepens our understanding of human identity and community and opens up new avenues for understanding the Christian theological tradition and its view of divine grace. I also believe that feminist theory has much to learn from theology, but alas, that topic awaits another time.[7]

Feminism is unique academically because it already inherently continues an activist project. Nonetheless, this situation between her academic colleagues, with whom she maintains an interdisciplinary conver-

7. Ibid., 2.

sation, and her church group, a receptive group for whom she relates the theory for liberating activist work demanded by feminism but with a Christian twist, evokes the constructive theological straddling of interdisciplinary and activism.

Looking at grace, sin, and the church, Jones reconstructs these key doctrinal loci to set forth a fully interdisciplinary activist theology. Charting feminist theory introduces the insights of another discipline—or perhaps an amalgamation of other disciplines that, in her view, at that point remained foreign to theology—and charts theology, especially as lived in the laity of the church. The doctrines serve as the landmarks on the map, and her reconstruction serves as the resurveying of the terrain. Jones' conception of constructive theology as a cartographic endeavor carries over to her editing work in *Constructive Theology: A Contemporary Approach to Classical Themes.* Constructive theology as cartography elegantly captures many of the key features of the method that have developed over the course of constructive theology's history. Above all it stresses constructive theology's contingency and unfinished quality, even in the view that what it describes may be outside of human subjectivity. Theology, as a map rather than as a direct copy of the terrain, stresses construction, revision, faithfulness to tradition, and the actionable nature of constructive theology.

Constructive Theology as Inductive Theology

Paul F. Lakeland takes on ecclesiology, the doctrine of the church. He claims,

> When you do ecclesiology, there really are only two possible ways to go. You can start with a definition of the Church and use it to evaluate where the Church is and where it is not, where it is faithful to the tradition and where it is not. Or you can start by looking at all the places that claim the name 'church,' prepare a composite description of them, and then formulate your more theoretical understanding of Church. You can work from above or below, deductively or inductively.[8]

Lakeland—in describing what he takes to be his constructive theological method—contrasts doing theology from different vantage points. To do theology "from above" correlates with how theology has tended to be done in a systematic or dogmatic mode. "Starting with a defini-

8. Paul F. Lakeland, *Church: Living Communion* (Collegeville, MN: Liturgical, 2009), 120.

tion" essentially means positing the unchangeable existence of something within Christianity, in his case, the church. From below, rather, means to examine contemporary manifestations of what might be the church and subsequently constructing a definition of church from those observations. The resulting inductive theology, he argues, should be a theology of the laity. Once again the characteristic non-clergy aspect of constructive theology arises. Lakeland doesn't dispute that church issued theology is important, but he asserts the cruciality of a parallel theology that arises from the laity.

Lakeland, and other Catholic theologians, must contend with extra issues when endeavoring to do theology constructively. Catholic theology, more than other Christian theologies, must be held accountable to tradition. The claim that inductive theology must be prioritized over deductive theology, which seems like a relatively benign claim, in fact rebels quite explicitly against the classic top-down movement of Catholic theology. Because of its very longstanding commitment to specific Greek philosophical systems paired with its doctrine of Apostolic succession, the Catholic church has a very clear investment in theology done systematically and according to the same philosophies that have been used for ages.

Lakeland's claim for inductive theology, then, is in fact quite provocative. It puts the impetus on the laity, everyday Catholics, to theologize the church as the community of Christ, as he calls it, "that community of faith distinguished by the experience that the loving care of God for us is supremely available in our intimacy with the story of Jesus Christ."[9] In order to define this community within the contemporary world, in a way that respects Catholic doctrine and tradition yet empowers the laity to participate, he harkens back to the usual constructive engagement with models and their reworking:

> The problem with inherited ecclesiology is not that its models and definitions are wrong but that over the centuries the models derived inductively have calcified and led to a deductive vision of the Church that, like all such deductive approaches, seeks to trim the really existing phenomenon—the Church today—to fit the images of the past. Sound theological reflection is always playing catch-up to the actual beliefs and practices of the Church. However, magisterial authority can sometimes give the impression that when it canonizes some development as the faith of the Church, it is necessarily for all time.[10]

9. Ibid., 25.
10. Ibid., 126.

Lakeland's interdisciplinary engagement is primarily with anthropology, from which he imports the technique of "thick descriptions"—a concept first developed as it is used today by Clifford Geertz, a canonical cultural anthropologist—but also with postmodernity generally. Thick descriptions—engaging in close readings of cultural practices and interpreting them symbolically in order to make sense of what a community's actions mean and say about that community—form the basis of Lakeland's inductive theology. By insisting that inductive theology must start with actual lived church experience, as witnessed and told by everyday Christians, Lakeland introduces the progressive, that is activist, strain that comes with constructive theology.

Constructive theology as inductive theology insists that, as a constructed system, Christian theology does best to be honest and forthright in what it intends to describe. Historical church declarations about theology, in this case, the church itself, don't hold much credence if they don't correspond to what is actually found there. Rather than asking whether Christian communitarian religious expressions fit some foreordained model, based on historical instances of the church that may or may not have ever actually existed, inductive theology looks to the experiences and practices of those who actually attend church, who live the Christian life, and who can most honestly articulate what "the church" means for them. Of course, as with other constructive theologies, these thick descriptions and subsequent theologies must be open to change as expressions of the church change.

Constructing a Definition and Method of Constructive Theology

All of the above models of constructive theology reveal something important about what I propose as a succinct definition of constructive theology as it has developed and as it exists today. Constructive theology is something different than liberal theology, but it owes much of what it assumes in its worldview, as well as the possibility of its very existence and early formulations, to liberal theology. It strives to liberate, yet it is not the same as liberation theology. Many liberation theologians are constructive theologians, but constructive theology would overstep its bounds to claim liberation theology as something under its own umbrella.

Constructive theology is undeniably academic, seeking to dialogue with, and importing insights from, other academic disciplines, often in a highly sophisticated intellectual form. Yet, perhaps unexpectedly, constructive theology makes a bid to be more practicable in churches than much theology derived from the church itself before it. As well, it is persistently concerned with being truly applicable in church contexts, challenging institutional theologies of churches and expanding the participation of laypeople in theological tasks.

The description of constructive theology as a meeting point between four major progressive theological schools has some merit given the way developments in each school are represented within the constructive theological tradition. It has elements of Chicago naturalism, process theology, Yale post-liberalism, Vanderbilt hermeneutics, and Union social justice. Constructive theology serves as a methodological home, centralized in the Workgroup on Constructive Theology, which takes the place of what historically might have been a specific institutional home. However, constructive theology has always been much more than these four schools, from the very beginning including theologians from all strata of theological education, and tracing its lineage to proto-theologians who had nothing to do with the twentieth century movements centralized there.

The above provide different perspectives on what constructive theology is, while the images of cartography and induction attempt to portray what constructive theology does. Cartography suggests a method that describes where one finds oneself, surveys the terrain, and decides whether the symbolic representation fits the reality or not. Maps are representations, not the real thing. As times change and as technology or techniques improve, maps require revision. The cartography metaphor captures many of the key aspects of constructive theology's method, including openness to change, the need for a theology that fits the age, and in Jones' engagement with feminism, interdisciplinarity and activism. Constructive theology as induction draws on philosophy, and Lakeland's specific project draws on cultural anthropology. The inductive process emphasizes constructive theology's mission to be theology that works for laypeople, in fact, drawn from the religious experience of everyday Christians. It also highlights the constructed nature of tradition, insisting that doctrine from the top down, that is from church hierarchy or traditional authority, has no more claim to being eternally valid than do timely, constantly revisited and revised theological claims. For Christianity today, in the light of postmodernism and contemporary world crises, it is more important that theology fit this specific moment than eternity.

In light of these descriptions of constructive theology, it's time to revisit the working definition proposed in the introduction:

Constructive theology is a method of doing Christian theology that takes seriously theological and church tradition as well as modern critiques of that tradition being something universal, eternal, or essential; it employs traditional themes and loci of theology in order to formulate useful, inclusive, fallible guidance for living as Christians in the contemporary world, against descriptions of a systematic theological system that pretend to unveil any true essence or essential reality of Christianity; and takes as its mode a good-faith engagement with parallel academic disciplines, often religious studies; an activist/crisis confrontation; or, ideally, both.

Constructive Theology Is a Method . . .

The most basic argument of this book is that constructive theology is, in fact, its own method of doing theology. "Constructive," as an adjective before theology, in the end, is not simply another word for systematic, and less so for dogmatic. Constructive theologians, beginning with proto-constructive theology, have been doing theology differently from other theological movements, but the same as one another. Constructive theology has developed, largely unbeknownst to constructive theologians themselves it seems, into a specific way of building theology seen as faithful to Christian belief, history, and tradition, and simultaneously called to be relevant and active in the contemporary world. Part of the uniqueness and the concreteness of this method has developed precisely because constructive theology, methodologically, engages with outside disciplines that have better defined methods than theology historically has. That is, its interdisciplinarity has both been a methodological principle and, through its various encounters, introduced methods from the social sciences, literary studies, philosophy, and even the "hard sciences." Furthermore, despite the complexity of constructive theologies and the dizzying variety, the method itself is relatively straightforward and holds throughout the history of constructive theology:

1. In the context of a relevant extra-theological insight or world crisis, identify the theological doctrine that most clearly speaks to that insight or crisis (or both).
2. Analyze the history of that doctrine, identifying its fissures and shortcomings. This is sometimes considered "deconstruction,"

especially by more postmodern, Derrida-influenced theologians. It could also be considered a Foucauldian genealogy or simply a history of the doctrine.

3. In dialogue with the relevant interdisciplinary insights and historical realities, propose redefinitions and reformulations, that is, reconstructions of that doctrine that are creatively faithful to both the doctrine and the matter at hand.
4. Evaluate in collaboration and dialogue and repeat.

The actual format of these constructive theologies has varied, but a few constants emerge.

Constructive theology values collaboration like no other theological movement ever has. The textbooks by the Workgroup on Constructive Theology are just the beginning of texts composed by multiple constructive theologians with the intent of producing either a work that deals with most or all theological doctrines or reflect from multiple angles on one. Constructive theology methodologically recognizes that individual works must be situated in a greater conversation. Although certain doctrines are almost entirely left out of the constructive theological tradition—and even then, constructive theology tends to work inordinately hard in cyclical periods on one or another specific doctrine, and so each doctrine will eventually have its day—each individual constructive theology acknowledges that a solitary, single-doctrine theology cannot adequately account for the whole of the Christian tradition. This approach requires both individual works, which take up specific individual doctrines and which can be read in tandem to provide a view of the greater theological whole, as well as the collaborative edited volumes that bring together voices in a conversation that includes most or all doctrines, but from many different perspectives.

. . . of doing Christian theology that takes seriously theological and church tradition as well as modern critiques of that tradition being something universal, eternal, or essential . . .

Constructive theology isn't radical. Its claims may be controversial or even provocative—it once faced stiff opposition—but constructive theology roots itself firmly in theological and church tradition. A contemporary tradition of radical theology does exist, in fact, arising out of death-of-God theology and postmodern deconstruction. Much more a specifically critical theology, radical theology tends to forego church and theological tradition and is much more heavily invested in philosophy than other disciplines, including theology itself. Radical theology often theologizes in spite of the church—or in order to suggest no forms of church—and tends not to recognize denominational or confessional differences as important. Constructive theology, on the other hand, emphasizes reimagining and mobilizing the church as it stands. It is not done from the standpoint of any single denomination or confession, but it also doesn't reject or diminish denominational or sectarian differences. In fact, as theology that greatly values plurality, theological pluralism as embodied in an ecumenical but denominationally divided church isn't necessarily seen as a great problem. Constructive theologies are left to demonstrate their own validity and value that is open to any denomination, but not minimizing those differences.

While constructive theology highly values church tradition and believes the churches are the communities that must be engaged and mobilized within Christianity, it is also intellectually critical of the church's history. Too often Christianity has sought to illuminate some fixed, stable idea of what God, the church, and Christianity at large, are. Even liberal theology has fallen into this trap, especially in its search for a historical essence, kerygma, or kernel—as if there was ever a single one of any of these things—of Christianity. Constructive theology argues that Christianity has always been diversely pluralistic. Further, theological claims, wherever they come from, including, and even especially, church leadership and theological elites, are constructed. As Kaufman argues, upon accepting the Kantian critique of knowledge about God, theologians must acknowledge that all our ideas about God are ultimately constructions, the foundational premise of constructive theology. Our constructions about God, regardless of the realities of God, are bound by culture, history, belief, and all of the demographic trappings that come with being enfleshed human beings doing theology. Therefore, church traditions and the theologies churches propagate are nonetheless constructions. And constructions are not objects of faith or confession, but something to be constantly reevaluated, deconstructed if needed, and reconstructed or expanded upon to increase inclusiveness, equality, and suitability in the ever-changing world.

. . . it employs traditional themes and loci of theology . . .

The use of traditional doctrinal loci is no small thing, and that method hasn't been universally appreciated even by constructive theologians. The Workgroup on Constructive Theology throughout its history has expressed ambivalence about theologizing within the doctrinal framework. And yet doctrinal loci are still employed almost universally by constructive theologians. As has been suggested, one key difference between systematic and dogmatic theologies and constructive theologies is that constructive theologies forego a preoccupation with touching on every single doctrine. As McFague noted in her theological "conversion," systematic theologians were often bent on producing their grand opuses, a theology that was comprehensive and coherent, showing how every doctrine can be logically synced with every other.

Constructive theology outright rejects such a pretense, and largely precludes the idea that a theology in which every doctrinal assertion could be logically systematized with every other is even possible. The theological loci are important because they provide entries into theologizing, suggesting ways to continue the theological conversation within the tradition. Furthermore, by using traditional doctrines, constructive theology is provided with the very things that need to be deconstructed and reconstructed.

. . . in order to formulate useful, inclusive, fallible guidance for living as Christians in the contemporary world . . .

Engaging with and critiquing tradition is not the end of constructive theology. Tearing down tradition accomplishes nothing without (re)construction in its wake. Constructive theology insists that upon identifying the parts of Christian theology, as encountered in Christian doctrine, that have hurt or that are no longer relevant, the next step must be to offer something in its place that is faithful to the tradition and also decidedly contemporary. Constructive theologies must be useful, though not simply a useful fiction, meaning that whatever constructive theologies prescribe must have an actionable element. They do not offer insights about God or Christianity that are simply meant to be accepted, assimilated, and confessed, but rather formulations of Christian doctrines that should have both a sophisticated intellectual pedigree and a clear call to action.

Inclusivity in constructive theology speaks both to its progressive nature, expanding what is viewed as the faithful community of Christians into groups that have historically been excluded from Christianity's center. It shows why such inclusion is in line with the Christian tradition and, arguably, God's will, and offers theology that is inclusive of many different theological viewpoints, across demographics, denominations, geographies, and experiences.

Finally "fallible" indicates the open-ended nature of constructive theology referenced so frequently. Constructive theology is thoroughly fallibilist in its understanding of theological proclamations. The constructive theological method allows for claims that are considered to be right, just, and faithful now, but which inherently remain open to further insight, new testimonies, or engagement with outside disciplines. The fallibilism of constructive theology goes both ways. It recognizes that Christian theology, despite presumed best intentions, has turned out to be wrong, or at least has become obsolescent, in many important instances. Christian theology has always been fallible. In the same way, constructive Christian theology today must have the humility to recognize that it too will likely be shown, in some way or another, to have been exclusionary, short sighted, or naïve of important intellectual and spiritual truths still to be encountered.

Relatedly, constructive theology is for contemporary living Christians. It presupposes no eternal validity or universality and it refuses to remain content with insights from the past solely based on their establishment. Like Jones's church study group or Lakeland's inductive ecclesiology from the standpoint of the laity, constructive theology holds itself accountable, above all else, to ongoing Christian lives and experience. This doesn't mean that it rejects insights from the past solely based on their antiquity. Rather, it retains what remains living and vital while dispensing with that which inflicts damage or has become irrelevant. It accepts the basic framework of theology, the concerns that have been and remain central to a full understanding of Christianity. It insists that what made those things vital in the past makes them at least as much so now as Christianity faces so many contemporary crises and encounters, so many other thought systems and ways of understanding the world.

Constructive theology, as it exists and is done today, has abandoned the primary theological contradiction as being the nonbeliever. Neither does all of it go with the liberation agenda of the nonperson, though all constructive theology does presume the importance of that preoccupation. Instead, it emphasizes ongoing relevance and practicability in working for understanding and justice on as many fronts as there are theologians in an ongoing multi-vocal dialogue.

. . . against descriptions of a systematic theological system that pretends to unveil any true essence or essential reality of Christianity . . .

This is the juxtaposition between constructive theology and systematic or dogmatic theologies. This is the "constructive" of constructive theology. Theology, it argues, should not, indeed cannot, be done in a faithful way that results in a once-and-for-all system. Dogmatic theology was built on the foundation of theology as part of a confession. It proclaimed what Christians, often in a particular denomination, should believe. Systematic theology, as a specific category of theology—distinct from dogmatic theology, though dogmatic theology is also done in a systematic way, that is in a comprehensive, doctrine by doctrine fashion—came to fruition in response to the Enlightenment and pressure to create wholly consistent and logical theological systems. Both presume the existence of a metaphysical reality that can be described when subjected to the right sort of educated, faithful scrutiny. Christianity, as the religion that points to a specific God and a specific act of redemption in Jesus Christ, according to dogmatic and systematic theology, must have a particular eternal form that applies to all Christians and their relationship with God for all time. Constructive theology instead accepts the Kantian critique of direct knowledge of the divine and eternal, and reconsiders the view of theology entirely. In its own twist, constructive theology accepts the critiques of the canonical atheists like Feuerbach that Christianity, as human beings know it, is imaginative—that's not equal to saying the same about God or God's work. The constructive response to such a critique is that there is in fact *no* "essence" of Christianity. Theology is through and through human words about God. Of course, this is acknowledged in dogmatic and systematic theology, yet they still pretend to speak for all time inasmuch as possible. Constructive theology flatly accepts that theological claims are always constructed and contingent; that any given theological claim may have been valid, may still be important, but nonetheless requires reexamination and reconstruction constantly in order to remain as faithful a witness between Christian life and Christian theology in a fallen world as possible.

Constructive theology is not dismissive of dogmatic and systematic theology. This is most clearly demonstrated by the ambivalence constructive theologians express in their inconsistent use of the term "constructive," often flip-flopping between "constructive" and "systematic." Constructive theology owes its existence to dogmatic and systematic theology, which have provided the framework and vocabulary with which constructive theology continues to choose to speak. Constructive theologians cite dogmatic and systematic theologians as authoritative—partly out of necessity given those are the available authorities to cite at all—but also because constructive theology does ultimately build something of a system. The system is simply a messy one, dispersed throughout a large number of individual theologians, often working collaboratively. The system is in flux, and is not internally coherent. All of its tenets are constantly available for reinterpretation. A fully realized system in the constructive theological tradition might use the theology proper of McFague, the theological anthropology of Hopkins, the ecclesiology of Lakeland, the hamartiology of Jones, etc. These thinkers will inevitably contradict or challenge one another in certain instances. But the fully realized account of Christianity arises and finds form in that very conversation, disagreement, and resonance itself.

. . . and takes as its mode a good-faith engagement with parallel academic disciplines, often religious studies, an activist/crisis confrontation, or, ideally, both . . .

As chapters three and four suggested, these are the key thematic drivers of constructive theology. Constructive theology utilizes concepts and insights from all sorts of academic disciplines. It comes, in its history, to reflect the makeup of religious studies, which in some ways has alienated theology from the academy by appearing to be a more legitimately objective way to study religion. Constructive theology opens theology from a primarily inward turned discipline, which holds its own judgment as normative for rigor and applicability, and accepts at least the techniques of other disciplines, especially philosophy, psychology, anthropology, sociology, and literary studies/hermeneutics. Theology takes a risk in turning to other disciplines. Already facing a credibility crisis, turning to other disciplines may seem to imply that theology lacks its own method or intellectual insights relevant to the academy at large.

It is important, then, that constructive theology doesn't simply dress up concepts imported from other disciplines in Christian clothing, as it were. It also interrogates and critiques the insights it borrows. The interdisciplinary nature of constructive theology must be double-edged. It mines other disciplines for ideas that help to strengthen and expand Christian theology in the contemporary world, using the latest analytical and critical observations available from any number of disciplines. At the same time, constructive theology must seek to send its own insights to the academy at large. This latter move has been less successful to this point: not many constructive theologians, in my experience, are being used broadly in other disciplines. Nevertheless, constructive theology has created at least the bridge by which this cross-fertilization could happen.

Constructive theology must also seek to effect real change in the world. That is, it has activist intentions. Whether that comes through redefinition and rehabilitation of theological doctrines, changing the world of language and symbol in which Christians operate, or whether that means calls to direct action, constructive theology, especially in its most recent iterations, is through and through an activist theology. And no realm in need of greater justice and equality is off limits to constructive theology. It continues to expand its purview, so far having done its most extensive work with feminism, race, and politics/class, with a growing body of work in queer/LGBTQ issues, and disability. As activist theology, constructive theology is also a true blend of Christian ethics and Christian theology, so much so that many people who are Christian ethicists have participated in the Workgroup on Constructive Theology. Again, as McFague remarked concerning her "conversion," theology historically has been kept separate from supposedly less respectable Christian ethics. The relationship between Christian theology and Christian ethics has always been somewhat in flux. Constructive theology in its contemporary form is never solely one or the other. There has always been an activist/ethical strain in constructive theology, but now it is a non-negotiable constitutive part.

Constructive theology, at its best and as a rule in the present, then, is a mix of these two. Constructive theologies can emphasize one or the other more or less. But the most successful and influential theologies employ both in a balance where incisive interdisciplinary critique informs and buttresses activist impulses in theology, and likewise, activism in constructive theologies reflects, affirms, and expands critical insights.

Reflecting on this definition and its analysis, it's helpful to revisit the non-negotiable characteristics of constructive theology in order to provide a summary. Constructive theology is:

1. Persistently open-ended. This quality of constructive theology is attested to by almost every constructive theologian, even extending to proto-constructive theologians in the early 1900s.
2. Based in the insight that Christian theology is constructed, that is, imaginatively and creatively produced human thoughts about God and God's work. Irrespective of the ontological or metaphysical status of God or what Christianity might be for God, constructive theology acknowledges that fundamentally, Christian theology is subject to the same complete lack of direct knowledge of God as all human discourse, and therefore theology is always contingent and constructed.
3. Almost always doctrinally based. There are a few exceptions, but even in those exceptions, the themes of doctrine are still engaged, even if not by their names. At the same time, constructive theology forsakes dealing with every doctrine, or in the usual hierarchy of them.
4. Suspicious of systems or confession-based theology, that is, systematic and dogmatic theology. Constructive theology acknowledges and is grateful for the debt it owes to these theological approaches, but insists that Christianity cannot be so logically or comprehensively codified, once and for all, by any one person or even one institution or specialized, elite group. Some constructive theologians are hesitant about this distinction, and systematic theology, especially, resists this split. But, to me, the differences in method are so pronounced as to be undeniable.

Evaluating Constructive Theologies

One of the biggest questions that arises with respect to constructive theology is how to evaluate the success of any specific constructive theology, given the volume and plurality of them that are produced. Dogmatic theology could be judged according to its faithfulness to belief, denominational or church tradition and doctrine, and overall coherence. Systematic theology could be judged by its reasonableness, comprehensiveness, and coherence. Constructive theologies come in such a variety and with so many different aims, it can be difficult to judge the value of one against another except on an intuitive basis, which is neither intellectually rigorous nor practicable.

The charge of relativism is often laid against constructive theology. From the conservative side, the complaint argues that if there is no final authority for constructive theology, like scripture or church tradition, and if all theological claims are fundamentally constructed and capable of being expanded upon or reconstructed, Christianity loses its distinctness amongst other religions and cultural systems. From the liberal side, some versions of constructive theology can seem to discount reason, specifically as it pertains to theology and particularly with respect to historical criticism, as well as experience, as abstracted intellectual insights rarely wholly reflect lived experience. Intuitively, many Christians may not recognize the constructed nature of cultural systems generally, least of all Christianity, when religion is so often thought to be about eternal, universally valid truths, especially Christianity as a "universal" religion. Constructive theology, it seems, faces questions of evaluation from both the academy and from the church.

In fact, this tension provides the means for evaluating individual constructive theologies. Specialists in the intersdisciplinary field should be able to recognize the concepts employed, as well as the particular ways they are used in the theology. Laypeople should be able to recognize an implementable call to action within the theology. And the theological community generally should be able to recognize the analysis and reconstruction of doctrine as both critically faithful to tradition and as a needed correction to the same. Constructive theologies will ultimately never be satisfying for systematic or dogmatic theologians, but it shouldn't seem like a foreign discourse entirely. Critically faithful to the tradition means both historically and discursively tenable. Deconstructive or genealogical analyses of doctrines privilege thick descriptions that focus on the effects of identify formation, power, and practical effects of doctrinal development rather than exhaustive historical research. The point is to illuminate how doctrines empower and marginalize today. In being recognizable and faithful to other disciplines, theology doesn't cede its right to self-evaluation. Rather, it emphasizes that irresponsible use of other disciplines' tools risks intellectual superficiality as well as loss of respect in the academy.

Constructive theologies are best evaluated on their applicability to contemporary Christian life, in churches or by laypeople or even by people who take Christian views of the world seriously from a non-religious or other religious standpoint, supported by truly rigorous intellectual analysis. Because of its ongoing, tenuous nature, constructive theology cannot afford to be sloppy on either of these fronts. To alienate itself from the church or the real lived life of Christians creates dead, self-congratulatory theology for a sequestered and ultimately miniscule community of theological specialists. To misinterpret, misuse, or simply slap theology on top of another discipline risks being escorted out of the academy entirely as derivative or extraneous, an attitude many in the broader academy already hold toward theology. Constructive theologies can be judged successful when they are patently open-ended dynamic constructions around doctrines based on serious intellectual rigor and suggest actionable norms. Having placed itself at the intersection of these important concerns, constructive theology is best evaluated by its faithfulness at that intersection to all of them. And that, as it happens, is also true of Christian witness generally.

Contemporary and Future Constructive Theology

Constructive theologians today are working in colleges, universities, and seminaries everywhere. Whether those positions are explicitly identified as "constructive" or not, the number of theologians who identify themselves or their work as constructive is huge. Progressive and liberation theologies everywhere have embraced the moniker "constructive," but the meaning of that adjective, until now, has been left relatively unanalyzed.

At this point in time, given the ongoing crises in the world and the continued efforts on the part of theology to assert its place in the academy, even as theology continues to shrink alongside religious studies and philosophy in universities, constructive theology only looks to get bigger proportionally. Constructive theology may grow to be the most apt resistance to the hegemony of conservative and fundamentalist theology in terms of the public understanding of Christianity in the United States. It reflects and bolsters contemporary movements for social change, including things like fighting white supremacism in the United States, the need for real action on the climate crisis and other ecological and environmental justice issues, and the ever-growing dominance of free market, capitalistic, predatory economics and neo-colonialism around the world. As academic disciplines have become more specialized, applying critical thinking and theory into more and more specific areas of inquiry, so has constructive theology.

Further, alongside religious studies, constructive theology has begun questioning the terms on which religions can have a genuine conversation, and in many cases, begun to question the construction of the very category of religion itself. Pluralism and multiplicity have grown in importance in constructive theology, queer studies has become a more pronounced voice, and the hard sciences have become, in some theologies, a bigger part. Finally, along with continuing postmodern examinations of identity, intersectionality has become a bigger and bigger theme, expanding and deepening constructive theology's engagement with injustices in the United States and beyond.

Methodologically, though there is still significant hesitancy to declare constructive theology something separate from systematic theology, systematic theologians have had a hard time finding a home in the Workgroup on Constructive Theology whenever they've been included.[11] While it's true that systematic theology can be said to have a constructive phase, that is, an individual systematic theologian's contribution to the system of Christian theology as received, systematic theology has a hard time accepting construction as the heart of doing theology.

It's easy to see why a theologian who believes theology should be done systematically might have a difficult time reconciling with constructive theology. Systematic theology, again, attempts to describe Christianity as a religious or faith system. Seeing Christianity as a system—or something that can be schematized systematically—is inherently at odds with a view that emphasizes the revisability of Christianity, indeed, the nonsystematic nature of the Christian religion. Christianity, as conceptualized in constructive theology, is messy, dynamic, pluralistic, historically complicit, but capable of continuous revivification and renewal. Systematic theologians may see constructive theology as not rigorous enough—though I've argued constructive theology has a new rigor in its interdisciplinarity—on account of its tentative, fallibilist nature; not faithful enough in that it seems to invite relativism and minimize the importance of rigorous reasonableness; and foreign as a method against the backdrop of dogmatic and systematic theologies that have a clear, historically supported framework.

In the near future it seems that the differences between constructive theology and systematic theology, as well as dogmatic theology, will become larger and more prominent. Constructive theology has signif-

11. Stephen G. Ray Jr., in conversation with the author, November 22, 2015.

icantly distinguished itself from systematic ways of doing theology. Again, it is collaborative, open-ended, fallibilist, and built on the fundamental premise that theology is a construction, not a description of something essential. Constructive theology has quietly become the most widely accepted method of doing progressive theology. Its importance, in contradistinction and as an antidote to conservative theologies, which get the most press in the contemporary United States, should be highlighted and affirmed. This isn't to say that systematic theology isn't important. Indeed it is. There's certainly something powerful about theological work that starts with the doctrine of God and ends with eschatology and accounts for every accepted, historically important doctrine along the way. It can remind us that there are many moving parts in Christianity, that one's view of any one doctrine necessarily affects every other important aspect of one's faith.

Nonetheless, constructive theology works better in the contemporary world, and does a better job of providing meaningful, intellectually rigorous, actionable theology in the present. Perhaps it is the limited nature of constructive theologies that makes this so. The applicability of a focused constructive theology gives it potential for immediate impact, availability to a wider audience, and as an entry into a wider intellectual discussion with other important fields. By highlighting the distinctiveness of constructive theology, it will be given more room to grow. Split off from the trappings of systematic theology, it will have a better chance at influencing other academic disciplines, and to dispel some of the anxieties laypeople feel when trying to crack open specialized academic theological works on their own. Constructive theology's method has distinguished it from dogmatic and systematic theology, and the force of that difference is becoming difficult, if not damaging, to ignore.

Rising Issues and Theologians in Constructive Theology

The Workgroup on Constructive Theology is in the process of intentionally orienting itself toward the future. The members of the group continue to be amongst the most well-known and influential theologians within the academy in the United States. It's impossible to get too far in theology today without encountering theologians who are part of the group or at least prefer to be called "constructive." A tide seems to be turning, and yet a fair amount of ambivalence about declaring the independence and novelty of constructive theology remains.

Nevertheless, constructive theology continues to move forward, even as it shares themes and methods that go all the way back to proto-constructive theologians, Bernard Meland, and the first instantiation of the Workgroup on Constructive Theology. Increasingly important issues include pneumatology, hamartiology, and dialogue with other religions.

Shelly Rambo's *Spirit and Trauma: A Theology of Remaining*, uses psychological theories around trauma to reconstruct pneumatology in a way that recovers Holy Saturday, while expanding the doctrine to include the "sur-vivre," or living beyond, of traumatic experiences. She relates the Holy Spirit, through trauma studies as encountered in psychology and literary studies, to traumatic events like the recent United States wars in the Middle East and Hurricane Katrina in New Orleans.

Stephen Ray reconstructs hamartiology, the study of sin, in order to show how the doctrine can be both destructive and important, especially as it pertains to social sin. Ray critically engages both the theological tradition around sin as well as theories of hermeneutics like that of Paul Ricoeur in order to "help readers understand how even the best-intentioned sin-talk can participate in needless and, in many cases, malicious harm to marginalized persons and their communities."[12]

Laurel Schneider has sustained a project on multiplicity within Christianity, which also opens paths for dialoguing with other religions. She, along with Catherine Keller, has popularized the term "polydox" within Christian theology—a term associated with Alvin J. Reines, a Jewish theologian—which has found traction with other theologians like Kathryn Tanner and Mary-Jane Rubenstein.

John Thatamanil has renewed comparative theology in a constructive mode, arguing "comparative theology emerges out of . . . vulnerability. It seeks to think through what we have learned from other religious traditions even as we strive to keep faith with our prior convictions. It is risky work, a labor of mind and heart that will require us to rethink our own convictions."[13] In some ways, the apparent endpoint of constructive theology may be exactly what many might have feared. If Christianity is ultimately a constructed entity, the conversation is thrown radically open. Christian theology can dialogue

12. Stephen G. Ray Jr., *Do No Harm: Social Sin and Christian Responsibility* (Minneapolis: Fortress, 2003), xi.
13. John Thatamanil, *The Immanent Divine: God, Creation, and the Human Predicament* (Minneapolis: Fortress, 2006), xii–xiii.

with anything, up to and including other religions, because ultimately its premises remain open to redefinition, rethinking, and recapitulation. This isn't at all to say that Christianity loses its distinctiveness. Instead, Christianity is revealed as having always been fundamentally diverse and dynamic. Constructions, despite the architectural metaphor, remain persistently open to reconfiguration. Theologies, viewed from a constructive frame, may be more like Lincoln Logs or an erector set than like the pyramids or a cathedral.

Ultimately, contemporary constructive theologians—while working in many ways on the cutting edge—nevertheless are doing something that, at this point, has been happening for one hundred and ten years. Harkening back to Silas McBee, James Ten Broeke, and Bernard Meland, constructive theology today calls for the same basic things as the first "constructive bases for theology" proposed by those early adopters. Ten Broeke wrote, "Every theological structure should be regarded, not as an end in itself, but as subservient to the needs and purposes of the religious life, for it was never intended to be anything but functional and instrumental, and, if the tool fits neither the subject nor the object to which it is to be applied it should be put away."[14] Aside from the somewhat archaic language, this is a statement that could have just as easily come from any constructive theologian today, and which is blatantly at odds with dogmatic and systematic ways of doing theology. Ten Broeke raised the question of whether new philosophies might serve as better structures on which to construct a new, relevant theology, a question pursued by constructive theologians as varied as Peter C. Hodgson, Catherine Keller, and Gordon Kaufman.

A presiding concern with "culture" is not entirely unique to constructive theology—Paul Tillich stands out as a firmly systematic theologian who is obviously very concerned with culture. But it is nevertheless a defining feature, and one that can be traced back to McBee, Ten Broeke, and especially Meland, who solidified the absolute necessity of seeing theology in its cultural context. "Culture," analyzing it, changing it, situating Christianity within it, is everywhere in constructive theology. Theologies are not universal frameworks existing somewhere "out there" and applicable to people regardless of context, but are fundamentally culturally bound, an insight that runs deep throughout the constructive theological tradition. That insight works its way into constructive theology by means of engagement with other aca-

14. Ten Broeke, *A Constructive Basis for Theology*, 8.

demic disciplines, again, a characteristic that first appears not as a novel thing in recent theologies, but in proto-constructive theologians who insisted on the importance of culture and other disciplines like psychology and the social sciences as they emerged—as well as philosophy, though philosophy's position as a conversation partner for theology goes back much further. As Youtz observed in 1907, today "current essays in theology may be roughly classified in two groups: first those which are seeking for an 'essence,' a 'finality,' or an 'ultimate principle of unity' which express an unresolvable *quantum* in all religion, or 'essential religion' seen in its lowest terms; second those which take current religious doctrines and try to translate them into the terms of the thought-life of today. They ask: What is the meaning or 'reality' of this or that doctrine for this age and generation? Or, What form will this truth take, consistently with the scientific and philosophical convictions of today?"[15] Again, this is a distinction that carries through today, and sets apart constructive theologies as the latter, though the term "translated" might better be "reconstructed." *The Constructive Quarterly* introduced the ecumenical, collaborative spirit of constructive theology, still embodied in the textbooks the Workgroup on Constructive Theology produces as well as the way individual constructive theologies must be situated in a larger theological conversation.

Constructive theologians often call for new ways of doing theology and making it relevant. A hard look at the tradition, however, reveals that constructive theology is not in fact a very new way of doing theology. The method has evolved over the course of one hundred years, and though the theologies may be new in the constructions they offer, and the issues they confront are new at least in their details (though systemically they're the same), the "way" of doing theology isn't actually all that new. Constructive theologies are still cutting edge within the field of theology, and the method of construction, based on reconsidering established theological doctrines, is done in many different ways by people from very different contexts and seeking different ends. But the basic premises of constructive theology are relatively established, and have simply been in need of explication.

This also isn't to say constructive theology doesn't face many criticisms from more "orthodox" or traditional theological viewpoints, or that its place in the academy, both within theology and further, isn't

15. Beckwith, *The Realities of Christian Faith*, vii.

in many ways controversial. Constructive theology has many forces to push against, to demonstrate its rigor, faithfulness, and applicability in many different contexts. But building on its history, it shows promise as an established method that bolsters progressive, justice-minded theologies in a culture and context where Christianity is so often viewed as reactionary, regressive, and in its worst cases, actively hurtful in so many places to so many people. Constructive theologies are more diverse today than ever, and they promise to only get more so. Nevertheless, the historical arc of the evolution of that theology, as well as how it works and what it continues to do today, is demonstrably straightforward. Constructive theology has a rich, unique past, and given its growing place in the theological academy, its future should be equally as provocative, important, and challenging.

Conclusion

Questions of theological method are always complicated ones. Theology doesn't invite method in the same way as the sciences, or even the social sciences do. As Kaufman argues, the object of theology, according to Kant and most epistemology after him, is off limits to direct human observation. There is no way to directly prove the veracity of theological claims through observation in the same way as scientific ones, and for that matter, neither can one prove the very existence of the object of study itself. The recognition in the contemporary United States of the magnitude of religious diversity in the world further complicates the matter in the midst of competing truth claims, all about a reality that cannot be demonstrated to the human mind in a straightforward, observable way. Constructive theology shares with the scientific method the ongoing reexamination and revision of its claim in light of ongoing discoveries and insights. However, its revisions are mostly done in a pragmatic way. Constructive theology judges its value on what it accomplishes in the world and whether the fruits of its practice can faithfully be called Christian or not.

Constructive theology is very clearly growing, and having a greater and greater impact in the theological academy. Interestingly, constructive theology has not engaged all that much with other disciplines within the purview of Christian divinity schools and seminaries like biblical studies and church history. Bible scholars have participated in the Workgroup on Constructive Theology at times, and the history of the church has been important for constructive theology, especially in historicizing the development of doctrines. But the participation of biblical studies has not been sustained in such a way that it has become a large part of constructive theology. There are indications that this is beginning to change, especially as certain segments of Bible scholarship begin to separate somewhat from historical criticism of the Bible. Again, the problem is not that constructive theology has a problem with historical criticism of the Bible. It presumes it as a necessary and important field. At the same time, drawing conclusions about the essence of Christianity based on historiography is something more characteristic of liberal theology. Constructive theology tends to prefer working with the text on its own received terms. Nonetheless, constructive theology could use to incorporate more engagement with biblical studies and church history, as well as other theological disciplines, into its conversation. Moving past historical criticism as normative for interpreting the Bible is an important part of constructive theology. But constructive theology—in addition to dialoguing with other academic fields—must culture the in-house discussion over how theological meaning is made, and how doctrines can be constructed drawing upon the entire available treasury of resources available to it.

Constructive theology today is the continuation of a project started over one hundred years ago, though those early practitioners are largely forgotten. Nonetheless, laying the groundwork was an important first step, and even if Meland and others never read Ten Broeke or *The Constructive Quarterly*, the work indicates the rise of the kinds of thinking and sorts of events that would come to shape constructive theology and preoccupy its work since. Constructive theology began as a few small attempts to reconcile Christianity with modern ways of thinking, especially philosophy in the beginning, and cultural forces that changed Christianity in the United States. Growing out of liberalism, its methods quickly became distinct as it confronted neo-orthodoxy in the guise of Karl Barth, as well as the sober realism of Reinhold Niebuhr. From McBee and Ten Broeke through Meland, constructive theology began to take shape, and its terminology began to solidify: culture, construction, reconstruction, meaning, hermeneutics, crisis, and all the rest. With Meland constructive theology found its first well-known standard bearer, who also for all intents and purposes coined the actual term itself "constructive theology," though of course he wasn't the first to apply "constructive" to theology. Meland, building on but ultimately departing from the theological naturalism of his mentors, incorporated process philosophy, social sciences, a new awareness of culture, and a rising sense of the interrelated, constructive, discursive nature of the human world in culture, religion, myth, and much more. Meland has remained so difficult to categorize as a theologian, between liberalism, post-liberalism, theologian of culture, constructive theologian, etc., because constructive theology has continued not to be recognized as a stand-alone variety of theology. Meland posits a new method, but it took the organization of the Workgroup on Constructive Theology to begin to form it as a viable, widespread alternative.

The first formulation of the premises of constructive theology and a proposed methodological prolegomenon came from Gordon Kaufman, especially in *An Essay on Theological Method.* Drawing on Kantian epistemology, Kaufman argued that direct knowledge of God is out of the question, even for theology. Getting straight the aims of theology and how one should go about intellectually engaging an object that is inaccessible to human cognition for Kaufman was imperative. Largely unacknowledged in constructive theology today, Kaufman's methodology, alongside the phenomenology of Farley and the pluralism of Tracy, in many ways serves as the foundation for constructive theologians through the present. It accentuates the constructed nature of all knowledge about God, the importance of traditional symbols, in constructive theology maintained through doctrine, and the necessity of constructing and reconstructing these doctrines or symbols. Kaufman, however, did not methodologically stay with constructive theology. Early in the Workgroup he disagreed with doctrine remaining the controlling framework for further theologizing. The method of constructive theology did not find a static, finished form in Kaufman, but many of his arguments still serve as the basis for constructive theology. The Workgroup on Constructive Theology dialogically developed the method that constructive theology employs today starting in 1975. Through collectively published works as well as the vast body of individually authored works, a method comes into focus. That method more and more takes on distinctive features, interdisciplinarity and activism, and is done in distinctive ways. Though present members of the group still voice misgivings about the separation of systematic or dogmatic theology and constructive theology, in practical terms, the break has been made. Systematic theology has given constructive theology many of its historical resources, symbols, and starting points for analysis and reconstruction. But systematic theology and constructive theology are simply not done in the same way. The growing use of the term "constructive" within theology broadly is not happenstance, but points to a burgeoning sense that a new variety of theology has arrived and is asserting its place. This assertion largely tracks historically with the growing influence of the Workgroup on Constructive Theology, which has served as a pan-institutional home for a very large number of the most influential progressively minded theologians in the United States. The membership of that group over the years reads as a veritable who's who of divinity school and progressive seminary theologians. The Workgroup has waffled on whether it intends to propose a method for doing theology throughout its history.

Throughout the development of the constructive theological method, two prominent themes emerge, which I've identified as the pursuit of being an interlocutor with other disciplines, religious studies in particular but not exclusively, and to be an activist variety of theology. The historical arc of constructive theology gives prominence to these two motivations in different weights, but both were to varying degrees present throughout. Early constructive theology much more sought to explore and validate its interdisciplinary interests. In order to be relevant and to claim a rigorous basis for reconstructing traditional Christian doctrines and symbols, constructive theology turned to other disciplines for their discursive analyses of human life, culture, and societies. These insights in turn ended up serving as the basis for constructive theology's strong swing toward activism as a reaction to liberation theology.

Immediately following *Reconstructing Christian Theology*, constructive theology struggled with its attempt to fully account for and embrace liberation theology. The activist principle of theology, the need to change the world from a Christian standpoint, took vast prominence. By the time the third textbook was published, the two themes of constructive theology had balanced out somewhat, with individual theologians emphasizing one or the other, but never losing sight of both. The fourth textbook presumes the importance and legitimacy of liberation theology.

Interdisciplinarity informs activism in constructive theology, and vice versa, making a claim both for what theology should be about and how it should be done, as well as what theology should be able to accomplish in the real world if done from a constructive standpoint. Through these themes and the method developed throughout its history, constructive theology can be usefully compared and contrasted with other ways of doing theology, and its distinctiveness asserted and affirmed as an important and relevant means of doing theology in the contemporary world.

The tradition faces questions about what it is and what may be next. Constructive theology is premised on the idea of ongoing reevaluation, rethinking, and reconstruction. Given that systematic theology has been the entrenched manifestation of theology in the academy and has managed to maintain the presence of divinity schools and the study of theology in the present higher education system is no small thing. At the same time, to truly assert its importance and to draw attention to the necessity of doing theology in the ways it proposes, constructive theology should declare itself to be something different and reflect more self-consciously on its methods, while continuing to propose the imaginatively constructive theologies that have become its hallmark.

At the very least, constructive theology must assert its independence, as it were, because it shows the most promise as theology that effectively responds to and contrasts with the fundamentalist, conservative theologies that in the popular imagination speak for all of Christianity in the United States. Constructive theology needs to demonstrate that Christianity continues to be relevant in the world, engaging imaginatively, rigorously, continuously, and in good faith with the current state of culture, justice, and (in)equality in which we find ourselves. Building on a much longer history than has been acknowledged, constructive theology promises to be a theology for the present and for some time in the future. Such an attitude affirms the importance of Christian theology, as well as the realistic possibility that constructive theology itself may someday be supplanted by a more relevant, more timely version of theology.

Construction and Relativism

One of the most persistent charges against constructive theology is that of its supposed relativism. If the Christian framework is simply a collection of symbols, in the constructive theological tradition, doctrines, that are open to, and in fact must be, reconstructed, what then is permanent about Christianity, especially when God in much of the Christian tradition is defined as impassible and Christianity as God's ultimate, unchanging action to save human beings? Gordon Kaufman, as a theoretical precursor of the method of constructive theology, started to answer this question in *An Essay in Theological Method*, "Though God himself may be conceived as radically independent, underived, self-contained reality—as alone having 'aseity'—with all other reality derivative, secondary and contingent, the *concept* of God cannot properly be understood to have that exalted status; it is shaped and affected by many considerations and must be qualified, defined, and redefined in very careful and complex ways if it is to be properly constructed."[1] Ultimately, that to which constructive theology points, is not considered to be relative. In fact, constructive theology makes a stronger claim than other, older ways of doing theology that God, that is, not the conception of God found in theology but God Godself, is absolutely whatever God is or is becoming—to acknowledge the strong process strain in constructive theology. To claim that theology can penetrate to what God actually *is*, in God's fullness and essence, in fact relativizes God because it makes God subject to human perception and description. To ignore the constructed nature of the concept of God in all theology subjects God to being made an object that, when scrutinized, is actually a formation of human thought and not Godself. It doesn't deny, necessarily, the possibility of revelation—as it has been critiqued—but instead denies that even such revelation allows for speech about God that is not essentially a construction of a concept. Kaufman casts constructive theology as essentially Kantian in epistemology.

Theologians and Christians throughout history have constructed Christianity. That admission in fact minimizes the relativism of God. It humbly acknowledges the nature of human speech about God while also recognizing the responsibility humans bear for making sure they never stop trying to get things right, while also recognizing that they never will. Fallibilism is not the same thing as relativism. The fallibilist nature of constructive theology holds that all conceptions of God could be, indeed are, in some way not fully true, and yet we might nonetheless be justified in holding those views. Fallibilism also requires continued engagement and inquiry to test whether what we say about God stands up to the purposes for which our conceptions are developed. If a conception of God cannot speak to the contemporary world, speak to the church, or hold its own in intellectual interrogation, it cannot finally be true speech about God, at least in an eternal sense. The scandal, perhaps, is that human beings have ever felt as if true descriptions of God have been possible. The idea of the *anologia fidei* ideally ensures that human beings recognize that no human speech can capture God in a one to one correspondence. Kaufman points out that in reality this attitude has seldom been the case, and God has been presumed to be a thing, objectified and codified in dogmatic and systematic theolo-

1. Kaufman, *An Essay in Theological Method*, 10.

gies.[2] While not all constructive theologians have followed Kaufman's turn to Kantian ethical practice as being the foundation of theology, it is nonetheless a precursor for the activist nature of contemporary constructive theology. For many, in fact almost all, constructive theologians, Christianity is more than an ethical system in need of a deontological guarantor. But it must nonetheless issue a call for right action and world changing.

Intellectual Rigor

Aside from relativism, the most common criticism of constructive theology is that it is not rigorous enough intellectually, usually either philosophically or theologically. This mostly reveals the anxiety of the accuser about changes in the academy generally, especially around postmodernism, and the reluctance to admit that Christianity could be a constructed system rather than a revealed, metaphysical one. In reality, when done well, constructive theology participates in some of the most intellectually rigorous dialogue that theology has ever been involved with.[3] The claims of theology should be accessible and verifiable, both academically and for laypeople who seek to live their lives according to them. By engaging whole-heartedly with other disciplines, constructive theology makes itself open to criticism from the outside, and for sure there are examples of constructive theologies that have been dismissed by the disciplines they embraced. Constructive theology is not based in revelation or piety, though it doesn't proscribe those things. But its multifaceted, pluralistic nature as a movement has been mistaken for lack of clarity or focus. In fact, the ongoing constructive efforts, open to correction and revision by the community at large, both academic and ecclesial, demands greater clarity, applicability, and intellectual thoroughness. This will only become increasingly true if other disciplines start to take more notice of constructive theology.

In trying to be interdisciplinary and intellectually rigorous, constructive theology does run the risk of doing neither well. But that needs to be considered on a case-by-case basis, and must be one of the primary ways of evaluating the quality of any particular constructive theology. Doing interdisciplinary work asks a lot of those who do it, more so in theology than perhaps most other disciplines because of the sheer length of theology's history. Going forward, constructive the-

2. Ibid., 27–28.
3. Ibid., 28.

ology can be more intentional about reaching out to experts in other fields, which runs the risk of finding out that theological uses of theories from other disciplines has been less substantial than thought. But the critique levied internally—from within the theological academy itself—seems unfounded and reactionary. Again, as Kaufman writes, and which goes to the heart of the accusation of lack of rigor from within theology, "There is no problem of how one can get into some charmed 'circle of faith' or 'theological circle' in order to do theology or to understand what is going on in theology. We are already there by virtue of speaking and understanding English. As regards its foundations, theology is no more parochial or exclusive than any other discipline."[4] Constructive theology fulfills the claim that theology must be an open discipline, rejecting claims that theology can only be done for or by the church, or in such a way as to be unintelligible to other academic disciplines. Theologies that insist on being "parochial or exclusive," or alternatively, disciplines seeing theology as such, ignore the burgeoning constructive basis of theology as embodied in constructive theology, as well as the historical fact that Christian theology has never truly been as self-contained as it seems or might like to think.

The Future of Constructive Theology

Today, divinity schools and seminaries around the country are confronting the evermore-apparent uniqueness of constructive theology as a mood and method for doing Christian theology. Positions explicitly called "constructive" continue to emerge in many places, even as a greater and greater number of faculty in "systematic" positions nonetheless identify as constructive theologians. Whether a hard split will happen remains to be seen. And even if it does, the basic interrelatedness of constructive, systematic, and dogmatic theologies will always remain. All three make important claims about the way theology should be done and about the nature and character of Christianity and God. Part of constructive theology's openness itself is openness to the different ways speech about God can happen. Constructive theology, then, in the current theological landscape, should not be viewed as a successor to dogmatic or systematic theology. Rather, it should be viewed as an important innovation, the importance and influence of which only looks to grow for the foreseeable future.

4. Ibid., 8.

Bibliography

Adams, Carol J., ed. *Ecofeminism and the Sacred.* New York: Continuum, 1993.

Anderson, Victor. *Creative Exchange: A Constructive Theology of African American Religious Experience.* Minneapolis: Fortress, 2008.

Armour, Leslie and Elizabeth Trott. *The Faces of Reason: An Essay on Philosophy and Culture in English Canada 1850–1950.* Waterloo, Ontario: Wilfrid Laurier Press, 1981.

Barth, Karl. *Church Dogmatics: A Selection with Introduction.* Louisville: Westminster John Knox, 1994.

_____. *Church Dogmatics, Vol. III: The Doctrine of Creation.* New York: T&T Clark, 1960.

Beckwith, Clarence Augustine. *The Realities of Christian Theology: An Interpretation of Christian Experience.* New York: Houghton, Mifflin and Company, 1906.

Bromell, David J. "Sallie McFague's 'Metaphorical Theology.'" *Journal of the American Academy of Religion* 61, no. 3 (Autumn, 1993): 485–503.

Chopp, Rebecca S. *The Power to Speak: Feminism, Language, God.* New York: Crossroad, 1989.

_____ and Mark L. Taylor, eds. *Reconstructing Christian Theology.* Minneapolis: Augsburg Fortress, 1994.

Connolly, Peter, ed. *Approaches to the Study of Religion.* New York: Cassell, 1999.

Dorrien, Gary. *The Making of American Liberal Theology: Crisis, Irony, and Postmodernity 1950–2005.* Louisville: Westminster John Knox, 2006.

Evans, James H., Jr., and Stephen G. Ray Jr. *We Have Been Believers: An African American Systematic Theology.* Minneapolis: Fortress, 2012.

Farley, Edward. *Ecclesial Man: A Social Phenomenology of Faith and Reality.* Philadelphia: Fortress, 1975.

_____. *Ecclesial Reflection: An Anatomy of Theological Method.* Philadelphia: Fortress, 1982.

Gruenler, R.G. "Constructive Theology." In *Evangelical Dictionary of Theology*, edited by Walter A. Elwell. Grand Rapids: Baker Academic, 2001.

Hodgson, Peter C. *Children of Freedom: Black Liberation in Christian Perspective*. Philadelphia: Fortress, 1974.

_____. *Jesus—Word and Presence: An Essay in Christology*. Philadelphia: Fortress, 1971.

Hodgson, Peter C. and Robert H. King, eds. *Christian Theology: An Introduction to Its Traditions and Tasks*. Minneapolis: Fortress, 1985.

Hopkins, Dwight N. *Shoes That Fit Our Feet: Sources for a Constructive Black Theology*. Maryknoll: Orbis, 1993.

Inbody, Tyron. *The Constructive Theology of Bernard Meland: Postliberal Empirical Realism*. Atlanta: Scholars Press, 1995.

Jones, Serene. *Feminist Theory and Christian Theology: Cartographies of Grace*. Minneapolis: Fortress, 2000.

_____ and Paul F. Lakeland, eds. *Constructive Theology: A Contemporary Approach to Classical Themes*. Minneapolis: Augsburg Fortress, 2005.

Kaufman, Gordon. *An Essay on Theological Method*. Missoula, Montana: Scholars Press, 1975.

_____. *Systematic Theology: A Historicist Perspective*. New York: Charles Scribner's Sons, 1968.

_____. "Theology as Imaginative Construction." In *Journal of the American Academy of Religion* 50, no. 1 (March, 1982): 73–79.

Keller, Catherine. *Apocalypse Now and Then: A Feminist Guide to the End of the World*. Minneapolis: Fortress, 1996.

_____. *Face of the Deep: A Theology of Becoming*. New York: Routledge, 2003.

_____ and Laurel C. Schneider, eds. *Polydoxy: Theology of Multiplicity and Relation*. New York: Routledge, 2011.

King, Robert H. *The Meaning of God*. London: SCM Press, 1974.

Lakeland, Paul F. *Church: Living Communion*. Collegeville: Liturgical Press, 2009.

McBee, Silas, ed. *The Constructive Quarterly: A Journal of the Faith, Work, and Thought of Christendom*, vol. 1 (March to December 1913). New York: George H. Doran Company, 1913.

McFague, Sallie. *The Body of God: An Ecological Theology*. Minneapolis: Fortress, 1993.

_____. *Life Abundant: Rethinking Theology and Economy for a Planet in Peril*. Minneapolis: Fortress, 2001.

_____. *Speaking in Parables: A Study in Metaphor and Theology*. Philadelphia: Fortress, 1975.

McFague TeSelle, Sallie. *Literature and the Christian Life*. New Haven: Yale University Press, 1966.

_____. *Metaphorical Theology: Models of God in Religious Language*. Philadelphia: Fortress, 1982.

_____. "Parable, Metaphor, and Theology." *Journal of the American Academy of Religion* 42, no. 4 (December, 1974): 630–45.

Meland, Bernard Eugene. *Faith and Culture*. Carbondale: Southern Illinois University Press, 1953.

_____. *Fallible Forms and Symbols: Discourses on Method in a Theology of Culture*. Philadelphia: Fortress Press, 1976.

_____. *The Reawakening of Christian Faith*. New York: Macmillan, 1947.

Miller, Benjamin. "Mythological Naturalism." *Journal of Religion* 22, no. 3 (1942): 270–87.

Morse, Christopher. *Not Every Spirit: A Dogmatics of Christian Disbelief, 2nd Edition*. New York: Continuum, 2009.

Pannenberg, Wolfhart. *Systematic Theology*, vol. 1. Grand Rapids: Eerdmans, 1991.

_____. *Theology and the Philosophy of Science*. Translated by Francis McDonagh. Philadelphia: Westminster, 1976.

Ray, Stephen G., Jr. *Do No Harm: Social Sin and Christian Responsibility*. Minneapolis: Fortress, 2003.

_____, and Laurel Schneider, eds. *Awake to the Moment: An Introduction to Theology*. Louisville: Westminster John Knox, 2016.

Rieger, Joerg. *Christ and Empire: From Paul to Postcolonial Times*. Minneapolis: Fortress, 2007.

_____. "Constructive Theology." In *Encyclopedia of Sciences and Religion*, edited by Anne L.C. Runehov and Luis Oviedo, 483–86. New York: Springer, 2013.

_____. *No Rising Tide: Theology, Economics, Future*. Minneapolis: Fortress, 2009.

Sanday, William. Review of *Contentio Veritatis: Essays in Constructive Theology*, by Six Oxford Tutors. *The Journal of Theological Studies* 4, no. 13 (October, 1902): 1–16.

Schneider, Laurel C. *Re-Imagining the Divine: Confronting the Backlash against Feminist Theology*. Cleveland: The Pilgrim Press, 1998.

Six Oxford Tutors. *Contentio Veritatis: Essays in Constructive Theology*. London: John Murray, 1902.

Tanner, Kathryn. *Economy of Grace*. Minneapolis: Augsburg Fortress, 2005.

_____. *Jesus, Humanity and the Trinity: A Brief Systematic Theology*. Edinburgh: T&T Clark, 2001.

_____. *The Politics of God: Christian Theologies and Social Justice*. Minneapolis: Augsburg Fortress, 1992.

_____. *Theories of Culture: A New Agenda for Theology*. Minneapolis: Augsburg Fortress, 1997.

Taylor, Mark L. *The Theological and the Political: On the Weight of the World.* Minneapolis: Fortress, 2011.

Ten Broeke, James. *A Constructive Basis for Theology*. London: Macmillan and Co., 1914.

Thatamanil, John. *The Immanent Divine: God, Creation, and the Human Predicament.* Minneapolis: Fortress, 2006.

Tillich, Paul. *Systematic Theology*, vol. 1. Chicago: University of Chicago Press, 1951.

Tracy, David. *Blessed Rage for Order: The New Pluralism in Theology*. New York: Seabury Press, 1975.

Walker, Corey D.B. Review of *Face of the Deep: A Theology of Becoming*, by Catherine Keller. *Journal of the American Academy of Religion* 75, no. 3 (September, 2007): 733–36.

Wieman, Henry Nelson and Bernard Eugene Meland. *American Philosohpies of Religion*. Chicago: Willet, Clark & Company, 1936.

Youtz, Herbert Alden, "Current Essays in Constructive Theology," *The American Journal of Theology* 11, no. 4 (October, 1907): 694–704.

Index